Praise for *The Faithful Departed*

"Philip Lawler's stunning book is a fresh look at the causes and consequences of the Catholic clerical sex-abuse scandal.... Lawler tells the story of the Church's role in advancing a culture of morality and excellence within the 19th-century immigrant community. But all of that good crashes into a mid-20th-century wall of indifference, amorality, and hostility to orthodoxy and 'the power of Faith.' ... Lawler places the blame squarely on the laps of the shepherds, the bishops who were more interested in their public image and meeting the mortgage payments, than the safety of souls."

> —Frank Keating, Governor of Oklahoma, 1995–2003; first chairman of the U.S. bishops' National Review Board

"*The Faithful Departed* is the best book-length treatment of the sex abuse crisis, its origins and larger implications, published to date."

> —Fr. Richard John Neuhaus

"[Lawler addresses] questions of deceit and complicity ... with a candor that is tempered but not compromised by discretion.... Every bishop and priest, and every Catholic who loves the Church and wants to know what went very wrong, should read *The Faithful Departed*."

> —*First Things*

"American Catholics and their bishops have not yet learned the lesson, Lawler thinks, and the evidence is with him."

> —Kevin Schmiesing, Acton Institute for the Study of Religion and Liberty

"The fearless and orthodox Catholic journalist Phil Lawler was at Ground Zero before the 2002 Geoghan trial set off the Great Unraveling. I can think of no one better able than he to explain what events in Boston and beyond mean for the Church's past, present and future. And not only the Catholic Church: what happened in Boston could happen in any church or religious body in which those in authority—aided and abetted by a docile laity—come to care more about using false piety to maintain power and position than doing the right thing."

> —Rod Dreher, columnist, *Dallas Morning News*; author, *Crunchy Cons*

"Lawler's masterful analysis is sobering and provides an urgent incentive for authentic renewal. If St. John Chrysostom is correct when he says that the road to hell is paved with the skulls of bishops, it would be a mistake for any bishop or priest to miss this book."

—Most Rev. Fabian Bruskewitz, Bishop of Lincoln, Nebraska

"If you don't read another book this year, read *The Faithful Departed: The Collapse of Boston's Catholic Culture*, by Philip F. Lawler.... I'm astounded by his clarity in defining 'where things went wrong,' resulting in the confused state of Catholicism and its vastly reduced influence in our nation today. He makes it clear right at the beginning that the scandal of sexual abuse and how it has been dealt with by our bishops—deadly serious though it is—is but a part of the picture."

—Fr. Christopher G. Phillips, *Atonement Online*

"Many Catholics understandably want to put the Long Lent of 2002 behind us. No one should do so without reading *The Faithful Departed*."

—George Weigel, Distinguished Senior Fellow of the Ethics and Public Policy Center

"Ten years before the headlines of Catholic clergy sexual misconduct began piling up, I interviewed Phil Lawler about a few 'isolated' abusers among Catholic clergy.... [He] thought that this might well mushroom into one of the worst scandals in American Catholic history. Fifteen years later we know he was right. If Phil Lawler had such good vision looking forward, imagine how clearly he sees the past in *The Faithful Departed*."

—Al Kresta, president/CEO, Ave Maria Radio; host, *Kresta in the Afternoon*

"Some in the Church dismiss the abuse scandal as 'old news.' It isn't. To understand the scandal's still-unaddressed causes and grasp the magnitude of its aftershocks, Phil Lawler's unflinching account is essential reading."

—George Neumayr, editor, *Catholic World Report*

"*The Faithful Departed* is a compelling pathology report of the dereliction of duty of bishops in Boston. It calls to accountability any man who dares to accept the call to Holy Orders. The historical facts alone will sting consciences. Lawler's masterful analysis is sobering and provides an urgent incentive for authentic renewal."

—Rev. Jerry Pokorsky, co-founder, *Adoremus*

"The most important work about the Church to appear in the last two decades."

—John Zmirak, *Inside Catholic*

THE FAITHFUL DEPARTED

The Collapse of Boston's Catholic Culture

PHILIP F. LAWLER

ENCOUNTER BOOKS

NEW YORK · LONDON

First American edition published in 2008 by Encounter Books, an activity of Encounter for Culture and Education, Inc., a nonprofit, tax exempt corporation. Encounter Books website address: www.encounterbooks.com

Manufactured in the United States and printed on acid-free paper. The paper used in this publication meets the minimum requirements of ANSI/NISO Z39.48 1992 (R 1997) (*Permanence of Paper*).

PAPERBACK EDITION ISBN 978-1-59403-374-2

THE LIBRARY OF CONGRESS HAS CATALOGUED THE HARDCOVER EDITION AS FOLLOWS:

Lawler, Philip F.
    The faithful departed : the collapse of Boston's Catholic culture / by Philip F. Lawler. — 1st ed.
    p. cm.
    Includes index.
    ISBN-13: 978-1-59403-211-0 (hardcover : alk. paper)
    ISBN-10: 1-59403-211-4 (hardcover : alk. paper)
    1. Catholic Church—Massachusetts—Boston.   2. Boston (Mass.)—Religious life and customs.   3. Boston (Mass.)—Church history. I. Title.
BX1418.B7L39   2008
282'.74461—dc22   2007045757

TABLE OF CONTENTS

You are the salt of the earth. But if salt has lost its savour, wherewith shall it be salted? It is good for nothing anymore but to be cast out and trodden on by men.

MATTHEW 5:13

PREFACE TO THE
PAPERBACK EDITION

Nearly a generation has passed since 1985, when Gilbert Gauthe was convicted of molesting boys while he served as a parish priest in Louisiana. Yet to this day, newspaper reports on the sex-abuse scandal in the Catholic Church routinely say that the scandal first emerged in Boston in 2002. Why?

By the 1990s, the high-profile prosecutions of Gauthe, James Porter, and Rudy Kos had made the American public painfully aware that some Catholic priests had abused young people. What emerged in 2002 and gave the burgeoning scandal an entirely new dimension was the realization that Catholic bishops had protected the abusers. What had been a story about the misconduct of a small percentage of American priests was transformed into a much more sensational story about the misconduct of the American Catholic hierarchy.

As I write this preface in the spring of 2010, a new set of stories, revealing clerical abuse in Europe and a sadly familiar pattern of bishops shielding the abusers, has prompted broader questions about the culpability of the Catholic hierarchy worldwide. Spurred on by critics of the Church and aggressive lawyers for abuse victims, many journalists have suggested that Pope Benedict XVI himself is ultimately responsible for the cover-ups. The criticism is misplaced, for reasons that I explain below. But the torrent of outrage directed at the Holy See demonstrates that the stakes in this debate are very high.

The dual pattern of abuse by priests and cover-ups by Church leaders that emerged in Boston in 2002 was stunning. But the scandal in Boston was not the first, nor was it the worst. The Archdiocese of Boston has paid out millions to settle the legal claims of sex-abuse victims, but nowhere near the $700 million paid by the Archdiocese of Los Angeles. The payments have forced draconian budget cuts for the Church in Boston, but the archdiocese has avoided bankruptcy, unlike seven other dioceses in the United

States. Prosecutors in Massachusetts considered filing charges against Church officials for concealing evidence of criminal abuse, but bishops in at least two other American dioceses were forced to sign legal agreements conceding that the established facts were sufficient to warrant criminal prosecution.

Yes, things were bad in Boston in 2002. But Boston was not alone. Things were bad all over the country during that year of relentless negative publicity that the late Father Richard John Neuhaus aptly characterized as a "long Lent" for the American Church. In retrospect, the debacle in Boston stands out not because it was the first or the worst, but for two other reasons that are rarely understood.

First, in Boston the head of the archdiocese, Cardinal Bernard Law, eventually accepted responsibility for the disaster and resigned. Dozens of other American bishops were equally culpable; dozens of others coddled predatory priests and covered up the evidence of their crimes. But while a number of bishops have stepped down after public revelations of their own misconduct, Cardinal Law is the only U.S. prelate who has resigned because of his failure to curb the misconduct of others.

Looking back now on the sequence of shocking revelations that became public in 2002, it is astonishing that the casualties among the American Catholic hierarchy have been kept so low—that only a single bishop was held fully accountable for the outrage in his diocese. Thousands of children have been molested; more than $2 billion has been paid to settle legal claims; thousands of parish churches and parochial schools have been closed down so that dioceses can pay off the costs of criminal activity; countless souls have turned away from the Catholic Church in disgust. And only one Church leader has lost his job.

Second, in Boston the Church fell into public disgrace at a crucial point in a long period of decline. The influence of Catholicism in the Boston area, once so overwhelming, had been waning for decades. Catholic thought was generally disregarded in public life, while Catholic politicians in Massachusetts rarely followed the dictates of Church teaching. But until 2002 it was still unthinkable that a public figure would launch a direct rhetorical attack on the Church. Now that changed. The sex-abuse scandal made it possible to criticize bishops directly, to scoff at their protests as the state legislature took new strides toward acceptance of same-sex marriage and the mandatory provision of abortifacient "emergency contraceptives" even by Catholic doctors at Catholic hospitals.

The political climate in Massachusetts shifted significantly once again in 2009 with the death of Senator Ted Kennedy. During his long public career, Ted Kennedy had held iconic status among liberal Catholics. He had been the most visible Catholic on the American political scene and the most influential among the many Catholic public figures who flouted the Church's teachings on a range of crucial moral issues including abortion, homosexuality, contraception, embryonic stem-cell research, and euthanasia. With his death, and with no younger member of the Kennedy clan stepping forward to take the Senate seat that the family had controlled for more than sixty years, a historic era was closing and a historic opportunity was opening.

An upstart Republican candidate, Scott Brown, seized the opportunity and startled the political world by winning the January 2010 special election to fill Kennedy's seat in the U.S. Senate. His victory rattled the comfortable liberal establishment in Massachusetts and demonstrated that the voters of the Commonwealth were prepared to shake off old habits and re-examine popular assumptions. The winds of political change were blowing across Massachusetts. It might have been an ideal time to reverse the years of drift into a reflexive anti-Catholicism in public life. There might have been an opening for a political candidate who proudly upheld Catholic teachings. But no such candidate was on the horizon. (Brown, who is not Catholic, opposes the Church's stands on abortion, contraception, and embryo research.) And if any such candidate had emerged, he would have found it necessary to rebuild a constituency starting from scratch, because loyal Catholics no longer have an organized political base in Massachusetts.

In neighboring Rhode Island, however, the end of the Kennedy dynasty took a very different form. Congressman Patrick Kennedy, the son of the late senator from Massachusetts, announced his decision not to seek re-election in 2010 shortly after a series of public clashes with Bishop Thomas Tobin of Providence.

In October 2009, when Congressman Kennedy lashed out at the American bishops for their opposition to a health-care reform proposal that included federal support for abortion, Bishop Tobin fought back with a public statement rebuking Kennedy. "I'm not sure whether or not you fulfill the basic requirements of being a Catholic," the bishop told the congressman. Later, Kennedy revealed that Bishop Tobin, in a previous private message, had asked him not to receive Communion since his public stands were so clearly at odds with his professed Catholic faith. Editorial writers thundered against the bishop, condemning what they saw as unwarranted episcopal interference in matters of public policy. But Tobin held his ground, pointing out that he was speaking not as a political actor but as a pastoral leader, explaining the requirements of membership in the Catholic worshipping community. Kennedy, despite his best efforts and the sympathies of the mass media, was unable to turn the bishop's public statements to his own political advantage.

Three months later, Kennedy announced that he would not run for reelection in 2010. Clearly it was not the bishop's rebuke that drove him out of public life; a precipitous decline in his popularity, as measured by local polls, prompted his withdrawal. Still, it was instructive that when a Catholic bishop took a firm stand and explained his position, the public understood. In January 2011, when Patrick Kennedy leaves Congress, Thomas Tobin will remain the bishop of Providence, his authority enhanced by his willingness to challenge a powerful politician. One can only wonder how differently American history might have played out if another Catholic bishop, in Boston, had been equally clear in rebuking another Kennedy, twenty or thirty or forty years earlier.

If Boston was neither the first nor the worst site of the clerical sex-abuse scandal, the city was still the most notable example of another, deeper social trend that I hoped to illustrate in *The Faithful Departed*: the decline of religious influence in public life. Nowhere else in the United States could one find such a conspicuous collapse of religious influence. In the space of a generation, the Catholic Church in Boston had dropped from a position of unquestioned dominance to one of public obloquy: from bully to whipping-boy. While Boston furnished a peculiarly vivid illustration, the same trend has been visible—if not quite so pronounced—in other American regions, too. The Catholic Church has beaten a retreat in the face of advancing secularism in nearly every corner of the United States. Nor is Catholicism the only faith to suffer such a decline.

The sex-abuse scandal did not cause this decline; the process was already well advanced before the ugly truths about clerical misconduct and episcopal dereliction were exposed to public view. But the public humiliation of Church leaders certainly accelerated the process. Any cleric who dared to speak out against injustices in society was open to an obvious, withering retort. Why should we listen to the clergy, the critics of Catholicism asked, when Church leaders themselves had tolerated such grotesque injustices? The argument was unanswerable. To restore their credibility,

Church leaders had to eliminate the charge of hypocrisy; they had to remove the scandal.

For most of a decade now, since they tackled the issue at a meeting in Dallas in June 2002, the American Catholic bishops have been struggling to put the scandal behind them. From time to time they have announced their success in doing so; the scandal, a past president of the bishops' conference informed the media, is now "history." And the "zero tolerance" policies approved at that Dallas meeting have in fact succeeded in curbing sexual abuse of children by Catholic priests. Complaints of molestation have dropped, and when credible new complaints have been raised, the accused priests have been promptly removed from ministry rather than shuffled off to a new parish to begin their predation again. In that respect, the Dallas policies have been successful.

Still, the credibility of the American bishops remains impaired because the sexual abuse of children by priests was only one aspect of the scandal. Again, by the mid-1990s the American public was fully aware that some Catholic clerics had molested children. The series of revelations that began in Boston in 2002 brought something new to the fore. It was horrifying that some priests had acted as sexual predators, but their misconduct, when it came to light, appeared to be personal rather than institutional. The dishonest responses by so many bishops, on the other hand, struck at the credibility of the Church as an institution. That is why reporters routinely cite 2002 as the year when the scandal was exposed. For the first time, the public learned that Catholic bishops had covered up evidence and lied to the faithful. That latter scandal, the scandal of episcopal mendacity, was not addressed by the Dallas policies, nor has it been addressed in the intervening years. Quite the contrary.

Instead of turning over a new leaf and offering a genuinely transparent explanation of the sex-abuse problem, the U.S. bishops have continued to fudge key facts. They have, for example, sought to camouflage the evidence of another serious problem: the influence of homosexuality among the clergy. In their bid to obfuscate the evidence, they have had some eager professional help. Researchers from the John Jay College of Criminal Justice, commissioned by the United States Conference of Catholic Bishops to study the problem, announced in 2009 that homosexuality was not an important factor, despite the fact that the overwhelming majority of complaints against priests involved relations with teenage boys. "Some Catholic leaders have contended that because 80 percent of the abuse victims were male, the crisis must have been caused by gay priests acting out," the John Jay study explained. "But Dr. Terry said she found that abusers were confused about their sexuality and had poor social skills, but had no pattern of homosexual behavior." Dr. Karen Terry, the lead researcher, went still further, saying: "Someone can commit sexual acts that might be of a homosexual nature, but not have a homosexual identity." Thus the John Jay report, strongly endorsed by the U.S. bishops' conference, asked readers to believe that priests who engaged in homosexual acts were not necessarily homosexuals. And since the priests who molested teenage boys were not necessarily homosexuals, it followed, by a sort of manufactured tautology, that homosexuality was not an important factor in their story.

Such blatant manipulation of the available evidence might draw approving nods from social scientists whose work is governed by the canons of political correctness. But ordinary American Catholics are unlikely to find the argument convincing. Father Neuhaus spelled out the point carefully, taking painfully small logical steps to ensure that no one could fail to follow him: "Between men who want to have sex with adolescent boys and men who do not want to have sex with adolescent boys, the former are more likely to have sex with adolescent boys."

The Dallas policies provided the American bishops with a set of standards by which they could judge their progress toward the eradication of the sex-abuse scandal. But again, those policies did not address the injured credibility of the bishops themselves. So when members of the American hierarchy proudly announced that they were in full compliance with the Dallas Charter, cynics could point out that the announcement was coming from the same bishops who had proven themselves untrustworthy just a few years ago.

The Diocese of Rockville Center, New York, for instance, announced in late 2009 that it had reached full compliance with the Dallas norms. *Newsday* explained that achievement:

> Last year an audit found that, while the diocese passed virtually every aspect of the 13-article audit, it failed in one part of one article. Of five parishes audited, one did not take sufficient action to train church volunteers in "safe environments"—or at least did not produce proper documentation showing it did so, church officials said.

Here, "full compliance" meant filing the appropriate paperwork. Once the forms had been duly entered in the docket, the problem was considered resolved. But what if those documents were not accurate? What if important facts had been omitted? What if someone filling out the forms had been dishonest? The process by itself could not ensure the honesty of the people involved.

At the same time that the Rockville Center diocese announced its achievement of "full compliance," archdiocesan officials just a few miles south in Newark, New Jersey, announced that they were pulling Father Michael Fugee off his assignment as a hospital chaplain after learning something about his past: he had been convicted in 2003 of criminal sexual contact with a young boy. The conviction had been overturned on appeal and the priest had entered a "pretrial intervention program." Nevertheless, seven years after the Dallas Charter had stipulated that a priest credibly accused of sexual abuse should be removed from ministry, this priest—who had been convicted in a court of law—was still on active duty. Would anyone in Newark, learning about this case, be reassured to hear that the archdiocese was in compliance with the terms of the Dallas Charter? Of course not. The process cannot inspire confidence if the people carrying out that process are still under suspicion.

The credibility of American Church leaders might have been restored if, at their meeting in Dallas or sometime thereafter, the bishops had held themselves accountable for their own misconduct—not only for their negligence in allowing predators to remain in ministry, but also for their dishonesty in hiding the problem. What might have happened if one doughty bishop had announced that some of his colleagues, having been exposed as liars, had lost their moral authority and should resign? No American bishop rose to make that demand. To this day, no prelate has said, for the record, that some of his colleagues betrayed their responsibilities so thoroughly that they could no longer be considered fit to act as successors to the twelve apostles.

One diocesan bishop has no power over another; Bishop X cannot require Bishop Y to resign. But he can ask him to resign; he can exhort him to resign; he can explain why resignation is the only honorable option. Or short of demanding a resignation he can acknowledge that at a minimum Bishop Y needs to come clean, to acknowledge his guilt and to make amends. Even that has not happened in the American case.

Interestingly enough, when the sex-abuse problem exploded onto the headlines in Ireland early in 2010, one bishop did say—in public, repeatedly, for attribution—that bishops who participated in a cover-up of sexual abuse should acknowledge their wrongdoing. While he did not explicitly call for resignations, when Archbishop Diarmuid Martin of Dublin said that some of his colleagues should reconsider their status, his meaning was unmistakable. "Everybody has to stand up and accept the responsibility for what they did," the archbishop said. An open admission of guilt, he reasoned, would be far better than a lengthy trial in the court of public opinion as the evidence gradually piled up. Explaining his preference for bishops to come forward and admit their dereliction of duty early in the process, Archbishop Martin said, "I would much prefer to be in that situation than to be hunted or pushed."

Bishops are understandably reluctant to criticize their brother bishops. Such public criticism of a colleague is an extreme measure, to be used only in extreme circumstances: when an institution is in crisis, when its credibility is in jeopardy, when revelations of corruption make it imperative to demand reform. Archbishop Martin seemed to think that the Church had reached that point in Ireland in 2010. The Church in the United States reached the same point nearly a decade earlier.

The sex-abuse scandal in Ireland produced results quite similar to those that emerged in Boston. In Ireland, too, the Church had long enjoyed a position of complete dominance in society, but gradually lost that position late in the twentieth century. The scandal gave critics of Catholicism an opportunity to unleash all their hostility, seizing the offensive and working to silence the public voice of the Church.

Because a general distaste for the Catholic faith had been growing for years in Ireland, many observers were inclined to blame Church doctrine for the scandal, to suggest that the Vatican was ultimately responsible for the misbehavior of Irish clerics. That analysis was misguided. In Ireland as in the United States, the teachings of the Church had never left any room for doubt that the sexual abuse of children is gravely immoral, and the Code of Canon Law had given Church leaders ample authority to discipline priests who were guilty of such immoral behavior. The bishops, however, chose not to exercise their proper disciplinary authority.

But in Ireland, unlike in America, the bishops quickly recognized that they should be accountable for the unchecked misconduct of their priests. Within a few weeks after the first public report on sexual abuse in the Archdiocese of Dublin, four Irish bishops had offered to resign. In the United States, by contrast, a full decade of similar revelations involving scores of dioceses produced only one resignation, that of Cardinal Law. The

American hierarchy still has not come to terms with its own culpability in the scandal.

Following on the abuse revelations that shook the Church in Ireland, the crisis has quickly spread across Europe, with a steady barrage of news stories exposing molestations and cover-ups in Germany, the Netherlands, Spain, Belgium, and France. Inevitably the questions have been raised: Was there an organized worldwide campaign, orchestrated by the Vatican, to protect abusive priests from civil prosecution? Was Pope Benedict involved?

These questions were, and are, valid and understandable. But the discussion has been complicated by a series of inaccurate media reports that have offered confused accounts of decisions that Cardinal Joseph Ratzinger made before his election as Roman Pontiff. Flawed reporting and ignorance of the Canon Law that governs internal Catholic affairs combined to produce analysis that criticized the future Pope for decisions that he had not made, and questioned why he had failed to take disciplinary action in cases that were not under his jurisdiction while he was prefect of the Vatican's Congregation for the Doctrine of the Faith.

Eventually, through the haze of hasty media reports, a clearer picture of past Vatican policies has emerged. While there was no worldwide conspiracy to protect predators, there was a distinct tension within the Vatican. Some powerful Church officials showed a remarkably imprudent sympathy for accused priests, and an equally questionable desire to protect the Church from negative publicity—even at the risk of danger to children. These officials condoned the lax policies of many diocesan bishops; together they formed a protective web for priests accused of molesting children.

But even as some Vatican officials helped conceal the evidence of clerical misconduct, others pressed for strong disciplinary action. In case after case, the latter group was led by Cardinal Ratzinger. In 2001, when the exploding scandal in the United States had finally drawn attention to the high costs of concealment, Cardinal Ratzinger won a signal victory: he persuaded Pope John Paul II to adopt new policy guidelines requiring bishops to report all clerical abuse to the Congregation for the Doctrine of the Faith, which would now expedite disciplinary proceedings. Under Ratzinger's leadership the Congregation began removing abusive clerics from priestly ministry on a schedule completely atypical of the Vatican's usual leisurely pace; cases were resolved at the rate of roughly one a day. Still, Cardinal Ratzinger—who now saw the damage done by priestly abuse

quite vividly detailed in the dossiers that crossed his desk—was not satisfied. On Good Friday in 2005 he spoke passionately about the need to purge
the "filth" from the Catholic clergy.

Just one month after that outburst, Joseph Ratzinger was installed as
Pope Benedict XVI. It is no coincidence that within weeks the Vatican permanently suspended from priestly ministry two powerful clerics who had
used their influence to dodge abuse charges for years prior to Benedict's
election: Father Marcial Maciel, the founder of the Legion of Christ, and
Father Gino Burresi, whose reputation as a mystic had won him an enthusiastic worldwide following.

Benedict XVI has shown his determination to end the abuse scandal,
but the Pope cannot accomplish this mission alone. He will need the active
cooperation of the diocesan bishops, who are primarily responsible for the
conduct of their priests. To bring the discussion back to the American case,
he will need a zeal for reform within the U.S. hierarchy.

To influence society, the Catholic Church must speak with authority.
To speak with authority, the Church must have credible leadership. To
restore its credibility, the American hierarchy must do more than follow the
terms of the Dallas Charter. The protection of children is necessary but not
sufficient to inspire public confidence. The bishops must demonstrate a
willingness to speak out—not to protect their own status or to polish their
public image, but to tell the truth, rally the faithful, and spread the Gospel.

Had the American bishops used their authority in that way over the
years, the sex-abuse scandal would never have arisen. Sexual abuse by clerics, as I argue in this book, is a symptom of a deeper disease within the
Church. The failure of Church leaders to begin the necessary reforms is a
clear indication that the disease persists. The problem has not been
resolved; the crisis of the American Church continues.

THE GOOD
OF THE CHURCH

Governor James Michael Curley wanted a lottery. It was the spring of 1935, the Commonwealth of Massachusetts was facing a budget crunch, and Curley saw the lottery as a painless alternative to tax hikes. At the State House on Boston's historic Beacon Hill, most legislators agreed. Debate had been perfunctory. Support for the proposal was overwhelming; passage of the enabling legislation seemed assured.

Then on May 20, Cardinal William O'Connell weighed in. "I am opposed to a state lottery," announced the powerful head of the Boston archdiocese. A lottery would bring "out-and-out gambling" to Massachusetts, he said, and this would be "a tremendous source of corruption and demoralization."

Within twenty-four hours the lottery was dead.

On May 21 the House of Representatives—where majority support for the measure had previously been unquestioned—voted 187-40 against the legislation. Prior to the vote, one lawmaker after another took the rostrum to explain that when he had spoken earlier in favor of the lottery, he had not fully considered the implications. Governor Curley admitted that he could not withstand the political juggernaut and dropped his plan. The most prominent Boston politician who kept fighting for the initiative was tagged with the dismissive nickname "Sweepstakes" Kelly. The idea of a state lottery would not be taken seriously again in Massachusetts for nearly thirty-five years.

That display of Cardinal O'Connell's clout was dramatic, but not terribly unusual. The cardinal had single-handedly turned the political tide against child-labor restrictions that he saw as tinged with "Bolshevism." He later crushed a move to legalize the distribution of information about birth control. When politicians asked what "Number 1" thought of a proposal, they were referring not to the governor or the mayor, but to the cardinal.

In 1937, Curley was again the victim of the cardinal's influence. Running to regain his post as Mayor of Boston, he faced spirited opposition from Maurice Tobin. On election day, the Tobin forces placed a front-page ad in the *Boston Post*, quoting Cardinal O'Connell's lament: "The walls are raised against honest men in public life." The ad was framed to suggest that the cardinal was endorsing Tobin, and despite frantic last-minute protests from Curley's supporters, O'Connell did nothing to discourage that impression. Tobin rolled up a comfortable margin of victory.

The political power that Cardinal O'Connell enjoyed was not merely the product of his formidable personality. His stature reflected the public dominance of a robust community that, after generations as a scorned minority, had grown to become the single most important social influence in Boston. Soon Catholics would account for the majority of voters in Massachusetts.

Among those Catholics, about 80 percent attended Mass every week and heard the doctrine of the Church proclaimed in sermons regularly. Many attended parochial schools, where their attitudes toward the world were shaped by the Sisters of St. Joseph and other religious orders. When the Holy Name Society organized a parade, 10,000 men marched through the streets of downtown Boston. A growing number attended Catholic colleges; Boston College and Holy Cross were attracting some of the brightest young men from the families of Irish and Italian immigrants. Lay Catholics joined the Knights of Columbus, the Women's Sodality, and the Altar Guild. They met their future spouses at CYO dances and Newman Club social hours. They identified themselves readily as Catholics, and on religious matters they identified Cardinal O'Connell as their leader.

In 1948 Catholics became a majority in the lower house of the state legislature; in 1958 they captured the upper house as well. Moreover, Catholic social influence was still on the rise. When Cardinal O'Connell died in 1944, he left his successor with 323 parishes: ninety-eight more than O'Connell had inherited when he took the reins of the archdiocese in 1907. Boston's new Catholic leader, Archbishop (later Cardinal) Richard Cushing, quickly embarked on an even more aggressive building campaign, in Boston and out into the distant suburbs, throwing up new Catholic churches and rectories, new schools and hospitals.

The engine of Catholic growth was running smoothly. Catholic parents had large families and sent their children to parochial schools. From there, the religious orders attracted enough young women to supply teachers for the next generation, and the seminary drew enough young men to staff the parishes. When Cardinal Cushing announced that he hoped someday to ordain one hundred new priests for the Boston archdiocese in a single year—a level that no diocese in the world had ever reached—his ambition did not seem unrealistic. As the number of annual ordinations crept up through the '60s and '70s and into the '80s, it seemed to be only a matter of time before it broke into the three-figure category. By every available measure the Church was still rapidly growing, and Catholic influence in the Boston area was still increasing.

And now?

In 2006, the Catholic proportion of the population within the geographical area covered by the archdiocese dipped below 50 percent for the first time in since World War I. Among those Catholics about 35 percent now attend Mass in any given week; the number who attend *every* Sunday (as required by Church law) is much lower.

The Boston archdiocese has sharply contracted, giving back the gains of the past generation. There are 298 parishes in the archdiocese today: twenty-five *fewer* than Cardinal Cushing inherited in 1944. More than sixty parishes have been closed since 2002, as part of an unprecedented "reconfiguration" designed to ease a steadily mounting deficit in the archdiocesan budget. The palatial residence built for Cardinal O'Connell has been sold, along with the adjoining grounds. Twenty parish church buildings have already been sold, and a dozen more will soon go on the market. Still the deficit looms, and unless there is some unexpected reversal of current trends more parishes will be closed within the next decade.

There are more Catholics in Greater Boston (in absolute terms) than there were a generation ago. But the affluent young Catholics of the early twenty-first century have not been visiting their parishes often enough, or tossing enough money in the collection baskets, to pay the heating bills on churches that their working-class ancestors sacrificed to build.

Nor are they sending their sons to the seminary or their daughters to the convents. In 2006 just five men were ordained to the priesthood for the Boston archdiocese: one-twentieth of the figure that Cardinal Cushing had set as his goal. Even if every parish could pay its own bills, the archdiocese would necessarily not have enough priests to staff them. The corps of clergy is aging as well as shrinking. Elderly priests are being asked to postpone retirement; there are not enough younger priests to replace them. And this problem is quickly becoming acute; in 2004 there were 130 parishes with a pastor above the age of seventy.

Since most of them are not regularly *practicing* their faith, or *supporting* their faith, it would be unrealistic to expect today's Catholics to identify with the *teachings* of their faith—especially when those teachings clash with the norms of popular culture. (Younger priests have been cautioned by their seminary instructors to *avoid* preaching about doctrine, particularly controversial doctrine, and so perhaps many Catholics do not even *know* what the Church teaches.) Sure enough, Catholics divorce and remarry, obtain abortions and sterilizations, use birth control and *in vitro* fertilization techniques, all at rates indistinguishable from those of their non-Catholic neighbors.

In the mid-twentieth century Catholics had established their own distinct culture in Boston. That culture molded their attitudes toward social and political life, and since Catholics were a majority, their cultural influence thoroughly shaped the society in which they lived. Now somehow that Catholic culture has dissipated.

Although they are no longer an absolute majority, Catholic voters still command by far the largest religious bloc among voters in Massachusetts. Yet the state's Congressional delegation in Washington is rock-solid in support of legal abortion. Self-identified Catholics still constitute a majority of the politicians in both chambers of the state legislature. Yet in recent months the legislature has repeatedly passed bills that the Catholic bishops opposed—in more than one case, *without a single dissenting vote*.

The collapse of Catholic influence was most painfully evident in 2004, when Massachusetts became the only state in the Union to give homosexual partnerships the full legal status of marriages. To be sure, the decision in favor of same-sex marriage was made by the state's highest court, but it took effect only after a legislature dominated by self-described Catholics acquiesced in the decision.

What happened?

How did the Catholic faith, which had built up its public influence so steadily during the twentieth century, lose all that influence within the span of a generation? That is the question this book seeks to answer.

The most obvious answer is that the sex-abuse scandal that shook the Boston archdiocese in 2002 sapped the credibility of the Catholic hierarchy. The faithful, according to this explanation, would no longer follow the orders issued by bishops who had allowed their priests to prey on altar boys.

That theory seems compelling at first glance. There can be no doubt that the prestige of Catholicism has suffered enormously as a result of the scandal. But as an explanation of how the Church lost public influence, the theory fails in two respects. First, the decline in Catholic clout was underway long before the first shocking stories of sexual abuse hit the headlines. Second, the sex-abuse crisis hit several other cities before it struck Boston. If the scandal itself could cause a major shift in political alignments, we should have seen the same changes in other communities. But the "People's Republic of Massachusetts" is unique.

Clerical abuse was not a factor in the presidential election of 1972, when Massachusetts was the only state in the Union to cast its electoral votes for George McGovern, a candidate too liberal to suit the voters of the other forty-nine states. The scandal still had not touched public consciousness in 1986, when Massachusetts voters decisively rejected two proposed constitutional amendments: one that would have allowed restrictions on abortion and another that would have authorized public aid to parochial schools. Before the first stories on priestly pedophilia crept into the headlines, Massachusetts had already completed its transformation from a bastion of social conservatism to the most liberal state in the nation, with the Catholic community of Boston in the vanguard.

It has become commonplace to say that the sex-abuse scandal that has shaken the foundations of American Catholicism first erupted in Boston in 2002. That too is inaccurate. The first hints of an emerging scandal had been dropped more than fifteen years earlier, and other dioceses had already been hit by devastating lawsuits before the focus of national attention shifted to Boston.

In 1985 the US bishops received a confidential report on sexual abuse by clerics, warning them that there was "simply too much at stake for the Church" for the hierarchy to ignore the issue. It was 1998 when the Diocese of Lafayette, Louisiana, was ordered to pay an $18 million legal judgment brought on by the multiple molestations of the former priest Gilbert Gauthe. That same year a Texas jury ordered the Dallas diocese to pay over $100 million (later reduced to $31 million) to the victims of another former priest, Rudy Kos. Even in Massachusetts, the revelations about disgraced priests like John Geoghan and Paul Shanley in the Boston archdiocese had been preceded, nearly a full decade earlier, by the trial of James Porter, a defrocked priest who had molested dozens of children while serving in the adjacent Fall River diocese.

In 1985, the issue of sexual abuse by clerics was a prominent issue for U.S. bishops and Catholic prolates.

[handwritten annotation: 2002 was the watershed year for the cleric sexual abuse scandal. Boston was its focal point.]

Still it is true that 2002 was a watershed year. During that year American Catholics shuddered over one ugly revelation after another, as the breadth and the depth of the scandal became ever more devastatingly apparent. And as the tragedy unfolded that year, Boston occupied center stage.

In one sense it was almost happenstance that gave Boston this central role. A Massachusetts judge was the first to order the public release of Church records that had previously been confidential, thereby providing the public with undeniable evidence of priests' misconduct and bishops' complicity. When other dioceses were later exposed to the same scrutiny, the results were depressingly similar. After those first staggering disclosures in Boston, the revelations elsewhere sounded familiar, and therefore less shocking. But since the pattern of corruption that was first exposed in Boston has subsequently come to light in other cities, it is not unreasonable to fear that the collapse of a traditional Catholic culture, now so evident in Boston, may be coming soon to other American cities.

In Boston, too, the crisis took on added drama because a powerful prelate became the target of public outrage about the scandal; ultimately Cardinal Bernard Law resigned in disgrace. Although many other American bishops have subsequently been forced to step down because of revelations about their *own* behavior, to date Cardinal Law is the only one who has been ousted because of a failure to curb *other* clerics' misconduct.

Once the cardinal had resigned, and reporters at the *Boston Globe* had pocketed their Pulitzer Prize awards for the investigative series that led to his downfall, public interest in the scandal began to evaporate. The tawdry facts of the case were too painful; readers tired of the story, and wanted closure. Cardinal Law's resignation provided a convenient sort of punctuation, and the public gaze turned to other subjects.

The cardinal stepped down, and the headlines gradually stopped. So it would not be unnatural to conclude that this one man, Bernard Law, was the source of the problem. But that conclusion is wrong. In hastily accepting it, most observers have missed the opportunity to probe deeper into the real reasons for the tragedy that has shaken the Catholic Church.

Convenient though it may be to cast Cardinal Law as the leading villain in the nationwide drama of sexual abuse, that characterization is grossly unfair. The cardinal was steadfast in upholding Church teachings, and critics of those teachings were fond of depicting him as a stern, unyielding dogmatist, impervious to human feelings. But those of us who saw him at work in Boston—who knew about the countless late-night hours he devoted to visiting the sick, the hundreds of unexpected phone calls he made to comfort the bereaved, his willingness to let paperwork pile up on his desk while he helped a troubled soul work through a personal problem—could never recognize him as the callous tyrant depicted in so many headline stories.

Furthermore, if Cardinal Law had been unusually malicious, or uniquely incompetent in handling the crisis, then his behavior should have been markedly different from that of other American Catholic bishops. It was not. He did what other bishops had done, were doing, and would do. All those bishops who had shirked their responsibility were guilty, but Law's guilt was exposed first.

In fact, in retrospect the resignation of an influential cardinal is the only aspect of the story that makes Boston's role unique. The *dimensions* of the scandal in Boston are not especially remarkable; other dioceses have shown the same pattern of protecting predatory priests and ignoring the suffering of their victims. But the *response* to the crisis, in a region where the Church was already suffering from dwindling attendance at Mass and widespread indifference to Catholic teachings, makes Boston's experience a fascinating case study.

To understand the impact of the sex-abuse crisis, one must first understand the nature of the scandal—or rather, to be more accurate, of *three* scandals that emerged simultaneously. Yes, there are three scandals—closely intertwined, but easily distinguishable—that have combined to ravage American Catholicism at the dawn of the twenty-first century. For the sake of convenience we can conflate these three problems, making use of a single rubric, the "sex-abuse crisis," as I do throughout this book. But at the outset it is important to distinguish among them.

1. The first scandal is the sexual abuse of young people by Catholic priests. The depravity of the priests' behavior, the betrayal of a fundamental trust that had been placed in them, the corruption of innocence: all these factors made their crime repellent, and the public exposure of their hypocrisy understandably caused a nationwide sensation. Still, as difficult as it is to overstate the harm done by these priests, it is necessary to keep their crimes in some perspective.

Although the absolute *number* of priests engaged in this vile activity was shocking, the predators composed only a very small *percentage* of the priests serving in the US. Their sins, loathsome as they were, are still understandable. Anyone who accepts the Christian understanding of Original

Sin realizes that all of us are capable of the most degrading, vile transgressions. And while we expect priests to adhere to a higher code of ethical behavior, every Catholic moralist knows the principle *Corruptio optimi pessima est*: the corruption of the best is the worst of all. Furthermore, Church leaders have finally recognized the scandal of clerical abuse and taken aggressive action to remove predators from the priesthood. From all available indications, the sexual abuse of minors by Catholic priests is much less widespread today than it was ten or twenty years ago.

2. The second scandal is the prevalence of homosexuality among Catholic priests. When the first stories about clerical misconduct began to emerge, ordinary Catholics began asking questions about the sexual predilections of American priests, and they naively continued to ask those questions, no matter how frequently they were told—not quite accurately—that the issue under discussion was pedophilia rather than homosexuality. The answers to their persistent questions suggested that the number of Catholic priests with homosexual inclinations was far out of proportion to the number of homosexuals in society at large. Moreover, there was circumstantial evidence that homosexual priests formed an influential clique that actively discouraged priests from exposing their colleagues' peccadilloes. The existence of such a "lavender mafia" could help to explain why Church officials failed to discipline priests who molested children.

When leaders of the US bishops' conference traveled to Rome in April 2002 to discuss the crisis with top Vatican officials, they acknowledged the importance of grappling with the influence of homosexuality, especially in the seminaries, where the habits and attitudes of future priests are formed. But even before they left Rome, the American bishops were backing away from that recognition, retreating in the face of critics who would not countenance any criticism of homosexual priests. The question of homosexual influence soon was removed from the agenda of the American hierarchy, and in their later public statements the leaders of the US bishops' conference actually sought to *deny* what they had acknowledged during those talks in Rome, arguing, against all available evidence, that the sex-abuse crisis could *not* be attributed primarily to homosexual priests.

3. The third scandal is the abdication of authority—or worse, the complicity—of American bishops when they were confronted with the evidence of clerical abuse. The bishops could have, and should have, ensured that a priest who molested children or traduced adolescents would not have the opportunity to commit that crime again. Instead, as the dreary public

revelations of the last decade have shown, scores of American bishops chose to ignore complaints about abuse, to conceal the evidence that was brought to their attention, and to give predatory priests one opportunity after another.

The first aspect of the scandal, the sexual abuse of children, has been acknowledged and addressed. The second aspect, the rampant homosexuality among Catholic priests, has been acknowledged but *not* addressed, and later even denied. As a result the homosexual influence within the American clergy is even stronger today than it was before the sex-abuse scandal erupted. But the third aspect of the scandal has never even been acknowledged by American Church leaders.

While a small *minority* of American priests has been involved in sexual abuse, a clear *majority* of bishops was party to the cover-up. The priests who have been found guilty of sexual abuse have been removed from ministry, but the bishops who betrayed their own sacred trust by countenancing sexual abuse remain in office. Whereas the misconduct by priests has been acknowledged and addressed, the administrative malfeasance of American bishops has still not been acknowledged—at least not by the bishops themselves—and not remedied. For all those reasons the third scandal, the scandal of episcopal misconduct, is today the most serious of all.

When they gathered in Dallas in June of 2002 to devise a nationwide response to the sex-abuse scandal, the American bishops devoted their attention exclusively to the first of these three interrelated scandals. Efforts by a few isolated bishops to recognize the other important dimensions of the scandal—the influence of homosexuality and the negligence of bishops—were quickly rejected. Consequently the policies that the bishops established, promising prompt suspension of any priest credibly accused of molesting a child, did nothing to restore public trust in the hierarchy itself. Bishops who showed an icy insensitivity to the suffering of young victims and who lied repeatedly to conceal their own guilt remain in power today. Even those bishops who were themselves caught up in compromising sexual activity have been allowed to resign quietly, preserved from public criticism by their colleagues—or have even been allowed to remain in office despite clear evidence of personal wrongdoing.

In short the US bishops have responded to these crises by protecting each other. But *why* have they done so? Why has there been no move—not even by a reforming minority—to root out the corruption that has been so clearly exposed in the American hierarchy?

For that matter, when they first encountered the evidence that priests were abusing children and corrupting adolescents, why did so many bishops fail to take prompt and decisive action? What possible incentive did they have to cover up the evidence of such appalling crimes?

Certainly there is nothing in the teaching or traditional discipline of the Catholic Church to justify such a lackadaisical response to clerical abuse. Catholic morality is notoriously strict in regard to sexual sins. And very few passages in the Gospels are as strongly worded as the one in which Jesus condemns those who corrupt innocent youth: "It would be better for him if a great millstone were hung round his neck and he were thrown into the sea" (Luke 17:2).

For centuries Church leaders acted on that understanding. St. Basil, a fourth-century pioneer of monasticism in the Eastern Church, ruled that any monk who molested young men should be monitored for the rest of his life to ensure that he never had the opportunity to repeat his crimes. St. Peter Damien wrote in his *Book of Gomorra* (1096): "We conclude that just as the sacrilegious violator of a virgin is deposed by law, so the prostitutor of a spiritual son must be barred from his ecclesiastical office by every means possible." The *Code of Canon Law*, the Church's internal legislation, reflects the wisdom that the Church has accumulated through twenty centuries of observing human frailty; the Code sets out a procedure to be followed when priests were accused of sexual abuse and stipulates harsh penalties for those who are found guilty. But in practice the American bishops almost never invoked the provisions of canon law in recent years; they handled the priests' transgressions informally—even when the same priests were accused again and again.

In some ways it would seem easier to explain this remarkable failure of leaders by starting with the premise that the American bishops were moral monsters: that they had no interest at all in the welfare of young people or the teaching of the faith. But even that extreme hypothesis does not afford a satisfactory explanation. If a bishop were motivated by nothing but the basest sort of cynical self-interest, he would *still* have every incentive to remove a priest who threatened to molest children. That priest was likely to create problems; a purely selfish bishop would want to be rid of him.

So the question persists: Why did Church leaders ignore the clear message of the Gospel, the undeniable thrust of Catholic moral teaching, and the institutional wisdom that had been collected over 2,000 years and codified in Church law?

The few prelates who have bothered to explain their conduct have said that they thought were acting for the good of the Church. Now at first glance, that explanation is simply incredible. How could "the good of the Church" possibly be served by the exploitation of children, by betrayal and lies? The Catholic Church sees herself as the mystical Body of Christ; how could it be helpful to the body to ignore a cancerous growth within?

Clearly, any bishop who tolerated abusive priests, covering up the evidence of their crimes, was guided by a very strange, unhealthy understanding of his own pastoral responsibilities. These prelates were, at best, protecting the public *reputation* of Catholicism. But the engine of the Church runs on God's grace, not on public acclaim; the Church has been most vigorous at times when the faith was held in contempt and even openly persecuted. The Body of Christ does not need a clumsy public-relations campaign. As St. Augustine tersely put it, "God does not need my lie."

The effort to keep ugly secrets from public view would make more sense if the Church saw herself as a purely human institution, depending on public support for her strength. If some isolated scandal arose within a local branch of the Rotary Club, we might all agree to keep the matter quiet, to preserve the club's image. Rotarians are good people, after all, and their clubs do a great deal of good work within the communities. If they ever lost their reputation for these good works, the Rotary Clubs would be doomed, because they have no other source of strength.

Not so with the Catholic Church. Anyone who embraces the faith—or even understands Catholicism from an outsider's perspective—knows that the Church relies on Christ, and models herself after a Savior who died in ignominy. Faithful Catholics should never allow superficial concerns about public perception to trump an unmistakably clear moral imperative. Yet many American bishops did exactly that.

Nor were they alone in doing it. Scores of the priests who have now been convicted as molesters were known to the police years ago, but never formally charged with any crime. Police and prosecutors sloughed off their own responsibilities many times, accepting a bishop's promise that the offending cleric would be "taken care of" and agreeing to keep the case quiet. These law-enforcement officials evidently believed, as the bishops believed, that pressing charges would not be good for the Church; and since the Church was a pillar of the community, it followed that prosecution would not be good for the community.

How did public officials come to such an understanding? They learned it, I will argue, from their pastors, and ultimately from their bishops. For more than a generation, the American hierarchy has done its best to convey the impression that the Church is a noble civic institution—that the demands of Catholicism will *never* clash with the claims of a democratic government. (You might say that this argument is the ecclesiastical equivalent of Charles Wilson's belief that "what was good for our country was good for General Motors, and vice versa.") When Church-state conflicts did arise, many Catholic leaders were quite willing to sacrifice the claims of their faith in order to minimize the conflict and preserve their privileged status as community leaders.

Yet again, the most conspicuous examples of this attitude have been shown in Massachusetts. In the 1950s, an Archbishop of Boston discouraged a priest from his energetic public preaching of a defined Catholic dogma because some people found that dogma offensive. A decade later the same archbishop—now a cardinal—announced that Catholic legislators should feel free to vote in favor of legislation that violated the precepts of the Church. In 1974 his successor encouraged Catholic parents not to send their children to parochial schools. And in 1993 yet another Boston archbishop instructed the faithful that they should not pray outside abortion clinics. In each of these remarkable cases, the Archbishop of Boston obviously thought that he was serving the cause of community peace. But just as obviously, he was yielding ground, and encouraging the Catholic faithful to yield as well.

And to what end? Today the bill for the sex-abuse scandals has come due, and the Church is paying a frightful cost—in public stature as well as in cash—for the bishops' pastoral failures. With their efforts to preserve the Church from criticism, they succeeded only in bringing down much greater obloquy upon the Church. If Church leaders had acted decisively and forthrightly to discipline the priests who molested young people, and to remedy the defects in clerical discipline that had allowed this sort of aberrant behavior, the faithful might have been shocked, but at least the public revulsion would have been directed where it belonged: at the erring individuals. Instead, by becoming silent partners in the scandal, the bishops have jeopardized the credibility of the Catholic faith itself.

The bishops made a fool's bargain. They were prepared to sacrifice the essential elements of the Catholic faith: the moral teaching, the clerical discipline, even the loving care for the faithful. In return, they hoped to prop up the prestige of the institutional Church. But whatever prestige the Church enjoys is based on public respect for those essential elements of religious faith. When the disgraceful stories eventually hit the headlines, the bishops could no longer fall back on the conventional respect they had once taken for granted. They were willing to sacrifice their apostolic mission to preserve their prestige; in the end they were left with *neither* mission *nor* prestige.

Critics of Catholicism, seeing this disaster as evidence to support their own views, have often observed that the bishops erred by devoting their attention to the institutional Church rather than the needs of the faithful. That explanation is misleading because it assumes that the Catholic *faith* can somehow be separated from the Catholic *Church*. It cannot.

The Catholic Church *is* an institution. To draw a distinction between an abstract body called "the Church" and the individual persons who hold the faith is to deny a fundamental tenet of the faith passed down from the apostles: that the Catholic community forms a single body, united across time and space. Like any other organization comprised of human beings, the Church has concrete needs: for buildings in which to worship and administrative structures to organize activities and resolve conflicts. The buildings and the bureaucracies may come and go; the man-made structures may change with time. Yet these structures belong to the Christian community—which is to say, they belong to all believers.

Has the leadership of the Catholic Church served the interests of that community of believers? Of course there could be as many different answers to that question as there are different ways to define the interests of the Christian faithful. Someone who disagrees with Church teaching on one or more key points might believe that the faithful would best be served by a change in doctrine. Or to take a more extreme case, a zealous Protestant who sees the Vatican as the Whore of Babylon would presumably argue that Catholics would all be better off it they simply left the Church. These might be reasonable arguments, which should be addressed reasonably: but not here. This book is not primarily a work of apologetics, and I do not directly address the arguments of those who reject Catholicism, in whole or in part, on theological or ideological grounds. My goal, instead, is to help the reader understand the interests of the faithful from an orthodox Catholic perspective. Whether or not he accepts the Catholic faith, a fair-minded observer should see the logic of judging the Church by the standards she has set for herself, in authoritative statements like the *Catechism of the Catholic Church*.

Christianity is an incarnational religion: a faith that teaches that the birth of Jesus Christ did not abolish human nature, but raised it to a new dignity. Some religions disdain the body; they see the concrete world as an illusive trap, ensnaring souls that should be liberated to enjoy some sort of disembodied bliss. Not so the Catholic Church, which has always insisted that the spiritual world cannot be neatly severed from the physical world and has always venerated those who, like Mother Teresa of Calcutta, devote themselves to serving the material needs of others. The spiritual mission of the Church is inextricably linked to her worldly mission.

Still it is only natural to make some common-sense distinctions between the sacramental life of the Church and the pedestrian work of the bureaucracy—between the missionary who preaches the Gospel and the diocesan clerk who handles the paperwork. Every believing Catholic supports the life of prayer, but the routine work of the ecclesiastical bureaucracy is not easy to love.

In everyday English usage, Catholics make this distinction—often without noticing it—by referring to the Church as "she" or as "it." "She" is the spotless Bride of Christ; "it" is the administrative machinery. "She" is the community of believers at prayer. "It" is the jumbled collection of buildings and budgets. "She" is a living body of faith. "It" is a deadening bureaucracy. For most practical purposes this distinction may be useful (and attentive readers will notice that I use it throughout this book), but it must be handled with care.

Consider, for example, my own relationship with my wife. I am very happily married. Leila is my best friend, the love of my life, my soul-mate, and my spouse. She also does the cooking. Each year I claim her as a dependent on my income-tax return. The woman who serves dinner is not different from the woman I married; the woman who affords me a tax exemption is the same one who bore our children. There is only one person here, playing different roles; there is no distinction to be made. But if I were to begin thinking of my wife *primarily* as a cook and a tax deduction, our marriage would quickly be in trouble.

So too with the Catholic Church. The "institutional Church" that critics disdain cannot be neatly separated from some idealized, disembodied community. There is only one Church, indivisible. But it would be foolish to pretend that the Church does not have different facets: different faces that she shows to the world. Some aspects of life in the Church have transcendent purpose and infinite value. Others are merely necessities and undeniably mundane; they have meaning only insofar as they serve the transcendent purpose. If Church leaders concentrate on the mundane to the exclusion of the transcendent, the faith will suffer.

In Boston, the faith has suffered.

The thesis of this book is that the sex-abuse scandal in American Catholicism was not only aggravated but actually *caused* by the willingness of Church leaders to sacrifice the essential for the inessential: to build up the human institution even to the detriment of the divine mandate. I argue that in Boston, Catholic culture lost first its integrity and then its power because Church leaders made the same fatal mistake, offering their first fealty to the church that is "it" rather than the Church that is "she." If my thesis is correct—if American Catholicism has been corrupted because Church leaders were pursuing the wrong goals—then it should not be surprising that the results have been most disastrous in the Boston archdiocese, where Church leaders had been most successful in pursuing those goals.

In 2002, when the sex-abuse scandal was in the headlines daily, Senator Rick Santorum, a Republican from Pennsylvania, made an interesting observation about the turmoil in Massachusetts. "When a culture is sick, every element in it becomes infected," the conservative lawmaker said. "While it is no excuse for this scandal, it is no surprise that Boston—a seat of academic, political, and cultural liberalism in America—lies at the center of the storm."

Santorum's effort to draw a causal link between liberal attitudes and sexual abuse drew howls of outrage from his ideological rivals. (The outrage arose nearly three years after the publication of the column in which Santorum made that statement, but the tardiness of the response—obviously timed to damage the senator's re-election campaign—is irrelevant to our purposes here.) They pointed out, quite accurately, that sex-abuse scandals have been exposed in many more conservative communities, so that liberalism cannot be the cause.

Still Senator Santorum was more than half right. Liberalism did not *cause* sexual abuse. But at least in Massachusetts, the triumph of political liberalism in the late twentieth century was not unrelated to the emergence of the sex-abuse scandal early in the twenty-first. Both trends were symptoms of the same underlying cause: a corruption that began when Church leaders betrayed their primary responsibilities.

What has happened in Boston can happen elsewhere. Throughout this book I will offer comparisons between the situation in Massachusetts today and the situation that other Catholic communities are facing, or may face in the near future. In Dallas, in Philadelphia, and in Los Angeles (to name only a few cities), the full dimensions of the sex-abuse scandal have not yet been explored, and the results could ultimately be as catastrophic as they have been in Boston already.

And what has happened to the Catholic Church can happen to other religious denominations. This book should serve as a cautionary tale. Any conservative Christian body, fighting to preserve the integrity of the Gospel message against the advance of secularization, should be wary of the same dangers. The faith will always face resistance, and Church leaders will always be tempted to tailor their messages to suit the latest fashions. But when the quest for public affirmation takes precedence over the demand for integrity to the apostolic tradition, the results are predictable. The church that caters to public opinion may enjoy a short burst of superficial success, but in the long run it will lose both integrity *and* popularity.

The harshest critics of the Church might say that the steady erosion of Catholic influence in Boston was caused not by strategic errors on the part of Church leaders, but by the inadequacy of their message. Enlightened believers (they might say) threw off the shackles of Roman authority to embrace a more modern approach. But it is only fair to point out that not even the most vociferous anti-Catholic bigots ever envisioned the sex-abuse scandal; no one suggested that the disintegration of Catholic authority would occur in this spectacular fashion; so no one should claim that the debacle has vindicated his theory.

No doubt there are many people rejoicing at the demise of Catholic influence, in Boston and elsewhere. Many people would argue that the Catholics of the early twenty-first century have come to a new maturity, adopting a more modern approach to the faith. But that argument, too, begs the question. If the model of Catholicism that prevailed in the mid-twentieth century is no longer valid, what is the best model for public Catholicism today?

If the Church should have *any* public influence, what should that influence be? To say that the Church should accept the norms of secular society on the most hotly contested issues of our day—such as abortion and contraception, divorce and same-sex marriage, sterilization and *in vitro* fertilization, stem-cell research and assisted suicide—is to say that Catholicism should have no public influence at all. Even those anti-Catholic bigots who embrace that view, if they are honest, should admit that their recent advances in these political debates have come not when they defeated the Catholic opposition in intellectual combat, but when their rivals left the field without a fight.

Again, in recent decades the rout of Catholic social thought has been most complete in Greater Boston. In the space of my lifetime, from 1950 to the present, Catholic influence in public life has plummeted, from a position of seemingly absolute dominance to one of near-universal contempt.

No, the collapse of Catholicism in Boston did not *begin* with the sex-abuse crisis of 2002. That crisis itself was the manifestation of corruption that had begun long, long ago. The corruption was evident decades ago, when Cardinal O'Connell—the same powerful prelate who could scuttle a popular legislative initiative with a single statement—learned that a prominent priest was engaged in gross sexual misconduct. The cardinal chose to leave that priest in office, and cover up the evidence of his transgressions. No doubt he told himself that he was acting "for the good of the Church."

PART I

THE CATHOLIC CENTURY

1

THE IRISH
CONQUEST

In the "city upon a hill" envisioned by Boston's founders, there was no room for Catholics.

Before setting sail from England in 1630, the Puritan settlers who would establish the Massachusetts Bay colony had already agreed upon their mission, which they saw in distinctly religious terms. John Winthrop—who had already been elected leader of the group, and would be the first governor of Massachusetts—explained that mission in a famous speech, delivered before boarding the *Arbella* for the trip to the New World. It was a short speech—not quite 550 words—that began and ended with citations from Scripture. In the memorable central portion, Winthrop underlined the religious significance of the colonists' effort:

> For wee must Consider that wee shall be as a Citty upon a Hill, the eies of all people are upon us; soe that if wee shall deale falsely with our god in this worke wee have undertaken and soe cause him to withdrawe his present help from us, wee shall be made a story and a byword through the world, wee shall open the mouthes of enemies to speake evill of the wayes of god and all professours for Gods sake; we shall shame the faces of many of gods worthy servants, and cause theire prayers to be turned into Cursses upon us till wee be consumed out of the good land where wee are going.

More than three centuries later, President Ronald Reagan cited Winthrop's speech in his own farewell address. But Reagan altered the original text a bit. He inserted an adjective, making it "a *shining* city upon a hill." More significantly, he used Winthrop's phrase to inspire his own somewhat different vision of the ideal American community. The outgoing president explained:

I've spoken of the shining city all my political life, but I don't know if I ever quite communicated what I saw when I said it. But in my mind it was a tall proud city built on rocks stronger than oceans, wind-swept, God-blessed, and teeming with people of all kinds living in harmony and peace, a city with free ports that hummed with commerce and creativity, and if there had to be city walls, the walls had doors and the doors were open to anyone with the will and the heart to get here.

There are strong similarities between these two visions; Reagan rightly considered himself an heir to the Puritan founders' legacy. But there are differences, too. Both men saw the prospects for a glorious, prosperous future. On the one hand, Reagan envisioned the prosperity that flowed from the society's open, confident, welcoming attitude; his was a city of builders and entrepreneurs. Winthrop, on the other hand, sought to inspire his followers by reminding them of the fearful costs of failure; his was a community of stern moral reformers. Rather than depicting a "shining" city, Winthrop thought it more important to remind his people that they had enemies.

And who were those enemies? To put it simply, they were Catholics.

The original Massachusetts colonists had left England to escape the influence of an established church that they regarded as thoroughly corrupt. They were dubbed Puritans because of their desire to "purify" the Church of England, eliminating even the slightest hint of popish influence.

Notice, now, that the Puritans were campaigning against the lingering traces of Catholicism. Decades of brutal persecution—first under Henry VIII, then under Elizabeth I—had eliminated the Roman Church from English public life during the sixteenth century; the country's few remaining faithful Catholics had been driven underground. For the Puritans that was not enough. They still saw reflections of Roman ritual in Anglican church services, and heard the echoes of the Catholic liturgy in the Book of Common Prayer. They were determined to erase any vestigial belief in the sacraments, any deference to an ecclesiastical hierarchy.

For decades the Puritans and their Nonconformist allies had fought in a tense struggle for control of England's churches. Now, recognizing that they had lost that battle, they were setting sail for a new country where they could establish a religious community in line with their own ideals. When he spoke of the enemies who would laugh in triumph if the Massachusetts Bay colony collapsed, John Winthrop was undoubtedly referring to leaders of the Church of England. But those English ecclesiastical leaders had become the

Puritans' enemies only because they had not made the definitive break away from the Catholic tradition. The Church of England was corrupt, but the ultimate source of that corruption (as the Puritans saw it) was Rome.

Once they were settled in the New World, safely beyond the reach of their English rivals, the Puritans could shift their priorities to face the greater threat. The leaders of the Church of England were now thousands of miles away, and the Pope in Rome was only a bit further. Particularly mindful of the growing Catholic influence in neighboring Quebec, where French Jesuit missionaries were setting out to convert the Indian tribes, the founders of the Massachusetts colony now concentrated on the papist threat. In 1647 the colony passed legislation barring the presence of any "Jesuit or ecclesiasticall pson ordained by ye authoritie of the pope."

Catholic priests were not only loathed by the colonists, but dreaded, because the Puritans were convinced that the Roman Church was a tool of the devil, enjoying access to dark supernatural powers. The grim faith of the colonists, with its emphasis on the sinfulness of man, left plenty of room for fear of the unknown and charges of diabolical activity—as events in Salem (a seaside community north of Boston) proved in 1692. But even before the infamous Salem witch trials, Goody Glover was hanged on Boston Common, convicted of witchcraft primarily because she was discovered to be a Roman Catholic.

Born and raised in Ireland, Goodwife Ann Glover and her husband were captured by Oliver Cromwell during his Irish campaign of 1649-1650 and sold into slavery in Barbados. After her husband's death there, Ann Glover made her way to Boston, where she worked as a maid. Described by a contemporary as "a despised, crazy, poor old woman," she was charged with witchcraft when the children of her employers fell ill.

Questioned closely by the Reverend Cotton Mather, the rector of Boston's Old North Church, Goody Glover denied that she was a witch, but admitted that she was a Catholic. Mather reported that the illiterate woman could recite the Lord's Prayer in Latin: clear evidence, he thought, that she was possessed. As she went to the gallows on November 16, 1688, Ann Glover once again identified herself as a Catholic. Witnesses to the execution saw her profession of faith as further evidence that she was indeed a witch. How could anyone who was *not* in league with Satan face death without repenting an alliance with the sinister powers of Rome?

The fierce anti-Catholicism of Cotton Mather endured for generations in Massachusetts, exercising a particularly strong hold on the intelligentsia.

Boston soon developed its reputation as a center for American academic life, and since higher learning was tightly connected with religious affairs—Harvard, for example, was established as a training-ground for the Puritan clergy—the schools did their best to inoculate young students against the evil snares of popery.

Thus in 1750 the chief justice of the Massachusetts colony, Paul Dudley, endowed a series of annual lectures at Harvard, to cover four religious topics. One of the lectures, Dudley stipulated, should be devoted to "the detecting and convicting and exposing of the idolatry of the Roman Church, their tyranny, usurpations, damnable heresies, fatal errors, abominable superstitions, and other crying wickednesses in their high places; and finally, [to show] that the Church of Rome is that mystical Babylon, that woman of sin, that apostate Church spoken of in the New Testament." (The Dudleian lectures continue to this day, although the explicitly anti-Catholic topic has been dropped.)

Church and state were inseparable in the earliest days of the colony, and Congregationalism was the official faith of Massachusetts until 1833. Even then, the impulse to do away with an established church came not from Catholics but from dissidents within the Puritan tradition, who were breaking away from the Congregationalists to set up their own Unitarian churches.

Catholicism, meanwhile, remained unknown and unwelcome in Massachusetts through the eighteenth century. Before the successive floods of Irish immigrants that washed ashore in the 1800s, the few Catholics who lived in the region were primarily of French-Canadian stock. When the Vatican finally established the Boston diocese in 1808, the first bishop, Jean-Louis Cheverus, was a French prelate, who would eventually return to his native land to become the cardinal-archbishop of Bordeaux.

Today, nearly two centuries after the diocese was erected, Boston is (at least in terms of ethnicity) one of America's most heavily Catholic population centers. But for several decades after the American Revolution, Boston trailed behind many other cities in establishing a clear Catholic identity. Maryland had welcomed Catholics during the colonial era, and the Baltimore diocese—the first in the United States—was erected in 1789, nineteen years before Boston. (To keep things in perspective, the Quebec City diocese was set up more than 130 years earlier, in 1674; and the Mexico City diocese was established in 1530, a full century before the *Arbella* crossed the Atlantic.) By the time the Church in Boston had grown enough to deserve the title of *arch*diocese in 1875, the Vatican had already accorded that designation to Baltimore, New York, St. Louis, New Orleans, and San Francisco.

The Irish potato famines changed the face of Boston forever. In 1800 the city's entire population was not quite 25,000; by 1900 the figure was over a half-million. The new arrivals were not all Irish, but the Celtic invasion was overwhelming. As early as the 1820s, the crowded ships were bringing 2,000 Irish immigrants to Boston every year. That figure soared during the 1830s to 1850s, and again in the 1870s and 1880s, at the peak of the successive Irish famines. In the year 1847 alone, the figures show over 37,000 new Irish-born residents settling in Boston, constituting one-third of the city's population at that time.

As a group these Irish immigrants were poor, ill nourished, and ill educated. They crowded into squalid tenement houses where disease spread quickly, where drunkenness and violence became commonplace. They clogged the city's waterfronts and strained the resources of hospitals and charitable agencies.

Boston's established gentry, the descendants of the Puritans, typically saw their new Irish-Catholic neighbors as a threat to public safety. The city's less affluent residents viewed the Celtic invasion with alarm for a different reason: Irish workers were now competing for their jobs. These social and economic factors mixed with the older Puritan theological hostility to create a virulent new form of anti-Catholicism.

The most famous manifestation of those powerful anti-Catholic sentiments came on August 11, 1834, when an Ursuline convent in Charlestown was burned to the ground by an angry mob. The incident illustrated the remarkable power of anti-Catholics prejudice among the people of Boston at that time.

The Ursuline convent had been established in conjunction with a school for girls, which enrolled some young ladies from Boston's leading non-Catholic families. In 1832 one young student, an Episcopalian girl named Rebecca Reed, announced her plan to embrace Catholicism and entered the convent. She left a few months later, complaining of the prison-like atmosphere in the institution, and wrote a sensational account of her experience that circulated briskly in Boston, reinvigorating old fears of sinister Catholic conspiracies. Late in July 1834 the flames were fanned by rumors that a nun had tried unsuccessfully to escape from the convent and was being held there against her will. Although Charlestown officials toured the convent at the mother superior's invitation and assured the public that all the nuns were living there voluntarily, the rumors still persisted.

At this tense point a prominent Presbyterian preacher, the Reverend Lyman Beecher (the father of Harriet Beecher Stowe, author of *Uncle Tom's Cabin*) appeared in Boston to deliver a series of fiery sermons condemning the growing Catholic influence in Boston. The next night an angry crowd formed outside the convent in Charlestown and began burning barrels of tar. The fire brigade was summoned, but the firemen joined the crowd of spectators, declining to intervene; the police never intervened. At their leisure the rioters broke down the doors, frightened away the nuns and their students, and torched the building.

The principal organizers of the arson attack were identified and eventually brought to trial, but despite evidence which one ringleader described as "sufficient to have convicted twenty men," they were acquitted by a jury of their (non-Catholic) peers, to the loud applause of courtroom spectators. Boston's Mayor Theodore Lyman acknowledged that public officials had failed to protect the Ursuline nuns and recommended that the Commonwealth of Massachusetts compensate the Church for the loss of the convent; that proposal was brought up repeatedly in the state legislature, and repeatedly defeated.

The Catholic population of the Boston area was growing at a prodigious rate during the early- and mid-1800s, but Catholic political power lagged far behind. In fact, the Know-Nothing movement, a nativist reaction against Catholic immigration, enjoyed its most spectacular successes in Massachusetts. In the elections of 1854, the Know-Nothings swept to victories in every available statewide office, every federal Congressional seat, and all but a handful of spots in the state legislature. During their brief stay in power, the Know-Nothings disbanded Irish militia companies and enacted a draconian ban on any form of public aid for private schools—a ban that remains on the statute books even today.

But demography is destiny, and Know-Nothings could not remain in political power when a Catholic majority gained the right to vote. As soon as the new immigrants had an opportunity to participate in the political process, they seized it, and the sheer size of the Irish immigrant population made the grosser forms of anti-Catholicism unsustainable.

While Irish immigrants were not the only Catholics in the Boston area, it is difficult to exaggerate the extent of Irish influence in the Church that was growing from a little frontier diocese into a leading center of

American Catholic influence. Boston's official Catholic newspaper was founded in 1829 under the aegis of Bishop Benedict Fenwick and was originally named *The Jesuit* in a nod to Bishop Fenwick's religious order. But within a decade it had been turned over to lay ownership, guided by Patrick Donahue, an enthusiastic supporter of the Irish nationalist Daniel O'Connell; the paper was renamed *The Pilot*, after the Dublin-based journal that circulated among O'Connell's followers. The Boston *Pilot* appealed to an Irish-immigrant readership throughout the United States; its popular "Information Wanted" advertisements helped Irish families to track down relatives who had disappeared in the post-famine diaspora. For decades the paper's readership was more national than local, and (if such a distinction could possibly be made) more Irish than Catholic. With a circulation that reached the astonishing level of 50,000 in the 1850s, the *Pilot* helped to cement Boston's reputation as an Irish-Catholic Mecca in Massachusetts.

Still the leaders of the old Protestant establishment, the scions of Puritan forbears, had not given up the struggle for primacy in Boston society. Gradually losing their grip on political power—especially in urban areas—they clung to their control over banks and businesses, the arts, and especially the schools.

Horace Mann, a Massachusetts resident, led the drive to establish public schools throughout the United States, motivated in no small part by the desire to ensure that the newly arrived Catholic immigrants would receive proper instruction in the civic virtues of the Protestant establishment. In Boston, as late as the early 1900s, the public schools still adhered to the dour religious outlook of the Puritans, and Catholic students were thrashed for skipping classes on Christmas Day.

Young people today, hearing about the era when books and plays were "banned in Boston," might be tempted to think that the censors were zealous Catholics; they would be quite wrong. The New England Society for the Suppression of Vice was founded in 1870 by staunch Protestants who feared that the burgeoning immigrant (that is, Catholic) population was detracting from the moral tone of the community. Later known as the Watch & Ward Society, the group reached the zenith of its power in the 1920s, under the direction of a man whose very name testified to the enduring power of the old establishment: Godfrey Lowell Cabot.

Members of Boston's social elite looked upon their Irish-Catholic neighbors as uneducated louts, prone to intemperance and violence. Many Irish Bostonians in turn saw the "Yankees" as censorious prigs. The Boston Brahmins were Anglophiles; the Irish immigrants came to America with ancient memories of British injustice, and saw their new rivals as a natural extension of their English oppressors. The constant sparring between these two groups—the Irish against the Yankees, the Catholics against the Protestants, the new immigrants against the old establishment—was an important factor (perhaps *the* important factor) in Boston's political and social life for the better part of a century.

When Catholics were a small minority, Church leaders discouraged any challenge against the Protestant establishment. Bishop John Fitzpatrick, who guided the Catholic community through the perils of the Know-Nothing era, urged Catholic immigrants to act like respectful guests in someone else's home, winning the respect of their adversaries by their irreproachable public conduct; the bishop himself reportedly discouraged the idea of raising the Boston see to the dignity of an archdiocese, fearing that the move could be seen as a challenge to Protestant hegemony.

Boston's first archbishop, John Williams, took the same conciliatory approach. He did not want to be named to the College of Cardinals; the city's leaders, he felt, were not yet prepared to accept a Prince of the Catholic Church. When he built the cathedral of the Holy Cross on Washington Street, a main thoroughfare in Boston's busy South End, he accepted—reluctantly, but with quiet dignity—the city's decision to build an elevated train line running directly in front of the cathedral's façade, so that for more than a century, until the "subway" system was finally re-routed underground, cathedral services were disturbed every few minutes by the clatter and shriek of the passing trains. More remarkable still, Archbishop Williams did not favor opening parochial schools; he encouraged the faithful to content themselves with the public-school system.

This deferential approach won the admiration of Boston's social establishment. Both Bishop Fitzpatrick and Archbishop Williams were awarded honorary Harvard degrees: the definitive stamp of Yankee approval. Irish and Italian Catholics began graduating from college and entering the professions. They gained acceptance, ordinarily, as long as they did not challenge the accepted social order. But while prominent, educated Catholics could now gain full respectability, their less fortunate followers still had to fight and scratch for economic opportunities. Employers still posted job openings with the initials "INNA" to signal that "Irish need not apply." And if the truth be told, even the most respectable Catholics never penetrated the top layers of city's social elite. Boston Brahmins still controlled the exclusive clubs and commanded the first pages of newspapers' society columns.

There was one field, however, in which the Catholic immigrants quickly ascended to the very top positions: politics. Irish Catholics, in Boston as elsewhere in America, showed a natural gift for political organizing. Irish politicians relished campaigning, and if they fought bitterly among themselves, they came together to support "their" candidate in any contest against a non-Irish opponent. Irish-Catholic politicians began capturing spots on Boston's city council and urban seats in the state legislature. In 1885, Hugh O'Brien became the city's first Catholic mayor.

"Politics, as a practice, whatever its professions, had always been the systematic organization of hatreds," wrote one of Boston's most perceptive social commentators in his autobiographical *Education of Henry Adams*, "and Massachusetts politics had been as harsh as the climate." The political contest was harsh because the stakes were so high. Not only did the Catholics and Protestants (mostly Democrats and Republicans, respectively) loathe each other, but the defenders of Boston's Puritan tradition were convinced that if the Irish immigrants came to power, they would use their public posts to serve their own private purposes—handing out civil-service posts to families and friends, steering building contracts to their political allies, driving the government toward bankruptcy with their profligate public spending.

Those fears were not unreasonable. Along with their zest for political combat, Irish politicians had brought a new style of government to America. The Democratic-party machinery that they set up in cities like Boston was based on patronage and personal favors. Ward bosses found jobs for breadwinners, intervened with the police when youngsters ran afoul of the law, mediated neighborhood quarrels—and expected payback on Election Day. Anyone who won public office was *expected* to use his influence on behalf of his friends, and the winners did not apologize for taking the spoils.

In fact the *failure* to help one's friends was seen as a sign of inconstancy—an indication that the man was not really fit for political leadership. Writing in 1985, Thomas O'Connor, a popular historian of Boston, told the story of a South Boston housewife who was told that a particular candidate was so honest that he would never use his office to enrich his own family. "Well, if the son of a bitch won't help his own sister," the woman remarked, "why should I vote for him?"

Old Yankee politicians, who regarded public service as a sacred trust, viewed this attitude with alarm and contempt. But the old Yankees were in a minority by the early 1900s, and the new Irish machinery was rolling to victory. In 1910 a populist named John F. Fitzgerald (the grandfather of the future President John F. Kennedy) became Boston's mayor. The flamboyant campaign style of "Honey Fitz," who often punctuated political rallies by singing "Sweet Adeline," charmed his Irish supporters and terrified his Yankee opponents.

But the guardians of Boston's old political establishment should not have wasted much time worrying about Honey Fitz, because a far more formidable enemy was already on the horizon: James Michael Curley.

Curley embodied all those traits that Republicans feared and despised in their bold new Democratic rivals. Curley was an unabashedly divisive figure, who styled himself as a sort of Irish tribal chieftain; he showed an absolute delight in outraging the Boston Brahmins and only a minimal interest in satisfying the needs of other ethnic groups. A gifted speaker, he frequently used his rhetorical powers to hector and bully his opponents. There was an air of potential violence about his early public campaigns; John L. Sullivan, the world's bare-knuckle heavyweight boxing champion, was a regular companion.

Curley made no bones about the fact that he rewarded his allies and punished his enemies. Nor was he scrupulous about his methods. After an initial term in the state legislature he won election to the Boston city council while serving a prison term for civil-service fraud. He never apologized for the offense that brought his conviction (he had signed another man's name on a civil-service exam); he proudly explained: "I did it for a friend."

Curley was elected Mayor of Boston in 1914, again in 1922, yet again in 1930, and one last time in 1945. He served four terms in the US House of Representatives, and one as Governor of Massachusetts. He governed as he campaigned: pleasing his friends, enraging his foes, polarizing the community. Angry opponents labeled him a rascal, and pointed out (quite accurately) that the home he bought across from scenic Jamaica Pond was obviously beyond the means of a man living only on the mayor's salary. Loving supporters replied that he was *their* rascal and lined up outside that home to meet with the great man and ask for favors.

James Michael Curley did not represent the Catholic Church. He made scores of enemies during his long public career, and dozens of them were at least as Irish and as Catholic as he was. The city's Catholic spiritual leader, Cardinal O'Connell, was definitely not a friend. And not even his most ardent admirers—and he has many, even today, a half-century after his death—could think of Curley as a likely candidate for beatification.

Still Curley's ascent to political power marked a watershed point for Catholics in Boston's public life, because no other public figure could have been more thoroughly unacceptable to the city's old guard. When he first ran for mayor, Curley launched a deliberate frontal assault on the old Yankee establishment. If he could win, flouting the standards of polite Protestant society, then Catholics need no longer worry about acting like polite guests in a Puritan community. Once in the past, the Puritans had run Boston, and community leaders could safely ignore the likes and dislikes of the city's few other residents. Now Curley set out to prove that his Irish-Catholic cohort ran Boston, and the old guard had no choice but to accept their new inferior status.

When Curley *did* win, the existing civic order was overthrown, and a new order indeed took its place. Since 1930, every mayor of Boston has been a baptized Catholic. One hundred years after the Diocese of Boston was erected, the city's Catholics had defeated the Boston establishment. More than that: Catholics had *become* Boston's political establishment.

2

UNDER NEW
MANAGEMENT

Bishop John Fitzpatrick did not want to be named an archbishop, and Archbishop John Williams did not want to be a cardinal. But William O'Connell, who took over the leadership of the Boston archdiocese in August 1907, suffered from no such reticence. Young, openly ambitious, and certainly not shy about confrontation, Archbishop O'Connell was a prelate nicely matched to the new assertive mood of Boston's growing Catholic community.

Militant and Triumphant: that is the title that James O'Toole, a local historian and sometime archivist for the Boston archdiocese, gave to his biography of O'Connell. That title neatly captures the spirit of the long (thirty-seven-year) reign during which this remarkable churchman, whose energy was surpassed only by his bulletproof self-confidence, became the unquestioned leader of Boston's Catholic community, and therefore the most powerful man in Massachusetts.

The story of how O'Connell *became* Archbishop of Boston is an important part of the overall tale. Born into a respectable working-class family in Lowell, a mill town north of Boston, he entered the seminary, left, and completed a bachelor's degree at Boston College before entering the seminary again, this time to stay. His academic work was distinguished enough to qualify him for further education in Rome, and there he began cultivating the Vatican contacts that would sustain him throughout his ecclesiastical career.

A decade after his ordination, Father O'Connell was a priest with a promising future. Talented and hard-working, with the clerical polish that comes from Roman training, he was clearly marked for advancement. Still it was a shock when, in November 1895, he was named rector of the Amer-

33

ican College in Rome: the institution where he had been a student just a few years earlier.

When the opening was announced, O'Connell had not been regarded as a likely candidate for the job in Rome. Different American prelates had their own favored candidates, and he was not one of them. But while the other contenders lobbied American bishops, the brash Bostonian called on his friends in Rome.

At the time the US hierarchy was torn by the "Americanist" controversy: a heated dispute that arose when some US clerics advanced the claim that the worldwide Church should adopt the democratic outlook of their country. (Pope Leo XIII would condemn the excesses of Americanism in his encyclical *Testem Benevolentiae* of 1899. In one of history's little ironies, the papal document denying that America has a privileged moral status was formally promulgated on January 22: a date that holds a grim meaning for active Catholic Americans today.) The Vatican was keenly aware of the potential for trouble if the American College—the conduit through which the most talented young priests in the country would pass—fell under the control of a rector who would encourage an attitude of independence from the Holy See. O'Connell made it unmistakably clear that he would align himself firmly with Rome. In effect he became the Vatican's candidate for the post at the American College, and when the American bishops had trouble choosing between their favorites, O'Connell won the contest.

Five years later Bishop James Augustine Healy of Portland, Maine, died. Once again O'Connell was not considered a leading candidate to succeed him. Once again the rivalries between US prelates, exacerbated by the charges of "Americanism," prevented the emergence of a single consensus candidate. But now Monsignor O'Connell was stationed in Rome, where he could press his own case more effectively. In 1901 he became Bishop of Portland.

Another few years passed, and another opportunity arose. Boston's Archbishop Williams was aging, his health was slipping, and the Vatican was looking for a coadjutor who could share the burden of leadership while being groomed to succeed Williams. By now his rivals in Boston were keenly aware that the aggressive young bishop in Maine would be angling for the job. But they were unable to stop him.

During his last two years in Portland, Bishop O'Connell spent more time in Rome, or on special assignments for the Vatican, than in Maine. He made good use of his friendship with Cardinal Rafael Merry del Val, who was now the powerful Vatican Secretary of State under Pope Pius X. He stressed his unswerving allegiance to the Holy See. And sure enough, despite heavy opposition within the ranks of the Boston clergy, and a distinct lack of enthusiasm on the part of Archbishop Williams, he was named coadjutor in February 1906. When Williams died the following August, O'Connell became Archbishop of Boston at the age of forty-seven.

Five years later there was one last successful campaign. Again making no effort to conceal his ambition, the archbishop sought appointment to the College of Cardinals. In 1911 he won his red hat. Since an American campaign for the papacy was unthinkable, at the age of just fifty-two he had climbed as high as he could go. Now the city's first cardinal —entitled to be addressed as "Your Eminence"—applied his enormous energy to the task of consolidating his pre-eminent position in Boston.

By any of the normal statistical indices he was successful. From the time of O'Connell's arrival in 1907 until his death in 1944, the number of priests serving in the Boston archdiocese leapt from 600 to 1,500; the number of nuns, from 1,500 to 4,500. The number of parishes in the archdiocese went from 225 to 323, and the student population at Catholic high schools soared from 792 to 10,567. His successor, Cardinal Richard Cushing, is popularly known as the great builder of the Boston archdiocese, but really Cardinal O'Connell deserves that title.

Immigration rates having slowed, the Catholic population of Boston now increased at a modest rate: from about 800,000 to somewhat over one million during the O'Connell era. But the *institutions* of the Church were growing at a dizzying pace, and it was the institutions to which the cardinal devoted his attention.

Cardinal O'Connell took great pride in his ability as an administrator. Under his leadership, he insisted (with an implicit slap at his predecessor) that the Boston archdiocese be well managed. Decisions were made smoothly and policies were implemented promptly—always, of course, with the cardinal himself calling the shots.

Pastors were expected to run their parishes the way the cardinal ran the archdiocese: efficiently, decisively, avoiding all friction. Pastors who handled these responsibilities well were accorded a great deal of autonomy; they could make their own decisions about parish finances, programs, and personnel, provided that they did not violate the general policies of the archdiocese. If a conflict arose between a priest and a parishioner, the archdiocese invariably sided with the pastor. So the system arose in which complaints from the laity were funneled first through the pastors, with priests protecting each other against any "interference" that came from outside the clerical ranks.

For years this system worked quite well. Parishes were built, schools were opened, religious orders and charitable agencies were founded and grew; tens of thousands of Catholics were baptized, educated, married, and buried each year. But there was a price to be paid for all this efficiency. Many Catholics came to rely on the system itself—to think of the Church as a series of effective programs rather than a conduit of God's grace.

The very efficiency of the O'Connell system made it possible for an unreflective Catholic to go through life without any real sense that the Church is, by her nature, a missionary organization. The ordinary lay Catholic would contribute to the missions, certainly, but he might not have any sense that he *himself* was called to be a missionary, to spread the Gospel in his everyday life.

At worst, the Catholics of the mid-twentieth century could come to think of the faith as an entitlement. That attitude was especially tempting to clerics, who could begin to think of "our" Church—"our" parish, "our" diocese—in much the same way that their cousins in the political world looked upon government institutions as their own possessions rather than as a sacred trust.

In politics that attitude leads to abuse of power; in religious affairs the tendency toward abuse is compounded. A religious minister speaks and acts in God's name, and a Catholic priest in particular is understood to administer the sacraments *in persona Christi:* acting as Jesus Christ. When a cleric falls into the error of thinking that he is acting on his *own* authority, he ceases to act like a minister and becomes instead an ecclesiastical bureaucrat.

Unfortunately the sort of system run by Cardinal O'Connell (and most other Catholic Church leaders) is slow to recognize and correct that grave error. It is no simple matter to measure the strength of a priest's interior life: to quantify the power of his prayer. It is relatively easy, however, to know whether a pastor is implementing diocesan programs on schedule. The system cannot discern how many souls the priest is saving, but it can account for the size of the weekly collections. So skillful administrators are rewarded and move up through the ranks, gaining more power and encouraging younger priests to imitate their efficiency.

In her book *The Long Loneliness,* the great Catholic lay activist Dorothy Day referred to this phenomenon as the "scandal of businesslike priests." It is no scandal, surely, if priests aspire to run their parishes well. But it *is* a scandal if that is their highest aspiration. Despite the spectacular growth of Catholicism in Boston during the O'Connell era, that scandal was beginning to emerge; the corruption of the clergy had already begun.

Years later, the writer Paul Wilkes spent several months following the life of a Boston priest for his book *Mysterious Ways.* In the course of his research Wilkes visited St. John's seminary, where Boston's priests are trained. The rector, Father Thomas J. Daly, explained that young men hear talks about celibacy, about living alone, about how to find psychological help when they need it. "But above all," Father Daly said, "they must be professional. That's very important; we must have professional men."

Those are frightening words, which illustrate a serious misunderstanding about the nature of the priesthood. That they were spoken by the rector of the seminary—the man most directly responsible for the intellectual and spiritual formation of Boston's priests—makes them all the more shocking.

A priest is not a professional, like a doctor or lawyer, who can take off weekend and vacation time and look forward to eventual retirement. Once ordained, a priest is a priest forever; he may rest, but he cannot stop being a priest. The priesthood is a *vocation,* not a profession: a calling from God, not just a line of work. And to say that a priest should be professional "above all" is to denigrate the importance of his prayer, his sacrifice, his striving to identify with Jesus Christ.

A businesslike priest, a professional priest, can run a parish. He can administer the sacraments, and with proper training he can explain the teachings of the Church. But can he set souls on fire? He will be respected as a representative of the Catholic faith. But can he give people a taste for the ineffable mystery that lies at the root of that faith?

At about the same time that Father Daly made that astonishing statement about "professional" priests, a future Pope was telling enthusiastic lay Catholics in Italy that the Church should never settle for a system that conveys the Church's moral teachings, but fails to spark spiritual excitement. Then-Cardinal Joseph Ratzinger, speaking to a crowd of 10,000 people at a rally in Rimini, Italy, said:

> In the Church today, it seems to me that we are experiencing the temptation—undoubtedly understandable in human terms—to be understood

even where there is no faith.... Everybody more or less can see that there is a need for the moral dimension, and so they offer up the Church as a guarantee of morality, as an institution of morality, and they do not have the courage to present the mystery.

The mystery of the faith, the mystical personal encounter with the God, is terribly difficult to explain to an unbeliever. But without it Christianity appears to the outsider—and worse, sometimes to the believer himself—as a series of propositions to be accepted and rules to be obeyed.

The system of pastoral management that Cardinal O'Connell developed had an answer for every question and a response for every argument. The cardinal encouraged the faithful to trust their pastors and their parochial schools. Once they had been properly instructed, he assured them, Catholics would have no cause for reticence. They need no longer feel inferior to their Yankee neighbors; they should be able to demonstrate the superiority of their faith with the certainty of a Euclidean proof.

In his biography of O'Connell, James O'Toole captures the essence of the cardinal's approach:

> As bearer of this militant message, O'Connell reminded Catholics that they need no longer be apologetic for their religion. They had a duty to assert themselves.... Supremely self-confident, O'Connell never doubted that there was a clearly identifiable Catholic position on everything or that he himself could and should state that position with "manly firmness."

He had all the right arguments; he had all the right policies; he had all the right programs. There is no irony intended here; Catholicism really was flourishing in Boston, and Cardinal O'Connell commanded tremendous respect even among non-Catholics. But like every successful administrator, the cardinal was tempted to take his administrative process more seriously than his fundamental mission—in his case (as the old Christian adage puts it) to be so busy with the work of the Lord that he could forget the Lord of the work.

Cardinal O'Connell succumbed to that temptation in at least one important case. That he yielded to temptation proves only that he was human. But the particular circumstances of O'Connell's failure are eerily familiar to anyone who has witnessed the scandal that enveloped the Boston archdiocese two generations later. Then as now, the problem began with a priest's sexual misconduct, but the damage was compounded by a prelate's choice to protect the miscreant and cover up the evidence.

William O'Connell had a nephew, James O'Connell, who followed him into the priesthood. The cardinal made his priest-nephew the chancellor of the archdiocese, giving him effective control over all the material assets of the church in Boston. That appointment was a fairly blatant display of nepotism, but by itself it did not threaten the integrity of the hierarchy in Boston. What followed did.

In his book *Militant and Triumphant*, O'Toole provides a detailed explanation of how the scandal unfolded. Father James O'Connell shared his uncle's residence, and he and a friend, Father David Toomey, enjoyed throwing lavish parties there. Their boisterous conduct raised eyebrows among the Boston clergy, but Cardinal O'Connell ignored the warning signs.

In 1912, Father James O'Connell struck up an acquaintance with a married woman from New York, Frankie Johnson Wort, and a romance began. She left her husband, traveled to South Dakota for a quickie divorce, and on her return trip she stopped in Indiana for a civil marriage ceremony in April 1913, in which she was united to a man who identified himself as James Roe, but was in fact Father James O'Connell. The couple bought a fashionable townhouse in New York, where Mr. Roe embarked on a moderately successful career in real-estate investment—subsidized, apparently, by funds he embezzled from the Boston archdiocese.

For several years thereafter, Father James O'Connell continued to serve as a priest and chancellor in the Boston archdiocese, while spending enough time in New York to pass as a married man with a normal professional career. It is not clear exactly when Cardinal O'Connell learned about his nephew's double life, but since he was so proud of his management skills, he must have realized fairly quickly that something was amiss, when his right-hand man was missing two or three days every week.

Meanwhile the younger O'Connell's friend, Father Toomey, was leading a very active double life of his own. In 1912 his dalliance with a young woman prompted a breach-of-promise lawsuit, which was settled quietly. In 1914 he met another woman, Florence Marlow, and lured her into a romantic alliance, claiming to be a layman with no religious affiliation at all. Showing his complete disdain for the sacraments of the Church, Toomey was re-baptized and married fraudulently, using a false name, and he too settled down to live in New York with his young lady.

Toomey, however, was not as discreet as James O'Connell, nor had he been prudent enough to inform his wife about his imposture. Curious about her husband's frequent trips to Boston, Florence Marlow followed him there in 1918, and caught him not only acting as a priest but also courting yet another woman. Outraged by the deception, she confronted Cardinal O'Connell and told him everything—about David Toomey and about his friend "James Roe."

By 1918, then, if not earlier, Cardinal O'Connell certainly knew that his nephew was masquerading as a married man. But he took no disciplinary action.

Rumors about James O'Connell's misconduct had swept through the Boston archdiocese and found their way to Rome. The Pope's representative in Washington hired a private detective who corroborated the charges. A prosecutor in Boston buttonholed the cardinal and warned him that criminal charges might be filed. Still he did nothing.

Why did Cardinal O'Connell fail to take disciplinary action against a priest who was blatantly violating his vows, almost certainly stealing from the archdiocese, and now causing a distinct threat of public scandal?

In a sworn deposition Florence Marlow said that the cardinal had told her he would not take action against his nephew "for the sake of his mother and father." But that explanation is inadequate; James O'Connell could have been removed from his post quietly—as indeed he was, many months later.

David Toomey (who by now had been discharged from the priesthood) claimed in 1919 that James O'Connell had been able to blackmail his uncle, because he had "proofs of the cardinal's sexual affection for men." That theory does offer a possible explanation for the cardinal's forbearance, which otherwise seems inexplicable. It would also underline the extent to which this scandal was a harbinger of things to come. But Toomey, who thought so little of his priestly and marital vows, is not a credible witness, and he offered no hard evidence to support his claim.

Still the cardinal's behavior does require some cogent explanation. Why did he protect his philandering nephew? The canon law of the Church—not to mention ordinary moral sense—called for action. Even the crudest considerations of his own self-interest should have prodded him to discipline James O'Connell, so that the young man's disgrace would not damage his uncle's reputation. Yet the cardinal continued to stall. Apparently there was something he found more frightening than gross immorality, more frightening than being exposed for sheltering a crooked priest.

Was James O'Connell threatening to expose some other festering scandal? Was the young chancellor—who had access to all the funds of the archdiocese—holding some financial leverage? Or was the cardinal so thoroughly captivated by the beauty of his own administrative machinery that he did not recognize the threat? We do not know the answer.

Finally, in May 1920, Cardinal O'Connell met with Pope Benedict XV, who told him that James O'Connell/Roe must be removed. By now nearly seven years had passed since his nephew began living as a married man; two years since an outraged woman had informed him of the alliance; one year since a private eye and a public prosecutor had confirmed the details. But *still* the cardinal delayed. It was only in November 1920, six months after his meeting with the Pope, that O'Connell finally approved a "leave of absence" for his nephew, and Father James O'Connell quietly disappeared from the scene.

The episode severely damaged Cardinal O'Connell's standing in Rome, and probably destroyed any chance he might have had of earning an appointment to a post in the Roman Curia. But he survived and continued to lead the Boston archdiocese for almost twenty-five more years.

Before, during, and after this unpleasantness, William O'Connell always carried himself with the dignity and aplomb befitting his role as a Prince of the Church. He may have been chastened, but he managed to avoid public disclosure of the scandal. He continued to live in his accustomed regal style: entertaining no questions about his authority, enjoying all the perquisites of his office.

Cardinal O'Connell was widely respected but not loved. His grand style provoked resentment; his penchant for ocean cruises earned him the sobriquet "Gangplank Bill." (One of his priest-secretaries, later to be an auxiliary bishop of Boston, was given the nickname "Splash Me" Minihan, because he allegedly heard that poolside order so often from his boss.)

Some of the priests who worked closely with the cardinal nourished the deepest resentments about his high-handed manners. Young curates assigned to the archbishop's residence seethed about the way he would order them to perform menial tasks, such as taking his dog for a walk. On April 22, 1944, when Cardinal O'Connell died in his bed, his household was thrown into disorder. Many hours passed before someone realized that the dog had not yet been taken out that day, and a conscientious young priest was given the assignment. He searched all through the house, to no avail. The dog was never found.

3

GOOD
NEIGHBORS

In 1944, the year Cardinal O'Connell died, America's top-grossing film was *Going My Way*. The next year it was *Bells of St. Mary's*. The image of Bing Crosby as a suave young Catholic parish priest was charming American audiences. Hollywood was in love with Catholicism.

In the years immediately after World War II, American popular culture embraced religious faith in general. A gentle support for faith was evident in the illustrations of Norman Rockwell, in radio dramas, and later in television comedies. Ordinarily the religion depicted in these warm portraits of American life was a vaguely defined non-denominational Christianity. But Catholics constituted the largest single religious group in the country now, and their faith was the most readily identifiable. The nuns in their habits, the Latin liturgy, the stained glass, the statues, the incense and candles all combined to provide the rich sort of setting that film producers appreciated.

Hollywood was on comfortable terms with Christianity in general and Catholicism in particular. Bible-based epics like *Ben Hur* played to enormous, appreciative audiences, while more specifically Catholic films like *The Song of Bernadette* encouraged popular devotions. Alfred Hitchcock flourished as a Catholic filmmaker, while Frank Capra directed a series of films extolling the Christian virtues.

Hollywood respected the influence of the Church, too. Producers may have chafed under the restrictions imposed by the Legion of Decency, and film stars may not have followed those standards in their own private lives, but the movie industry dared not defy the conventions. Studio executives were prudent businessmen who recognized the influence that the Church wielded over American culture.

Nor were films the only sign of Catholic cultural influence. Bishop Fulton Sheen emerged as a commanding presence on the radio, drawing an audience of up to four million for his show, *The Catholic Hour*. (Later, in the early days of television, then-Archbishop Sheen would become almost a cult figure, with thirty million viewers for *Life is Worth Living*.) A generation earlier another Catholic priest, Father Charles Coughlin, had won enormous audiences with his fiery speeches on social and political issues. Bishop Sheen took an entirely different approach, captivating his audience with his suave manner and his sound pastoral advice. He was a preacher, not a populist.

Bishop Sheen was also noted for bringing scores of converts into the Catholic Church, including prominent personalities like the columnist Heywood Broun, the industrialist Henry Ford II, the actress Loretta Young, and the violin virtuoso Fritz Kreisler. By presenting Catholic arguments clearly, to an audience no longer frightened by myths of papist perfidy, he was winning hearts and minds, and inspiring many other clerics to do the same.

A century or even a generation earlier, such conversions to Catholicism might have scandalized mainstream Protestants. But in this postwar era, Catholics themselves were entering the American cultural mainstream. They thought of themselves as ordinary Americans, and usually their neighbors felt the same way. The cruder forms of anti-Catholic bigotry were no longer socially acceptable. Non-Catholics generally had at least a rudimentary understanding of what their Catholic neighbors believed, and even if they did not share those beliefs they treated them with friendly respect. It was a time when a Catholic priest, wearing his Roman collar into a restaurant, might be reminded by a thoughtful Protestant waitress that it was Friday, and surely he didn't *really* want to order a meat dish.

Catholics throughout the country had established a strong, clear identity, and naturally that identity was strongest in the regions were the Catholic congregation was heavily concentrated, and the faithful had their own parochial schools, colleges, and social clubs. In Boston the gravitational tug of Catholic institutions was so strong that priests joked they were officiating at a "mixed marriage" when an Irish Catholic married an Italian or German Catholic. City dwellers, when asked where they lived, were likely to name a parish rather than a neighborhood: Holy Name rather than Roslindale; St. Brendan's rather than Dorchester.

The Catholic population was growing apace once again—not because of immigration now, but because the soldiers returning to civilian life after world War II were settling down and starting families. Large Catholic families were the norm during the years of the Baby Boom; a household with six or seven children was no cause for comment. These children were soon crowding into the parochial schools, which would have been overwhelmed if they had not been amply staffed with nuns. By the early 1960s there were close to 6,000 nuns in the Boston archdiocese, most of them working in the Catholic schools.

To lead the Church in Boston during this era, when the world seemed to be at peace with American Catholicism, the Holy See chose a priest who was at peace with the world. Archbishop Richard Cushing, a gregarious native of South Boston, was a clerical populist. The contrasts between the new archbishop and his predecessor, in personality and pastoral style, were remarkable.

Cardinal O'Connell had studied and worked in Rome and had carefully nurtured his contacts with Vatican officials. Archbishop Cushing had never spent any substantial length of time in the Eternal City. (He had been a very promising seminary student, an obvious candidate for study at the North American College in Rome. But his student years had come during World War I, when German U-boats were threatening trans-Atlantic shipping, and Cardinal O'Connell had judged it safer to keep his young charges at home.) He never developed close contacts at the Vatican—not even after his elevation to the College of Cardinals. He never even mastered Latin, and he came home early from the Second Vatican Council, frustrated by his inability to follow the debates.

O'Connell had exploited his contacts in Rome to win unexpected appointments, first in Portland and then in Boston. Cushing, however, was the leading candidate to be named the new Archbishop in 1944, since he was the single auxiliary bishop in Boston, yet the Vatican waited six months to make the appointment. O'Connell had been named a cardinal just four years after becoming Archbishop of Boston; Cushing waited fourteen years to receive his red hat. Like so many of his Irish Catholic contemporaries in the fields of business and politics, medicine and law, Richard Cushing was a local boy who had made good, earning his own promotions without outside help.

Where O'Connell had been a remote, authoritarian figure, who cultivated an image of polished *Romanitas*, Cushing was an affable man with an informal style, who was perfectly at home mugging for the cameras and munching peanuts at a baseball game. O'Connor had sought to enlighten American Catholics by exposing them to the more sophisticated thinking of Rome. Cushing felt that Rome could learn a great deal from the practical wisdom of Americans.

The notion that the Church should learn from the American experi-ence was not a new one; the same idea had led to the debates over the "Americanist heresy" in the late nineteenth century. But now that the US had emerged as a superpower, the same attitude (if not the full-blown ideas that had drawn Vatican condemnation) became more widely accepted. Americans were the leaders of the free world, teaching other countries—especially the countries of shattered Europe—the virtues of democratic plu-ralism. Why shouldn't the Vatican absorb the same lessons? American Catholics had learned to thrive in a non-Catholic environment; why could-n't the Church do the same?

In the Boston area the environment *was* largely Catholic. Neverthe-less some successful Catholic scholars and executives were beginning to think that the old Catholic attitudes were too narrow, too insulated, to give full scope to their new ambitions. Among these aggressive young Catholic laymen, by far the most prominent and powerful was a man who would become a close associate of the new archbishop: Joseph Kennedy.

A man of consuming ambition, Joe Kennedy displayed a curiously mixed attitude toward his own cultural and religious background. He was fiercely proud of his Irish-Catholic heritage, but scornful of the drudges who remained mired in the Irish ghettoes of Dorchester and South Boston. He complained bitterly that prejudice against Irish Catholics had limited his political prospects, yet he himself was openly disdainful of old-school Irish-Catholic politicians, including his father-in-law, former Boston Mayor John "Honey Fitz" Fitzgerald.

Kennedy did not let Church teachings inhibit him in his professional or private life; he was a ruthless businessman and a noted philanderer. But he maintained a sparkling image as an active Catholic layman, and cultivated friendships with leading Church officials. He had won influence with Presi-dent Franklin Roosevelt by opening a channel of communication with the Vatican Secretary of State, Cardinal Eugenio Pacelli, the future Pope Pius XII, and successfully reining in the fiery radio preacher, Father Coughlin. Now he assiduously groomed his ties with the new Archbishop of Boston.

In 1946, Kennedy donated $640,000 to the archdiocese for the con-struction of a hospital named for his eldest son, Joseph Jr., who had died in World War II. Not coincidentally, the hospital was to be located in the dis-trict where another son, John F. Kennedy, was running for his first term as a US Congressman. At the time, Kennedy's gift was the largest single dona-tion the Boston archdiocese had ever received. There would be more gifts to come in future years, as the Kennedys burnished their reputation as Boston's leading Catholic family.

John F. Kennedy's political career had a profound effect on Catholicism in America: an effect that is analyzed in some detail in the next chapter of this book. For present purposes it is enough to note that Archbishop Cushing had formed an important and highly visible public alliance with a layman who was conspicuously Catholic but not at all religious.

Joe Kennedy, like many successful Catholics of his generation, saw the Catholic Church as a public institution and as the object of his personal loyalty; he kept those two spheres, public and private, strictly separate. He never disputed the teachings of the Church, but if he ever saw the Church as an authoritative body—as the repository of truth about the human condition and the ultimate arbiter of moral law—he left no evidence of those sentiments. He was unabashed about exploiting Church influence for political purposes, but he would never use his own considerable influence to further the public interests of the Catholic faith.

From the perspective of non-Catholics, and especially anti-Catholics, this attitude toward the public role of the Church was quite welcome. Catholics like the Kennedys might profess some unusual beliefs and cling to some odd traditions and practices, but as long as they did not seek to impose their views on the wider community, who could object? So it was that in post-war Boston, the most prominent members of the Catholic community struck an effective truce with the public enemies of the faith.

Archbishop Cushing, again, had entered into a comfortable alliance with Joe Kennedy. He may not have fully approved of the latter's compartmentalization of the faith, but he did not denounce it. Unlike his predecessor, Cushing was not anxious to do philosophical battle with the surrounding society. Quite on the contrary, he quickly grew impatient with any discussion of deep philosophical and theological questions.

Hearty and outgoing by nature, Archbishop Cushing found it easy to like his fellow men, and be liked by them in turn. He generally thought the best of his neighbors, and assumed that men of good will would agree on important matters. Long before Vatican II propelled Catholics into the world of ecumenical affairs, Cushing was a practical believer in inter-faith dialogue. At a time when eyebrows were raised if a Catholic married outside the faith, the archbishop's beloved sister Dolly had married a Jewish man, Dick Pearlstein. Cushing became close friends with the Pearlstein family and played down the importance of their religious differences. In his sole major address during the deliberations of Vatican II, then-Cardinal Cushing gave an emotional defense of a draft statement on religious freedom, demanding that the Catholic Church profess her respect for all faiths and endorse freedom for all religions.

It is not surprising, then, that the most important conflict of the Cushing era was the clash between the archbishop and a priest who preached that there can be no salvation outside the Catholic Church.

Father Leonard Feeney was a gifted preacher, a popular poet, and a prolific author. The Oxford-educated Jesuit made a particular impression on a group of earnest young Catholics who had founded a new institution in Harvard Square called the St. Benedict Center. In 1944, the leaders of the Center asked the newly installed Archbishop Cushing whether he could arrange for Father Feeney's appointment as their chaplain, and the archbishop—who had been equally impressed by the Jesuit priest and his admirers at Harvard—was happy to oblige.

At first the partnership seemed ideal. The St. Benedict Center became a beehive of activity. Father Feeney's regular lectures regularly drew overflow crowds. Scores of Harvard students began to take a keen interest in the Catholic Church. Dozens of Catholics contemplated a vocation to the priesthood or religious life; dozens of non-Catholics asked to be baptized.

In fact, the parade of converts became a source of consternation for Harvard administrators. Avery Dulles, the son of Secretary of State John Foster Dulles, had caused a mild shock among the Yankee patricians who still ruled Harvard when he entered the Catholic Church in 1940. (Dulles eventually became a Jesuit priest and an acclaimed theologian; in 2001 he was elevated to the College of Cardinals.) The zealous Father Feeney drew the attention of several other Harvard students from families of the same elite social standing. A crisis arose with the conversion of Temple Morgan: a descendant of John Jacob Astor and relative of J. Pierpont Morgan, whose grandfather had donated the ornate gate that forms the principal entry to Harvard Yard. Archbishop Cushing was invited to dinner at Lowell House—then the preferred residence for Harvard's social elite—where concerned deans told him their misgivings about the intense sectarian activity at the St. Benedict Center.

To be fair, the intensity was unmistakable. Many of the students who congregated at the St. Benedict Center were veterans returning from World War II. Having witnessed the horrors of war and survived the face-to-face encounters with death, they were unusually earnest in their pursuit of answers to ultimate questions about the meaning of life. The answers given by Harvard faculty members often struck them as facile and superficial; they were much more satisfied with the answers provided by Father Feeney and the Catholic tradition to which he introduced them. As time passed they became contemptuous of what they saw as the breezy relativism that prevailed on campus, and they dug deeper into the solid foundation of Thomistic and Augustinian thought. They grew more and more convinced that the Catholic Church held the ultimate truth, while institutions like Harvard were avoiding it.

These ardent young Catholics experienced their own crisis in 1945, with the atomic bombing of Hiroshima and Nagasaki. The members of the St. Benedict Center saw these bombings, with their massive and deliberate destruction of innocent civilian life, as morally unjustifiable. They waited expectantly for some booming condemnation of this heinous act, from Church leaders if from no one else. Catherine Goddard Clarke, a former Wellesley College faculty member and founder of the St. Benedict Center, relates that when "no strong voice arose," the members of the tight-knit group in Harvard Square agreed that "someone had to tell the truth before it was too late."

For Father Feeney's followers, the mandate to "tell the truth before it was too late" entailed opening an offensive on two fronts. First, they condemned philosophical relativism as morally dangerous, and began to treat Harvard, where that relativism prevailed, as a hostile power. Students associated with the St. Benedict Center began to withdraw from Harvard—sometimes without having consulted their parents, and in a few cases abandoning their studies just a few weeks before they would have received their degrees. This radical behavior quite naturally redoubled the concerns of Harvard's administration.

At the same time that they denounced relativism, the Center's members questioned why Church leaders were not issuing similar denunciations—why the Catholic hierarchy appeared to be preserving its neutrality during a great moral battle. They concluded that the Church's leaders had made too many concessions to the spirit of the age and grown too timid in proclaiming that the Church alone holds the ultimate truth. Ultimately they narrowed their focus to a single doctrine which, they observed, Catholic leaders were no longer willing to proclaim: the dogma that there is no salvation outside the Church.

Extra Ecclesiam nulla salus: That became the battle-cry of the St. Benedict Center and the banner that Father Feeney carried into battle with his ecclesiastical superiors. That doctrine was, and is, a clear and authoritative teaching of the Church, although the interpretation that Father Feeney gave to that doctrine is far more stringent than what other Catholic theologians would accept. For years Feeney asked officials of the Boston archdiocese and the New England Jesuit province to affirm that doctrine; for years they ignored his pleas. Setting aside the question that he considered crucial, they told him that the real issue was whether or not he would obey legitimate Church authority.

As the passionate zeal of the St. Benedict Center became disruptive, the Boston archdiocese stepped in to douse the flames—without directly answering the challenge that Father Feeney and his followers had raised. First the archdiocese issued a directive that students must not be encouraged to withdraw from Harvard. Then in 1948, his Jesuit provincial instructed Father Feeney to report for a new assignment at Holy Cross College in Worcester. When Feeney questioned the transfer, his provincial, Father John McEleney, told him that the decision had come down from "higher authorities." Although he declined to be more specific, McEleney was clearly referring to Archbishop Cushing, to whom he had appealed for advice on "this delicate matter."

Despite his vow of obedience, Father Feeney refused to accept the new assignment, saying that to do so would appear to vindicate the charges that he was teaching something contrary to Catholic doctrine. As a consequence of his disobedience he was suspended from priestly ministry. He was told that the suspension was punishment for his "grave offense against the laws of the Catholic Church." But Archbishop Cushing promptly confused the issue, and confirmed Feeney's fears, by telling reporters that the Jesuit priest had been disciplined for "teaching ideas leading to bigotry."

Father Feeney was now locked into an unhappy position from which there was no easy exit. His superiors said that he must agree to obey their orders before they would agree to discuss his doctrinal concerns; he insisted that he could not accept their orders until they, by addressing his doctrinal concerns, proved that they represented the legitimate authority of Catholic tradition.

The battle escalated, and in light of the tolerant attitude that Church leaders would adopt toward dissident theologians of the next generation, it is remarkable to see the ferocity with which the Boston archdiocese pressed its offensive. Father Feeney was expelled from the Jesuit order. His poetry disappeared from the pages of Catholic publications, and all reference to him in the *Catholic Almanac* was removed. The St. Benedict Center was placed under interdict. Professors who were actively associated with the Center were fired from their posts at local Catholic colleges. The Feeneyites were reviled and condemned. In an astonishing display of pettiness, when a member of the little group died, the Boston archdiocese not only refused to allow a Catholic funeral Mass, but even urged the Catholic director of a funeral home not to make arrangements for the burial. Finally, in February 1949, Father Feeney was excommunicated from the Catholic Church.

The official cause for Feeney's excommunication was "grave disobedience of Church authority." But the public perception of the case was quite different. Especially when he and his followers began preaching on Boston Common, excoriating the enemies of Catholicism, he became identified as a renegade who had gone far beyond the confines of Catholic orthodoxy. He was perceived, as he had feared he would be, as a heretic— ironically, because he would not cease proclaiming a defined dogma of the Catholic Church. The message that he carried into the public square was seen as utterly unacceptable; *Life* magazine referred to him as "America's hate priest."

In 1974 an elderly Father Feeney was finally reconciled with the Church. His followers of the St. Benedict Center, now living in rural Still River, Massachusetts, were also reconciled. But the "Feeneyites" were never required to retract their public statements on their favorite dogmatic issue: *extra Ecclesiam nulla salus*. When he was welcomed back into the Catholic Church, Father Feeney was asked to recite any accepted formulation of Catholic faith. He chose the Athanasian Creed, which begins: "Whosoever will be saved, before all things it is necessary that he hold the Catholic faith." His followers were assured, as they swore their fealty to the Church, that they could continue to proclaim that doctrine, in the stringent form that Father Feeney had taught it. The end of the Feeney conflict confirmed the judgment of the great Catholic apologist Frank Sheed, who had observed many years earlier that Father Feeney had been "condemned but not answered."

Father Feeney's reconciliation came only after Cardinal Cushing's death in 1970. The intervening years had seen a cataclysmic change in the Catholic Church, brought on by the changes of Vatican II, and an ironic reversal in Cushing's role. Once seen as a populist within the Church, in his later years Cardinal Cushing came to be perceived as an authoritarian figure, resisting the rebellion of the 1960s. Having devoted so much of his energy to the cause of religious freedom, he was appalled and outraged in March 1966 when, as he spoke to an audience of Boston pastors about the message of Vatican II, the meeting was picketed by angry students from his own archdiocesan seminary, who demanded the liberties that, they insisted, Vatican II had promised.

In his earlier years as archbishop, Cushing had been successful in silencing a Jesuit who preached an unusually strict form of Catholic doctrine. By the end of his life, he found himself powerless to forestall the political ambitions of another Jesuit, Father Robert Drinan, who was every bit as recalcitrant as Feeney in his defiance of Church authority, and challenged Church teaching as well. Despite the disapproval of the aging cardinal, Father Drinan sought and won a seat in the US House of Representatives, where he became a prominent defender of unrestricted legal abortion on demand.

Cardinal Cushing could not reconcile himself to the revolutionary changes that he himself had helped to set in motion. For the last several years of his life he was subject to bouts of depression, aggravated by chronic health problems that included asthma, emphysema, and an evident weakness for alcohol. His optimistic outlook on American society had been shattered by the assassination of President John F. Kennedy on November 22, 1963.

When the President's widow Jacqueline later announced her plans to marry Aristotle Onassis, conservative Catholics were appalled. How could this very prominent Catholic widow marry a divorced man? Cardinal Cushing's response was revealing. Rather than affirming the teaching of the Church he expressed his deep and abiding sympathy for the Kennedy family. "Why can't they leave her alone?" he complained.

Why indeed? Why couldn't the Catholic Church just leave her faithful alone? The Cushing era had begun at a time when even non-Catholic Americans recognized the cultural influence of the Church. It ended with even a Catholic prelate questioning whether the Church should have any influence at all on the public actions of the Catholic faithful.

4

Personally Opposed, But . . .

Cardinal O'Connell had been revered because of his august position, but his personality and his administrative style were not calculated to win friends. He commanded the respect of his followers, but could not win their love.

Cardinal Cushing, on the other hand, was genuinely loved by the people of Boston—Catholics and non-Catholics alike—but he was not always respected. Everyone seemed to have a favorite anecdote about "the Cush" and his foibles. The laughter was generally sympathetic; the cardinal's immense popularity protected him from direct public criticism. Indeed when the sweeping cultural changes of the 1960s produced a new attitude of hostility toward the Church, the cardinal's personal standing camouflaged some of that hostility as well. Cushing himself remained a beloved figure, but public respect for his office as Archbishop of Boston was steadily eroding.

For Boston's Catholic leaders, who had held such a commanding position in public society, public attacks on the Church came as a shock. Just a few years earlier such attacks would have been unthinkable. How had the influence of Catholicism fallen so far and so fast?

The question is sharpened by the fact that roughly halfway through the Cushing era, Catholics had been enjoying their greatest public triumph in the United States, and especially in Boston. In 1964, for the first time, Roman Catholics became the single largest religious bloc in the US Congress—a distinction that they have held to this day. And of course in 1960 Boston's delighted Irish Catholics had seen one of their own, John F. Kennedy, elected to the White House.

Kennedy's election seemed at the time to constitute the definitive proof that Catholics had overcome the last barriers to their success in American public life. But a closer examination of the 1960 election, and the way it was achieved, shows something quite different. John F. Kennedy captured the presidency not by defeating anti-Catholic prejudice but by exploiting it.

Consider the situation that faced the Massachusetts senator just a few weeks before the November 1960 election. Kennedy was running neck-and-neck with his Republican opponent, Richard M. Nixon. In the Southern states of the Bible Belt, he faced implacable opposition from fundamentalist Protestants; anti-Catholic groups were distributing hundreds of thousands of leaflets questioning whether a Catholic could ever be considered a truly loyal American, in light of his fealty to Rome.

When he rose to address the Greater Houston Ministerial Association on September 12, Kennedy was speaking as a supplicant. A political candidate in the final stages of a tight campaign is not in a position to challenge popular prejudices; he is hoping to gain support or—as in this case—to curb opposition. Kennedy could not realistically hope, in a short speech, to erase generations of fundamentalist suspicions about the Catholic Church. He had a more pragmatic goal: simply to remove the issue of Catholicism from the presidential campaign.

"I believe in an America where the separation of church and state is absolute," Kennedy told the Baptist ministers in Houston. It should be understood, he continued, that "no public official either requests or accepts instructions on public policy from the Pope, the National Council of Churches, or any other ecclesiastical source." But of course his audience was not worried about the National Council of Churches. The ministers in Houston were concerned about the influence of the Catholic hierarchy, and delighted with Kennedy's statement that in his vision for America, "no religious body seeks to impose its will directly or indirectly upon the general populace or the public acts of its officials."

"I do not speak for my Church on public matters," Kennedy said, "and the Church does not speak for me." He reminded his audience that he was the Democratic candidate, not the Catholic candidate, for the presidency. And he promised that if he won the presidency he would make all decisions "in accordance with what my conscience tells me to be in the national interest, and without regard to outside pressures or dictates." His personal religious beliefs, he assured skeptics, were his own private affairs; they would not influence public policy.

The reassurances that Kennedy gave to his Protestant audience were not entirely original. In 1826, addressing a joint session of the US Congress,

Bishop John England of Charleston, South Carolina had insisted that "the tribunal of the Church has no power to interfere with my civil rights." The bishop underlined his patriotism by adding: "I would not allow to the Pope, or to any bishop of our Church, outside of this Union, the smallest interference with the humblest vote at our most insignificant ballot box."

At first glance Bishop England's argument looks very similar to Senator Kennedy's, but there is a critical difference. Bishop England was speaking as an ecclesiastical official, promising that he would not allow Roman authority to interfere in the civic affairs of the young American republic. Kennedy was speaking as a Catholic layman and an elected public representative, telling his Protestant audience that he would not let Church authority shape *his own* views on public affairs.

Nor was Kennedy addressing his remarks only to those issues in which the Catholic Church might have some special political interest, such as the question of US diplomatic representation at the Vatican or the taxation of parish properties. When he promised to be guided only by his own conscience, Kennedy said that he was speaking about "birth control, divorce, censorship, gambling, or any other subject"—highlighting those topics on which the teachings of the Church did not match American popular attitudes. He was signaling, therefore, that he would not consider the Church teaching on these issues as definitive.

But if Catholic teachings were not Kennedy's final frame of reference, what was? The candidate's promise was to govern by his own conscience. But how was his conscience formed? What sort of decisions would it dictate? Kennedy's speech did not give his Houston audience any way of predicting his policies. Or did it?

Laws often reflect a moral consensus in society—such as the universal consensus that murder is wrong. Up until the early twentieth century, American laws restricting birth control and divorce reflected the general agreement that these practices were inherently objectionable. By the time of Kennedy's speech in Houston, that consensus was severely eroded, and pressure was building for changes in the laws that remained on the books. It is certainly true that the Catholic Church strongly held to the old principles that had once been so widely held, but the Catholic Church was not alone. Many other Christian, Jewish, and secular groups still upheld the same principles. When he indicated that he would not be guided by Catholic teaching, Kennedy was implicitly distancing himself from that old moral consensus. The sexual revolution had not yet begun in earnest, and in 1960 there was still a broad agreement in America that abortion is wrong, and that marriage is the union of a man and a woman. But when the moral consensus on those topics broke down, Catholic politicians would follow Kennedy's logic to distance themselves from Church teaching on those issues as well.

In his Houston speech Kennedy did not directly challenge the authority of the Church. Instead he assured the Greater Houston Ministerial Association that he would be guided by his own conscience rather than by any Church teaching. That message was reassuring to Protestant ministers, whose theological views were based on the presumption that every believer can follow his own interpretation of the Bible. But Kennedy's message was—or at least should have been—unsettling to Catholics who believed that a properly formed conscience will adhere to the teachings of the Church.

At the time most American Catholics were not attuned to the theological and political implications of Kennedy's speech; it was enough that the Catholic candidate had successfully quieted the anti-Catholic opposition. From the perspective of fundamentalist Protestants, however, the Houston speech was much more than a campaign gesture. They had wanted assurance that the Catholic Church could not influence public policy. They received that assurance from the man who was identified (despite what he said in Houston) as the Catholic presidential candidate.

When he promised not to let Church teachings interfere with his judgment and asserted the primacy of his own conscience, Kennedy could speak persuasively to Protestant ministers, because on every important public issue of the day, he *opposed* the stance taken by American Church leaders. Senator Kennedy, the presidential candidate, opposed plans to open diplomatic ties with the Holy See; he supported public funding for birth-control programs; he opposed taxpayer support for parochial schools and even volunteered to his Houston audience that such aid would be "unconstitutional."

The top issues on the political agenda in 1960 did not pose the same grave moral choices as today's debates over abortion, same-sex unions, and euthanasia. But even in his allusions to the less divisive issues of his day, Kennedy was signaling to his audience that he would *oppose* the influence of the Church. Thus in his address at Houston he gave his anti-Catholic critics everything they wanted, clearly hoping to eliminate any incentive they might have for opposing his candidacy.

Today Kennedy's Houston speech is often cited as a model of how Catholic politicians should approach the potential conflict between Church teachings and individual freedom. In fact, the speech provided a victory of historic proportions for anti-Catholic forces. Perhaps it is noteworthy that the speech was reportedly drafted by John Cogley, an influential Catholic journalist of that era. Later Cogley renounced his faith and eventually confessed that he had ceased to be a believing Catholic in 1957—three years before the speech was written.

Again, the concessions that Kennedy made to anti-Catholic sentiment in his Houston speech were not generally recognized at the time. Catholic voters still saw him as one of their own and cheerfully gave him their unquestioned support. In fact the speech helped to remind Catholic voters of their ties to the Democratic candidate.

Monsignor Francis Lally, the editor of Boston's archdiocesan newspaper *The Pilot*, would point out in 1962 that the presidential campaign had generally not called attention to Kennedy's Catholicism. On the contrary, the image carefully molded by his political strategists had emphasized Kennedy's graduation from Harvard, his service in the US Navy, and his ties to the country's financial and intellectual elites. "All this," Monsignor Lally wrote, "made a picture with almost no touches that most Americans would recognize as traditionally Catholic."

Nevertheless Kennedy *was* a baptized Catholic, and that was enough to forestall unwanted questions about the compromises he had made at Houston. The Democratic contender probably calculated—correctly—that no American bishop would criticize a Catholic candidate too forcefully, no matter how consistently that candidate staked out his opposition to the Church.

Perhaps the Kennedy campaign had learned from the experience of Supreme Court Justice William Brennan, who had made his own effort to distance himself from Church teachings during his Senate confirmation hearings in 1956. Brennan's public remarks on the supremacy of the Constitution had provoked the wrath of one Catholic newspaper in Brooklyn, but a promising young cleric in Washington, DC—the future Archbishop of New Orleans, Philip Hannan—came to the nominee's defense, arranging for favorable coverage in the local Catholic papers. Brennan sailed through the confirmation process—and, seventeen years later, became the moving force behind the *Roe v. Wade* decision that overthrew all state laws restricting abortion.

As candidate and later as President, Kennedy maintained his consistent opposition to Church positions on public support for contraception and diplomatic ties with the Vatican. But it was his clash with Church leaders on public aid to parochial schools that he drew public criticism from Catholic leaders. The Jesuit magazine *America* charged in 1962 that President Kennedy's policies imposed "harsh economic sanctions upon millions of parents who, in the exercise of their religious liberty, choose to educate their children in parochial schools."

Government aid to Church-run schools could be seen as a pocketbook issue; obviously Catholic parents would prefer to have their children's education subsidized by taxpayer funding. But *America* magazine was careful to frame the question as a matter of justice, noting that Catholic parents were forced to pay twice—as taxpayers to support the education of *other* children in public schools, then again as parents to support their *own* children's education in parochial schools.

In 1961, the question came to a head in Washington, as some American bishops voiced public opposition to President Kennedy's education program because it would not benefit the parochial schools. Back in Boston, Cardinal Cushing refused to criticize his old friend's proposal. "While I am not convinced that the Constitution forbids all subsidies to private education," Cushing said, "I feel that as long as the majority of the American people are against such use of taxes, Catholics should try to prove their right to such assistance but neither force such legislation through at the expense of national disunity nor use their political influence in Congress to block other legislation of benefit to education because they do not get their own way." Unlike the editors of *America*, Cardinal Cushing's statement framed the issue exclusively in terms of Catholic financial interests; he ignored the more sweeping moral question about equal justice.

With such unwavering from his own archbishop, President Kennedy successfully maintained the position that he had established in Houston. While asserting his fidelity to Catholicism, he opposed the public interests of the Church time and again, offering the odd explanation that he could not allow his private beliefs to influence his public performance.

That explanation is odd because if Kennedy really did set aside his personal beliefs, what principles *would* guide his decisions? If he simply followed public preferences he would be a glorified pollster, not a political leader. But if he held to some *other* set of ethical principles that trumped his Catholic beliefs, then his ultimate loyalty was not to the Church.

Kennedy's argument was not intellectually coherent. But it was politically successful. He quieted the anti-Catholic opposition. He won the election. He escaped without a rebuke from the American bishops. His strategy worked, and in the years since 1960 many other Catholic politicians have followed the same winning plan.

Campaign tacticians admired the Houston speech because it proved politically expedient. Protestant fundamentalists liked it because it conceded the force of their argument against Catholic Church influence. Secularists liked it because it removed religious principles from public debates. Catholic Church leaders at first accepted Kennedy's argument, perhaps reluctantly, because they hoped to see a Catholic elected to the nation's highest office. But as the years passed, more and more liberal Catholics endorsed the argument put forward by Kennedy in Houston. By drawing a distinction between Church doctrine and private conscience, they could avoid a protracted battle with secular culture; they could expand their own political influence without making the sacrifices that their faith might ask of them.

American Church leaders avoided battles frequently during the 1960s. When the federal government introduced massive subsidies for artificial contraception (subsidies that were expanded during Kennedy's presidency), the American bishops fought a strictly limited campaign. They did not oppose the contraceptive programs as a whole; they asked only for exemptions, so that Catholic institutions were not required to supply the contraceptives. The Catholic Church teaches that contraception is inherently immoral: an offense against natural law. If that is true, then it is seriously immoral for *anyone* to use contraceptives, and it is immoral for Catholic taxpayers to support their use—whether or not the users are Catholics. But the bishops based their political efforts on the much more restricted argument that it is wrong for *Catholics*—Catholic doctors and Catholic institutions—to be drawn into the campaign to encourage use of contraceptives.

That argument suggested the same artificial distinction that Kennedy made in Houston: the distinction between private beliefs and public actions. By failing to mount a principled resistance to *all* public support for contraceptive programs, the American bishops had given their tacit support to the logic of the Houston speech.

In the coming decades new fronts would be opened in America's culture wars, and Catholic politicians would refine the explanations they offered for opposing the teachings of their Church. In an important 1984 speech at Notre Dame, New York's Governor Mario Cuomo took a bold step beyond Kennedy's Houston argument. He explained that while opposed to abortion as a matter of moral principle, he could not impose his private beliefs to influence his decisions as a government leader. So he would allow the killing of unborn children and support public subsidies for the slaughter.

Cuomo's speech set a new standard for liberal Catholic politicians. To this day, Catholic campaigners explain away their support for legal abortion by saying that they are "personally opposed, but . . ."

Yet Cuomo was not the first prominent Catholic to offer that argument. That dubious distinction belongs to Cardinal Richard Cushing.

In 1965, the Massachusetts legislature was debating a proposal to repeal a statewide ban on the sale of contraceptives. Cardinal O'Connell had squelched a similar proposal a generation earlier, and Cushing might have done the same by issuing a clear moral imperative to the Catholics who composed a solid voting majority in the legislature. But he did not. Instead the cardinal told a radio audience that while contraceptive use was immoral, "I am also convinced that I should not impose my position— moral beliefs or religious beliefs—on those of other faiths."

Cardinal Cushing went on to acknowledge that Church leaders had opposed legalized contraception in the past. "But my thinking has changed," he said, "for the simple reason that I do not see where I have an obligation to impose my religious beliefs on people who just do not accept the same faith as I do." To Catholics serving in the legislature the cardinal gave this simple advice: "If your constituents want this legislation, vote for it."

The Catholic opposition to contraception is based on natural law arguments, not on any esoteric beliefs. A non-believer can recognize the force of the Church's argument on the integrity of marital relations without accepting Catholic doctrine on theological issues such as the Trinity, the Eucharist, or the authority of the Roman Pontiff. Rejection of birth control is not a matter of sectarian policy; many Evangelical Protestants and Orthodox Jews hold the same views. In fact, until the past century nearly all Christians opposed contraception, and the law that Massachusetts lawmakers repealed in 1965 had been passed in 1899, long before Catholics became a significant force in the state legislature.

Yet Cardinal Cushing conveyed the impression that opposition could be motivated *only* by religious faith, and since he could not expect others to accept his faith, he would not expect them to oppose contraception. In effect the cardinal severed the connection between the Church's stand and the natural law reasoning behind it; his statement implied that the ban on contraception was an arbitrary rule, applicable only to members of the Catholic Church.

With his public statement on this issue, the cardinal opened the way for the legalization of birth-control use in Massachusetts. How could secular defenders of the contraceptive ban be expected to risk their political careers, when the Archbishop of Boston had conceded the fight? How could they be expected to advance cogent, non-sectarian arguments for the ban, when the cardinal had virtually denied that any such argument existed?

But the damage done by Cushing's statement endured long after the political contest on Beacon Hill in 1965. Years later, when the subject had switched to abortion, liberal politicians introduced the same logic that the cardinal had advanced, claiming that it would be immoral to impose their private beliefs on others who did not share their faith. Arguments based on natural law, embryology, and political history were swept aside. Liberal Catholics framed the abortion issue exclusively as a sectarian issue, and improbably claimed the moral high ground as defenders of religious freedom.

One such campaigner was Father Robert Drinan, a Jesuit law professor who proved remarkably skillful in exploiting the rhetoric of religious freedom during a political career that spanned ten years as a highly partisan Democratic member of the US House of Representatives. When Drinan first considered running for Congress in 1970, his Jesuit superiors in Rome forbade it. Undaunted, Drinan proceeded with his plans, and when the head of the Jesuit order pressed him to withdraw from the race, Drinan replied that he had secured Cardinal Cushing's permission for his political plans. (He had not.) By now the campaign season was well underway, and when officials in Rome insisted that he drop out, Drinan and his defenders in the US argued that his withdrawal at such a late date would be perceived as evidence of unwarranted ecclesiastical interference in secular politics. Before the argument between Boston and Rome was settled, the November election took place, and Father Drinan won his Congressional seat.

Father Pedro Arrupe, the superior general of the Jesuits, ordered Drinan to leave Congress after his first term. But with the connivance of his local provincials in Boston, the wayward Jesuit went through the same charade that had proven effective in 1970: he stalled, dissembled, invoked the cause of religious freedom, and ultimately ignored direct orders until he had won re-election in 1972. The stakes were higher in 1974, because the Jesuit priest had become one of the most ardent Congressional defenders of legal abortion, after the *Roe v. Wade* decision thrust that issue into the limelight. But Father Drinan, emboldened by his previous successes, fended off criticism from his Jesuit superiors in Rome and from Boston's new archdiocesan leader, Cardinal Humberto Medeiros, and won re-election in 1974, 1976, and 1978. Finally in 1980 the Vatican issued a flat, unambiguous order that all Catholic priests must withdraw from partisan political activities, and Father Drinan announced that he would step down.

To fill the seat that he was vacating, Drinan endorsed Barney Frank, a state legislator with a reputation for quick wit and liberal attitudes. Like Father Drinan, Frank supported unrestricted legal abortion on demand. But unlike Drinan—who would surely have cruised to victory and another term—Frank faced tough opposition in the Democratic primary election. Arthur Clark, a pro-life Catholic and mayor of the city of Waltham, had assembled a impressive campaign team, and within the waning days of the campaign, pollsters gave Clark a slight edge. Then the Archbishop of Boston weighed in, and everything suddenly changed.

On the Sunday before the primary election, Cardinal Medeiros issued a pastoral letter on the public responsibilities of Catholic citizens, to be read aloud at Mass in each parish of the Boston archdiocese. Without referring directly to the Congressional race, the cardinal made his meaning quite clear. "Those who make abortion possible by law cannot separate themselves from the guilt which accompanies this horrendous crime and deadly sin," he proclaimed.

Editorial writers howled in protest. The cardinal was trying to assert ecclesiastical control over secular politics, they charged; he was trying to impose his religious views on the voters. After a decade of conspicuous silence from the archdiocese about Father Drinan's support for abortion, the cardinal's last-minute intervention in this political campaign was certainly heavy-handed. And after fifteen years of indoctrination in the thinking that Cardinal Cushing had popularized, the voters of Massachusetts were inclined to side with the outraged editorialists, not with the archbishop. Support for Barney Frank surged in the last few days of the campaign, and he eked out a narrow victory.

After that disastrous foray into the political world, Cardinal Medeiros retreated into silence. And if truth be told, most of his potential allies were happy to see him on the sidelines. Pro-life candidates worried that if the cardinal became involved in their campaigns, they might suffer the same fate as Arthur Clark. The Archbishop of Boston—who just a few decades earlier could decide the fate of legislation with a single public statement—had been written out of the Massachusetts political equation.

In that ill-timed and ill-fated pastoral letter of 1980, Cardinal Medeiros offered a reasoned and reasonable explanation of why conscientious citizens—Catholic or not—should not support legal abortion. But the voters of Massachusetts were no longer prepared to listen to arguments put forward by Church leaders. They had been persuaded that religious beliefs were private, while political stands were public, and one could never influence the other. By the 1980s, Catholic politicians had grown accustomed to deflecting questions about abortion by explaining that they were personally opposed to the practice, but ... Catholic voters were equally accustomed to hearing that explanation, and most accepted it. Church leaders rarely challenged the argument.

Advocates of legal abortion quickly capitalized on the opportunity provided by the Catholic retreat. As the leading abortionist Bernard Nathanson would reveal after his dramatic conversion to the pro-life cause and the Catholic Church, strategists for the abortion lobby deliberately cultivated the notion that all public opposition to abortion was guided by the Catholic Church. The belief that a fetus is an unborn child, they argued, was based on a Catholic theological tenet, which non-Catholics could not be expected to accept. This argument *should* have been recognized immediately as a fraud. The humanity of a fetus is not a matter of theological speculation; it can be established by scientific tests. And opposition to abortion was never exclusively a Catholic affair; many thousands of others—notably including Evangelical Protestants, historically suspicious of the Roman Church—were active in the pro-life movement. Nevertheless the propaganda of the abortion lobby had a considerable effect, because so many Catholic leaders were conceding the major premise: that religious beliefs should remain private.

Today, this compartmentalization of religious beliefs is so widespread that even spokesmen for the Church regularly take it for granted that Catholic moral teachings are matters of internal Church discipline, applicable only to Catholics.

Consider, for instance, an editorial that appeared in the Boston *Pilot*—the official newspaper of the archdiocese—in June 2006. A few weeks earlier, faculty members at the Jesuit-run Boston College had protested the honorary degree awarded to Condoleeza Rice, the US Secretary of State, because of her involvement with the war in Iraq. After explaining that con-scientious Catholics differed in their views on that conflict, the *Pilot* edito-rial continued:

> As if to shore up their argument, some who oppose Rice's appearance are claiming she also holds some pro-abortion views. While that could have weighed into BC's decision, that too is certainly not an impediment to receiving an honor from the school, since the current position of the U.S. episcopate is that institutions should not honor Catholic politicians who support abortion. Rice, we note, is not a Catholic.

According to the logic of that *Pilot* editorial, it would be wrong for a Catholic university to honor a *Catholic* politician who supported abortion, but honors for a non-Catholic politician would be perfectly acceptable. The problem, then, would not be that the politician was complicit in the killing of unborn babies, but that a pro-abortion *Catholic* politician would be dis-regarding directives from the American hierarchy. Since non-Catholics are not subject to the bishops' authority, they would be excused—regardless of their involvement in the spilling of innocent blood.

Opponents of Church teaching on abortion (and on euthanasia, divorce, contraception, etc.) had argued for years that the Catholic position was nothing more than an exercise of power: an arbitrary rule, established at the bishops' whim, which should not be imposed upon the secular world. Anyone who read that *Pilot* editorial, and took it to represent the outlook of the archdiocese, would have to conclude by June 2006 that Church lead-ers in Boston shared that understanding.

PART II

SHIFTING FOUNDATIONS

5

THE CENTER
CANNOT HOLD

Important as it was, the privatization of religious belief was not the only radical change that affected American Catholicism during the 1960s. The youth rebellion that shook all of Western society caused lasting changes in popular culture, bringing a thoroughgoing suspicion of traditional beliefs and an exaltation of individual freedom. And while these changes altered popular culture, the Church herself saw profound internal changes following the Second Vatican Council.

Many fine studies of Vatican II have already been written, and in this book we need not repeat their arguments. For our purposes it is enough to make a few important points about the changes brought on by the Council. The changes were unsettling and even disorienting, particularly to the laity. The post-conciliar period saw a cataclysmic breakdown in traditional Catholic beliefs, practices, and discipline. With the lines of ecclesiastical authority badly blurred and often completely ignored, individual pastors had greater freedom than ever before. Yet with fewer Catholics retaining fundamental beliefs about the unique sacramental role of the priesthood, the legitimate authority of the clergy was waning. The net result was that priests had more scope for the arbitrary exercise of their influence, but less respect for their ministerial role; they had more power but less responsibility. It was a recipe for disaster.

Many conservative Catholics see Vatican II as the fundamental cause for the problems that wrack the Church today. That reasoning is simplistic. If the leaders of any institution gather to plan for the future, and their plans bring the institution to ruins, there must have been some problem before the meeting: some flaw in the leaders' thinking or in the way those leaders were chosen. A healthy institution does not self-destruct.

Still it is undeniably true that before the opening session of Vatican II in October 1962, everyone knew what Catholics believed, and what their faith demanded of them. Any informed American—Catholic or not— knew that Catholics were expected to attend Mass on Sunday, pray the Rosary, eat fish on Fridays, and, once married, stay married for life. Within a few years after the Council closed in December 1965, all those certainties were gone.

Contrary to popular opinion, Vatican II did not call for radical changes in the Church. The documents that actually issued from the Council did not question any old doctrines or propose any new ones; when the Council fathers did address doctrinal issues they invariably reaffirmed traditional beliefs. The Council did *not* lift the requirement for Catholics to attend Mass on Sunday and to observe some penitential practice (with abstinence from meat highly recommended) on Friday. The Council did *not* call for the abolition of the Latin Mass; in fact its liturgical directive called for the greater use of Gregorian chant. The Council did *not* encourage nuns to abandon their distinctive habits or authorize priests to remove statues from parish churches.

Nevertheless, shortly after the Council, all those traditions were called into question. Changes were introduced into nearly every aspect of life within the Church, as reforms mandated by "the spirit of Vatican II." Only rarely did this "spirit" match any of the Council's actual teachings; much more frequently, what was alleged to be the "spirit of Vatican II" clashed directly with the documents that the Council fathers had signed. Still the "spirit" held sway, and the changes continued. Frustrated conservative Catholics, brandishing copies of the Council documents, pleaded for an end to the uproar. But their pleas were ignored and the cyclone of change whirled onward.

To this day, the understanding of Vatican II is seriously marred in two respects. First, most Catholics think of the Council as marking a sharp break in the continuity of Church teaching. If Vatican II did not actually *change* doctrine, they believe, at least it caused a profound shift in the way doctrines are *interpreted*. Actually, as Pope Benedict XVI remarked, in a December 2005 address to leaders of the Roman Curia, the teachings of Vatican II can only be understood properly if they are read in the context of a constant, organic Catholic tradition—as natural developments in a stream of thought that has followed the same basic course for two thousand years.

Second, most Catholics think of Vatican II as a sort of super-council, whose teachings trump all previous expressions of Catholic orthodoxy. Again the reality is quite different. Church teaching does not change, and a doctrine, once it has been formally defined, is not subject to amendment. The sixteenth-century formulations of the Council of Trent may sound awkward to contemporary listeners, but the doctrines proclaimed by that Council are every bit as authoritative today as those of Vatican II. Each Sunday at Mass, Catholics recite a Creed that was approved by the Council of Nicea in 325. The fundamental truths have not changed.

Catholics believe that the Holy Spirit guides the deliberations of an ecumenical council, so that the formal teachings of the Church are preserved from error. But this divine guidance does not give the council fathers free rein to introduce new doctrines. On the contrary, the Spirit helps Catholic prelates to preserve the integrity of an ancient faith, handed down intact and essentially unchanged over two thousand years. Nearly a century before Vatican II, in 1870, the First Vatican Council explained: "For the Holy Spirit was not promised to the successors of Peter, that by his revelation they might make known new doctrine, but that by his assistance they might inviolably keep and faithfully expound the revelation or deposit of faith delivered through the apostles."

So it is absurd to speak of an up-to-date pastor as a "Vatican II priest," or to chide a more conservative Catholic for holding "pre-conciliar" attitudes—as if the Council had defined a new type of Catholic belief.

Why, then, were the practical results of Vatican II so thoroughly divorced from the Council fathers' intentions? Why was "the spirit of Vatican II" so different from the Council's teachings? The simple answer is that while proponents of radical change in the Church could not muster a majority among the bishops who met in Rome in the early 1960s, and thus could not dictate the contents of the Council documents, they were prepared to continue their campaign for change after the close of Vatican II. What they could not accomplish in the Council chambers, they managed to do in the European theology faculties, the Catholic journals, and the secular media. Having lost the conciliar battles, they declared victory—and persuaded sympathetic professors and journalists to ratify that claim.

The successful hijacking of "the spirit of Vatican II" was a two-step process. At the Council itself, liberal Catholics could not command majority support for their own preferred statements, but they could and did insert ambiguous phrases in the documents, which they could later cite as authority for their own novel ideas. Then when the Council ended, liberals called upon their own favorite witnesses—clerics who had participated in the Council discussions either as bishops or as experts and observers—to explain what the Council had *really* intended: the spirit rather than the letter of the law.

The Council urged Catholics toward a more active involvement with modern culture. Taken in proper context, the Council documents encouraged the faithful to transform popular culture through the influence of Catholic teaching. Liberal Catholics turned that formula on its head, suggesting that Catholic teaching should be transformed through the influence of popular culture.

By any reckoning, the Council had called for greater engagement between the Church and culture. Conservative Catholics read the Council's documents as exhortations to change the culture; liberal Catholics invoked "the spirit of Vatican II" as a mandate to change the Church. But the internal dynamic of progress favored the latter interpretation. In his excellent book on the changes in the Church, *Turmoil and Truth,* the British Catholic author Philip Trower used a memorable image to make the point:

> Six men are pushing a heavily loaded car which has run out of fuel. Three of them, who have been riding in the car, want to push it 20 yards to get it into a lay-by. The other three, who have offered to help, mean to push the car 50 yards and shove it over a cliff followed by the car owner and his two friends. Once the pushing begins and the car starts moving it is probable the car is going to come to rest more than 20 yards from the starting point even if it does not end up at the cliff's foot.
>
> Now let us imagine what a group of people watching from a nearby hilltop will make of the incident. They will start by assuming that all six men have the same intentions. The car is moving steadily forward. Then they see three of the men detach themselves from the back of the car, run around to the front and try to stop it. Which are the troublemakers? Those surely who are now opposing the process that has been started.

Thus conservative Catholics—those who upheld the traditional teachings of the Church, and even those of Vatican II—came to be seen as obstructionists, stalling the implementation of reforms. Conservatives, suspicious of secular encroachment into the affairs of the Church, were not prepared for a public-relations battle that was fought out in the major media. Their liberal counterparts, anxious to tear down the barriers that separated the Church from the outside world, leapt at the opportunity to court public opinion. American Catholics learned about the Second Vatican Council primarily through secular newspaper and magazines accounts, and these publications consistently offered the Whig interpretation of Church history.

Tradition-minded Catholics, confident that their Church could not and would not change in any essential respect, were caught off guard by the first excesses of post-conciliar enthusiasm: the theology teacher who brought Karl Marx into the classroom, the priests who omitted portions of the Mass. But they assumed that things would quickly be set right. Soon the bishops would realize what was happening and (or so the conservatives thought) step in to restore order with a quick, authoritative word. Those assumptions were mistaken. Many radical Catholics were ready to defy orders from the hierarchy. And bishops, conscious of the rebellious spirit that was cropping up around them, were not willing to issue the orders that might put their power to a test.

So the rout was on. Radical reformers tore at every aspect of Catholic life, questioning time-honored practices and beliefs. Catholic schools jettisoned their entire religious-education programs; the old reliable *Baltimore Catechism* quickly became a collector's item. In parochial high schools, religion classes became freewheeling discussion sessions, with students encouraged to reflect on the works of contemporary theologians who announced that "God is dead," or to analyze the verses of pop songs. Nuns replaced their habits with pantsuits, moved out of their convents to find apartments, and left the Catholic schools behind. Traditional practices like Benediction and the Forty Hours devotion fell into disuse; lay groups like the Holy Name societies and the women's sodalities vanished.

Before the Council, even an informed American Baptist knew that Catholics were expected to abstain from meat on Friday and attend Mass on Sunday. By 1970 many Catholics believed (incorrectly) that both requirements had been lifted. And even if they *did* realize that Sunday Mass was still obligatory, more and more Catholics chose to sleep late; attendance figures fell into a long, steep decline that has not yet halted.

Of all the changes that emerged in the 1960s and 1970s, the most striking and significant were the changes in the liturgy. The Mass—the central act of Catholic worship—was altered almost beyond recognition. The Latin that had been used in the Roman rite throughout the world was replaced by vernacular languages. The words of the prayers and gestures of the priest were simplified. Solemn old hymns were discarded and peppy new tunes written; guitars replaced organs. Even church buildings were radically changed to accommodate the new style of worship. Statues were pulled down and replaced with felt banners bearing emotional slogans. Altar rails were torn out to bring the congregation closer to the celebrant; altars themselves were turned around so that the priest faced the people—like a teacher facing his class.

As with so many other changes that were introduced in "the spirit of Vatican II," the sweeping changes in the liturgy went far beyond what the Council had authorized, and continued long after the Council closed. New prayers were added, new translations of the Scriptures introduced, new theories continually tested on unsuspecting congregations. Only rarely did the ordinary Catholic have any control over the liturgical innovations that occurred in his parish; more typically he would learn about the latest changes only when he arrived in church on Sunday morning. From week to week, year after year, bewildered parishioners did not know what to expect at Sunday Mass, and the experiments would continue whether or not they approved.

The constant liturgical experimentation had a corrosive effect on the faith of Catholics. Writing in 2006, forty years after the Council, the historian James Hitchcock observed:

> Sacred ritual always presents itself as divinely ordained, but the speed with which liturgical changes were introduced, the confusing and often contradictory things said about them, the way in which they were decreed by committees and bureaucratic offices, the continuing debates, the replacement of sacred liturgical books by discardable leaflets, the wholesale destruction of so much that was venerable, and the endless tinkering all had the cumulative effect of making the liturgy seem an all-too-human activity, not a divine action in which humans were privileged to participate but something that they themselves created. According to the cheerful rhetoric of the reformers, Vatican II had ushered in "the age of the laity." The practical results of the liturgical revolution were exactly the opposite. Yes, a handful of lay Catholics joined parish liturgy committees and became lectors or lay ministers. But the vast majority of lay Catholics were passive and helpless observers, unable to influence the changes that their pastors imposed upon them. Traditionally Catholics saw the liturgy as a mysterious action of the Holy

Spirit, in which priests filled a prescribed ministerial role. Now the liturgy came to be seen as the province of the clergy: not as the action of God but as something that priests themselves did for the benefit of the lay people in attendance. Facing the people, the priest himself became the central figure in the liturgical drama: the star of the show.

Lex orandi, lex credendi, reads the old Latin principle: the rule of prayer is the rule of belief. Because the Mass expresses and defines the fundamental tenets of Catholic doctrine, it is not surprising that at a time of radical change in the liturgy, there were profound changes in what Catholics believed, and the way they practiced their faith. In fact Monsignor Klaus Gamber, a German scholar whose studies on the liturgy drew the admiration of Cardinal Joseph Ratzinger (the future Pope Benedict XVI), argued that liturgical reformers were motivated by a desire to shape a new form of Catholic doctrine. In his book *The Reform of the Roman Liturgy*, Gamber wrote: "The traditional liturgy simply could not be allowed to exist in its established form because it was permeated with the truths of the traditional faith and the ancient forms of piety."

Liturgists argued that the changes introduced after the Council would encourage more active participation by the laity. They did not. Actually, in the years after the Council most members of the laity stopped participating at all. In 1958, a Gallup poll showed that three out of four American Catholics attended Sunday Mass regularly; by 2000 the figure was closer to one out of four.

With Mass attendance as the leading indicator, every other statistical index of Catholic practice and belief showed a similar decline between 1960 and 2000. Nearly half of the Catholic elementary and high schools in the United States closed. The number of Catholic marriages solemnized in churches fell by over 30 percent, while the number of marriages annulled by diocesan tribunals skyrocketed from about three hundred a year to nearly 50,000. The number of priests fell by about 20 percent, while the number of ordinations dropped by about 65 percent. Two-thirds of the country's seminaries closed. Teaching nuns, who had once formed the backbone of the massive Catholic education system, nearly disappeared. The total number of women religious fell by over 50 percent, but the teaching orders suffered a dizzying decline, from 104,000 in 1965 to about 8,000 today.

It was, in short, a disaster. In 1972, as the chaos spread, Pope Paul VI— who had enthusiastically championed the early Vatican II reforms—sadly admitted that something had gone seriously wrong. "We have the impression that, through some cracks in the wall, the smoke of Satan has entered the temple of God," he said. "We thought that after the Council a day of sunshine would dawn in the history of the Church. What dawned instead was a day of clouds and storms, of darkness, of searching and uncertainties."

With the worldwide Church in turmoil and traditional lines of authority breaking down, what mattered most to ordinary Catholics was the life of their own parishes. And there, again, the clergy reigned supreme. In Boston under Cardinal O'Connell, pastors could act as autonomous despots as long as they stayed safely within the boundaries of archdiocesan policy guidelines. Now those boundary lines had been erased, and pastors could run their parishes however they saw fit.

Up until the 1960s, when a new pastor was appointed to a Catholic parish, he might introduce a different style of preaching and a different method of conducting parish meetings, but the essentials of parish life—the Sunday Mass, the teaching in the parochial school, the advice given in confessions, the requirements for Baptism, and the programs for marriage preparation—would be unchanged. By the 1970s, the introduction of a new pastor could bring a complete transformation in all these areas, and lay people dismayed by the changes usually had no real choice but to move to another parish where they found the pastor's approach more congenial. Different parishes developed their own distinct personalities, emphasizing more "high" or "low" liturgy, liberal or more conservative preaching, traditional hymns or rock music. "Parish-shopping" became commonplace, with devoted families driving past several Catholic churches every Sunday to reach the one where they felt most comfortable.

From time to time bishops did impose some restraints on their pastors. But their orders were frequently ignored. One comparatively trivial example will illustrate the pattern: In 1988 the Boston archdiocese held a synod, bringing together parish and diocesan leaders to discuss the overall direction of the Church. Synod participants debated some controversial issues, and made some serious suggestions for reform. But one proposal generated universal enthusiasm: the synod members agreed that pastors should take up only one collection at each Sunday Mass. Everyone involved in the discussion agreed that this abolition of the dreaded "second collection" was an overdue reform—until someone pointed out that a nearly identical proposal had been proposed and adopted at the last archdiocesan synod, thirty-five years ago. In other words the second collection was *already* a violation of official archdiocesan policy. But over the years pastors had begun making exceptions to that rule—first occasionally, then more frequently, until finally there were second collections at every Sunday Mass. And sure enough, after the 1988 synod made its recommendation, the second collections ceased for only a few months before pastors began to re-introduce them.

Yet priests, while they had become the focal point of the Sunday liturgy and had unprecedented power to change the way their parishes functioned, were paradoxically losing the authority that they once enjoyed. The life of a Catholic priest commands reverence only when people value the sacramental life of the Church. As Catholic belief and practice slipped into desuetude, so did public respect for the Catholic clergy.

A decade before the Council, Father Feeney had argued for a strong affirmation by Church leaders that salvation is impossible outside the Church. His preaching may have caused resentment, but it certainly highlighted the importance of the Catholic priest, the minister of the Church's all-important sacraments. Within a generation even practicing Catholics had lost their confidence in the efficacy of those sacraments—and thus in the importance of the priesthood.

Indeed the question of salvation was rarely raised in the post-conciliar Church. Particularly in liberal Catholic circles, the top issues on the agenda were human rights, economic development, and personal fulfillment—admirable goals, but goals that could be fulfilled by an effective self-help program.

In 1995, speaking at a spiritual retreat for clergy, Father Raniero Cantalamessa, the official preacher of the pontifical household, described the state of the Catholic Church in Latin America by noting that Catholics there proclaim that "when we need a labor union we go to our parish priest; when we need the word of God we go to the Protestant pastor." The problem that he described was not confined to Latin countries; it was prevalent in the US as well. But in North America there were labor organizers to help workers form a union; the priest was not needed in that role, either.

After Vatican II, in parishes troubled by dwindling attendance and flickering faith, priests had more power but less authority. They could design their own liturgies and preach their own theological theories, but why were they doing it? If they did not represent the authority of a universal faith, what was the purpose of their work? Thousands of Catholic priests felt that they had been cast adrift. Many abandoned clerical life; many of those who remained were thoroughly demoralized. These unhappy priests had enormous freedom of action, but very little sense of purpose. They were dangerous men.

6

WAITING
FOR *ROE*

The sexual revolution of the 1960s and 1970s was a worldwide phenomenon. But it would be a mistake to assume that the social changes of that era simply swept across Boston the way they swept across so many other cities. Two centuries earlier the Boston area had been home to many of the leading political figures and the site of many of the important battles in a revolution that split the United States from the British crown. Now Boston again played a disproportionately large role in this new revolution that severed the link between sex and married life.

Dr. John Rock, a respected obstetrician who taught at Harvard Medical School, spent most of his life as a devout Catholic. Cardinal O'Connell officiated at his marriage, and Rock was a fixture at daily Mass in his parish in Brookline. But his deep concern for women with troubled pregnancies led him to begin exploring methods of contraception. In 1935 he was the only prominent Catholic to endorse a proposal that would have ended the Massachusetts ban on birth control. (The legislation was derailed by Cardinal O'Connell's intervention.) By the 1940s he had begun to teach his Harvard students about contraception, in a quiet contravention of the state law.

In the 1950s, Dr. Rock teamed with Gregory Pincus, whose research on contraception had the backing of Margaret Sanger, the founder of Planned Parenthood. Together Rock and Pincus supervised the groundbreaking studies that led to the development of the oral contraceptive pill, at a laboratory in Shrewsbury, Massachusetts.

When contraceptive pills came onto the American market—forever changing public attitudes toward sex, and procreation, and marriage—Dr. Rock was their most visible scientific backer. The fact that Rock was known to be a practicing Catholic made him an attractive spokesman for the birth-control movement, and he was dubbed with the ironic title "The Father of the Pill." Some devout Catholics denounced him, insisting that Rock's work was encouraging gross immorality. But Cardinal Cushing—as always, refusing to be drawn into a theological dispute—refused to take any action or make any statement that would convey his disapproval.

During the 1960s, Rock campaigned energetically for Church acceptance of the new contraceptive regimen. In 1968, when Pope Paul VI issued his encyclical *Humanae Vitae*, confirming the Church's traditional condemnation of artificial birth control, Rock was devastated. Eventually he stopped going to Mass, and died estranged from the Church.

Cardinal Cushing gave Rock free rein to promote the Pill, but most other American bishops fought against the public acceptance of birth control. In a statement issued in November 1966, the US bishops proclaimed:

> We call upon all—especially Catholics—to oppose, vigorously and by every democratic means, those campaigns already underway in some states and at the national level toward the active promotion, by tax-supported agencies, of birth prevention as a public policy, above all in connection with welfare benefit programs. History has shown that as a people lose respect for any life and a positive and generous attitude toward new life, they moved fatally to inhuman infanticide, abortion, sterilization, and euthanasia; we fear that history is, in fact, repeating itself on this point within our own land at the moment.

The bishops were fighting a losing political battle, however. Government support for birth-control programs was growing steadily, as was public acceptance of the Pill. Even within the Church the trend of opinion was clear. Leading Catholic theologians were devising arguments to defend the use of birth control, and by 1968 many conscientious Catholics had joined John Rock in thinking that the Church would eventually come around. When Pope Paul impaneled a special papal commission to study the issue, a majority of the members favored a change in Church teaching. But after much study and prayer the Pope concluded that he could not find a justification for that change, and with *Humanae Vitae* he affirmed that the use of artificial contraceptives could not and would not be accepted.

Humanae Vitae was a definitive statement, not simply another argument. But some of America's most influential Church leaders responded to the encyclical as if Pope Paul had encouraged further exploration of the issue. Cardinal Cushing announced to the people of Boston: "The matter is settled *for now*" [emphasis added].

[margin note: History of acceptance of birth control pills]

Within hours after the public appearance of *Humanae Vitae*, American Catholic theologians had organized a public statement of opposition to the Pope's stand. Open public dissent flourished, and the few brave bishops who punished dissenters soon learned that they would receive no backing from their American colleagues—or even, more remarkably, from the Vatican. In Washington, DC, Cardinal Patrick O'Boyle imposed canonical penalties on nineteen priests for their public rejection of the Pope's teaching. The priests appealed the disciplinary action, and after a lengthy process, three years later the Vatican Congregation for Clergy ruled that the sanctions should be lifted. Although the priests were required by that Vatican ruling to retract their public statements (which had served their purpose long ago), they were *not* required to profess allegiance to the Church's teaching. The Catholic author George Weigel termed this compromise "the Truce of 1968." The Vatican's decision, he observed, "taught theologians, priests, and other Church professionals that dissent from authoritative teaching was, essentially, cost-free."

Dissent from *Humanae Vitae* in particular was soon ubiquitous. Academic theologians assured their pupils that the Church teaching would eventually change—even as the successors to Pope Paul VI issued one statement after another confirming that teaching. Parish priests told married couples that they should follow their own consciences. Soon Catholic women were taking the Pill at a rate indistinguishable from that of their Protestant neighbors. For the first time in history, a majority of practicing Catholics were engaged regularly in an activity which their Church condemned as gravely sinful, and felt no remorse. Everyone knew that the Church forbade the use of contraceptives. Few people cared.

If theologians could freely dissent from *Humanae Vitae*, they could dissent from other Church teachings as well. And if lay Catholics could follow their own consciences regarding the use of birth control, they could make their own decisions on other moral issues—disregarding Church moral teachings when they saw fit. The teaching office of the bishops, already undermined by the confusion that followed Vatican II, was now almost completely removed from the realm of practical affairs and reduced to a sort of academic exercise. From time to time bishops would issue statements reaffirming traditional teachings, with no real expectation that these statements would have any practical effect on the lives of their faithful, let alone on government policies. Long gone was the day when a prelate's public statement could determine the fate of a legislative proposal; now bishops were content if their defense of Church teaching won the applause of a dedicated Catholic remnant.

In the realm of public policy, the debate on contraception was decided by the mid-1960s. Support for public subsidies of birth control—both for domestic use and for foreign-policy programs—was strong in both major political parties. Federal government support for contraceptive programs had been cautiously introduced by a Republican (Eisenhower) presidential administration, broadly expanded by a Democratic (Kennedy-Johnson) administration, and elevated to the level of a national-security priority under another Republican (Nixon) administration. Support for public subsidies of birth control—both for domestic use and for foreign-policy programs—was strong in both major political parties.

In August 1985, Archbishop Próspero Penados of Guatemala wrote to President Ronald Reagan, complaining that US officials "have been flooding Guatemala with hazardous artificial contraceptives, mechanical devices, and widespread sterilization programs for many years." The archbishop received no reply. By that time, opposition to federal birth-control programs was so weak as to be politically irrelevant, and the Guatemalan prelate's complaint failed to stir interest even among the pro-life officials of the Reagan White House.

By the 1980s, in fact, the battle lines of American public policy had moved to the issue of abortion, and conservative Catholics were fully occupied with their efforts to prevent federal subsidies for that practice.

At the time when *Humanae Vitae* appeared, it would have been unthinkable for a Catholic politician to endorse legal abortion. As late as 1971, Senator Ted Kennedy—who was later to become the Catholic politician most closely identified with the pro-abortion cause—wrote to a constituent that "legalization of abortion on demand is not in accordance with the value which our civilization places on human life." Senator Kennedy added that American culture should "fulfill its responsibility to its children from the moment of conception."

But even in those days, before the *Roe v. Wade* decision, the stage was already being set for a Catholic capitulation on the abortion issue. And Ted Kennedy should have been aware of the plot, because it was hatched under the auspices of his family. Most Americans were taken by surprise by the *Roe* decision, which struck down state laws restricting abortion. But the Kennedys were ready; for the better part of a decade they had been preparing their rhetoric for such an opportunity.

In July 1964, several liberal theologians received invitations to the Kennedy family compound in Hyannisport, Massachusetts, for a discussion of how a Catholic politician should handle the abortion issue. Notice now that abortion was *not* a major political issue in 1964. Ostensibly the meeting had been called to provide advice for Robert Kennedy, who was running for a New York Senate seat. But a candidate was not likely to face questions about abortion in 1964; the Kennedy planners had the more distant future in mind.

The participants in that Hyannisport meeting composed a Who's Who of liberal theologians, most of them Jesuits. Father Robert Drinan was there, as was Father Charles Curran (the leader in the dissent against *Humanae Vitae*; his writings on moral issues were later condemned by the Vatican). Father Joseph Fuchs, a Jesuit professor at Rome's Gregorian University, was on hand; so were the Jesuits Richard McCormick, Albert Jonsen, and Giles Milhaven. (Milhaven was later instrumental in the early public work of "Catholics for a Free Choice;" McCormick would become the Rose Kennedy professor of the Kennedy Institute for Bioethics at Georgetown University, and spend years teaching theology at Notre Dame.)

For two days the theologians huddled in the Cape Cod resort town as guests of the Kennedys. Eventually they reached a consensus, which they passed along to their political patrons. Abortion, they agreed, could sometimes be morally acceptable as the lesser of two evils. Lawmakers should certainly not encourage abortion, but a blanket prohibition might be more harmful to the common good than a law allowing abortion in some cases. And a danger to the common good would very likely arise if political leaders sought to impose their own private views on public policy.

The conference at Hyannisport offered a rare example of teamwork between academic theologians and practical politicians. The skillful operatives of the Kennedy family would round up the votes to end restrictions on abortion and eventually to provide public subsidies. The Jesuit theologians would provide protective cover for that effort, ensuring that Catholic colleges, universities, and theological journals gave a sympathetic reading to the politicians' public statements.

Thus the basic lines of "pro-choice" rhetoric were sketched out by Catholic theologians, at the residence of America's most famous Catholic family, nine years before the *Roe v. Wade* decision. The late President Kennedy had already laid the foundation for the argument that a Catholic politician must not attempt to enact his private religious views; now his brothers were prepared to take the next step forward. They were ready to explain that they were personally opposed to abortion, but . . .

Once the *Roe* decision was issued, and the question of abortion *did* become a hot political topic, liberal Catholics were ready with their reasons why Congress should not move to overturn the Supreme Court decision. The US bishops pleaded for Congress to act, but Catholic politicians held back. From 1977 through 1987 the Speaker of the House of Representatives, "Tip" O'Neill—a Catholic Democrat from Massachusetts and a Kennedy ally—saw to it that not a single vote was taken on any measure to restrict abortion.

As liberal Catholic theologians in the US did their utmost to obfuscate the moral principle involved—that the deliberate killing of innocent human beings can never be justified—the Vatican made every effort to clarify that issue. In a 1974 Declaration on Procured Abortion, the Congregation for the Doctrine of the Faith announced:

> It must in any case be clearly understood that whatever may be laid down by civil law in this matter, man can never obey a law which is in itself immoral, and such is the case of a law which would admit in principle the liceity of abortion. Nor can he take part in a propaganda campaign in favor of such a law, or vote for it.

Pro-life leaders quoted that Vatican document to liberal Catholic legislators, but they argued in vain. The defenders of legal abortion were now fully entrenched in their position, and—with respectable theologians still providing support in scholarly journals and newspaper editorial columns—insisted that their stand was in keeping with a carefully nuanced Catholic view.

Years passed, the number of babies aborted steadily rose, and the practice that had once been unthinkable gradually became accepted. In frustration, pro-life Catholics questioned why their bishops did not take action to discipline the wayward politicians. The Code of Canon Law stipulates that anyone actively involved in an abortion—the woman who procures it, the doctor who performs it, the man who pays for it—is subject to the penalty of excommunication. (The excommunication in this case is *latae sententiae*, which means that it takes effect immediately by virtue of the offense; there is no need for any public announcement of the penalty.) If this penalty is invoked for involvement in *one* abortion, conservative Catholics wondered aloud, how could it not apply to those lawmakers who, by their votes, allowed tens of thousands of abortion?

The bishops did issue regular public statements reaffirming the Catholic position, but abstract statements were not enough. As long as influential Catholics in Washington were working to preserve legal abortion on demand and escaping any form of ecclesiastical punishment, it was difficult for outsiders to believe that Church leaders took their own statements seriously. If innocent babies were really being killed, how could the bishops tolerate the lawmakers who promoted that killing? If the Church really did teach that abortion was *never* justified, how could the bishops fail to denounce the politicians who consistently justified the practice?

Abortion was a political issue, and most American Catholics were inclined to defer to the opinions of their own favorite political leaders—especially when those leaders were treated with scrupulous respect by the Catholic hierarchy. Eventually *Roe v. Wade* came to be seen as established law, rather than a shocking judicial decision. Among American Catholics, opposition to abortion gradually weakened. In 1992, a Gallup poll found that 70 percent of Catholics believed that they could, in good conscience, support a political candidate who favored legal abortion.

Pope John Paul II made another valiant effort to clarify the issue with his 1995 encyclical *Evangelium Vitae* ("The Gospel of Life"). "Abortion and euthanasia," the Pope wrote, "are thus crimes which no human law can claim to legitimize." Every Catholic is under a "grave and clear obligation to oppose" such laws, he said. Since a law allowing abortion is intrinsically unjust, "it is therefore never licit to obey it, or to take part in a propaganda campaign in favor of such a law or to vote for it."

Those were strong words. But a picture is worth a thousand words, and "pro-choice" Catholics had their picture. Just a few months before *Evangelium Vitae* was issued, Boston's Cardinal Bernard Law—a prelate known at that time for his frequent statements condemning legal abortion—had personally given Holy Communion to Ted Kennedy, at the funeral of the Senator's mother. Kennedy, the Senate's most vociferous opponent of any effort to restrict abortion, was apparently still considered a Catholic in good standing.

In Washington, by the 1990s the effort to overturn *Roe v. Wade* had stalled. Running as a pro-life presidential candidate in 2000, George W. Bush conceded from the outset that he had no plans to reverse the Supreme Court decision. Instead, once elected President Bush worked to enact incremental restraints on abortion, most notably a ban on the macabre procedure known as partial-birth abortion.

Before Bush entered the White House, the first legislative ban on partial-birth abortion had been stymied by a presidential veto. Congress had enacted the ban, but President Bill Clinton had rejected it. In the Senate, a vote to override the presidential veto was closely contested; with another seven pro-life votes the ban would have become law. But eight Catholic lawmakers—Senators Daschle of South Dakota, Dodd of Connecticut, Harkin of Iowa, Mikulski of Maryland, Moseley-Braun of Illinois, Murray of Washington, and both Kennedy and Kerry of Massachusetts—voted to sustain the veto. Thus the first federal legislation ever approved by Congress to stem the slaughter of unborn children was thwarted by the opposition of key Catholic legislators.

Like the priests who escaped punishment for their public dissent from *Humanae Vitae* under the "Truce of 1968," the Catholic politicians who voted to preserve partial-birth abortion suffered no adverse consequences for flouting Church teachings. Many bishops denounced the Senate vote, but no American bishop denounced the individual lawmakers responsible for that result.

The American bishops were ready to state the general principle: that a Catholic politician had a serious moral obligation to vote against abortion. But they were *not* willing to make a concrete application of that principle, and say that Senator Kennedy (or Senator Dodd, or Daschle or Harkin or Mikulski or Kerry) was guilty of a grave offense against the laws of the Church. By refusing to draw what appeared to be a natural, straightforward conclusion from the principles they had enunciated, the bishops lent credence to the argument that had been hatched in Hyannisport: that the abortion debate involved complicated moral judgments, and a vote in favor of legal abortion might somehow be justified by reference to some greater common good.

If the bishops would not denounce pro-abortion Catholic politicians, who would? Pro-life activists did, but since they were actively involved in the political battles their motives were suspect. Even when the pro-lifers cited the clear language of Vatican documents, their liberal adversaries charged that they were speaking as political partisans. And often they were; they were supporting pro-life challengers (usually Republicans) to the pro-abortion incumbents (who were usually Democrats).

Pro-life Catholics said that they held the only position consistent with the faith. Their "pro-choice" opponents said that the issue was actually more complex, and a Catholic politician could sometimes support legal abortion. This simple dispute cried out for a neutral arbiter, and the bishops were the obvious choice. But the bishops refused to settle the issue.

There was one other possibility. The Knights of Columbus, the world's largest Catholic fraternal organization, had impeccable credentials as a politically neutral Catholic group. There were hundreds of thousands of Knights enlisted in each of America's major political parties; the organization was certainly not partisan. Yet the Knights were proudly Catholic and staunchly pro-life; their adherence to Catholic teaching was also unquestioned.

Could the Knights settle the political issue, by expelling politicians who voted in favor of abortion? Membership in the Knights of Columbus was reserved to active Catholics in good standing. Pro-lifer activists in the organization argued that a Catholic politician who voted to support legal abortion had thereby shown his contempt for Catholic teaching and separated himself from the Church; he was no longer a Catholic in good standing.

In December 1990, the worldwide leader of the Knights of Columbus revealed that this intramural argument had been settled—not by a vote of the American members, but by an order from the Vatican. Virgil Dechant, the Supreme Grand Knight, said that his orders came from the Vatican Secretary of State. He quoted Cardinal Agostino Casaroli, as saying, in reply to the question of whether pro-abortion politicians might be excluded from membership, "Don't you dare make a move without the approval of Church authorities."

But "Church authorities" remained silent. The pro-abortion position was condemned, but the individual politicians who took that stance were treated as loyal Catholics in good standing. The only logical conclusion by someone standing aloof from the argument was that the bishops had accepted the Hyannisport argument: that under some circumstances, a vote for abortion—a vote in flagrant defiance of Church teaching—could be justified.

7

MOVING OUT OF THE CATHOLIC GHETTO

When the Democratic Party political machines took control of American cities early in the twentieth century, they were manned and governed primarily by Catholics. Immigrants or the sons of immigrants, the Democratic ward bosses won the allegiance of voters from urban working-class families, who were themselves mostly from immigrant stock.

At a time when Irish and Italian and German Catholics worked mainly at blue-collar jobs, it seemed natural to gravitate toward the political party that styled itself the champion of the workers. Particularly in the cities of the northeastern United States, Democratic party operatives controlled the labor unions, and the unions in turn provided funding and manpower for the Democratic machines.

Along with their partisan organizing functions, Democratic ward bosses performed a number of valuable social functions for poor and working-class families: securing jobs, finding housing, mediating disputes with neighbors or employers, even arranging dances at which young singles met their future spouses. In carrying out all these functions, the Democratic machine politicians developed deep and lasting bonds with the party faithful.

For our purposes in this book, it is also worthwhile to note that the ward bosses often interacted with Catholic pastors, who had traditionally carried out all the same informal tasks. The party began to supplant the parish as the focal point for the social life of the urban working-class family. For years that subtle transfer of allegiances went undetected, because the parish and the party worked smoothly together, and there was rarely any cause for conflict or competition.

The urban Democrats generally took a liberal stand on issues of taxes and social spending, but remained viscerally conservative on questions of social life and foreign policy. In Massachusetts that conservative strain was especially strong, and James Michael Curley once told Franklin Roosevelt that Boston was the most "Coughlinite" city in the country.

Curley was referring to Father Charles Coughlin, the fiery "radio priest" who had built up a nationwide following during the Depression with his speeches condemning the machinations of Wall Street tycoons and international bankers. Initially a strong supporter of the New Deal, Father Coughlin later turned against President Roosevelt, preaching his own blend of Catholic social thought and economic populism, arguing that capitalism and communism were equally dangerous forces. Although he was dogged by charges of anti-Semitism, Coughlin won the backing of many voters who were suspicious of both major political parties: the political forerunners of the third-party renegades who would back George Wallace and Patrick Buchanan in later years.

Father Coughlin's denunciations, and the prospect of third-party competition, troubled Franklin Roosevelt enough so that the President asked his most prominent Catholic ally, Joseph P. Kennedy, to try to tone down the priest's rhetoric. Coughlin, with his deep distrust of Wall Street, was not favorably disposed toward a man who had made millions by manipulating the stock market, and he rejected Kennedy's overtures. But Kennedy had the last laugh: joining forces with New York's Cardinal Francis Spellman, he appealed to the Vatican Secretary of State, Cardinal Eugenio Pacelli (later to become Pope Pius XII), and persuaded the Vatican to silence the radio priest.

Joseph Kennedy himself was a man of fairly conservative political leanings. His alliance with Franklin Roosevelt was marked by tension and occasional acrimony; Kennedy felt that the President underestimated his influence, while Roosevelt considered Kennedy too ambitious to be trusted. (They were both right.) In the years before World War II, as US ambassador to Great Britain, Kennedy was sympathetic to Prime Minister Neville Chamberlain in his efforts to avoid war with Nazi Germany. After the war he became a fervent anti-Communist, a supporter and friend of Senator Joe McCarthy. It is worth noting that his son, President John F. Kennedy, was a relatively conservative leader by today's standards. While in the White House, JFK went to the brink of nuclear war with the Soviet Union over the presence of missiles in Cuba, introduced a major tax cut to stimulate the economy, and committed the US to a military presence in Vietnam—a commitment that his younger brothers would later come to oppose.

But the Democratic party that had appealed to Catholic immigrants and produced the first Catholic President, changed dramatically over the course of the twentieth century, and the urban workers lost their controlling influence. The first major blow to the big-city Democratic machines came with the New Deal, and the realization that a distant and impersonal federal government could provide many of the services previously offered by the ward bosses. (That process is memorably described by Frank Skeffington, a fictionalized version of James Michael Curley, near the close of Edwin O'Connor's memorable novel, *The Last Hurrah*.) The second, fatal blow came with the McGovern Commission changes to the party structure in 1972. At the time, the McGovern reforms were depicted as a way to sap the power of big-city bosses like Chicago's Mayor Richard Daley. But in that process the changes effectively purged the urban Catholic operatives from the party leadership. The Democratic party veered sharply leftward, abandoning the blue-collar voters— socially conservative, patriotic, and disproportionately Catholic—who would be resurrected in the American political consciousness several years later as the "Reagan Democrats."

While the sociological complexion of the Democratic party was changing, the political leanings of the American Catholic hierarchy were shifting as well. The changes wrought by Vatican II had pushed Church leaders toward social engagement. Pope Paul VI, apparently convinced that the American hierarchy had become a haven for hidebound administrators, appointed a new apostolic delegate to the US, Archbishop Jean Jadot, who presided over the selection of more than one hundred new bishops between 1973 and 1980. These "Jadot bishops," as they were called, showed a strong penchant for liberal activism, and very little interest in traditional forms of piety.

Old-fashioned devotions were being jettisoned anyway, and theologians were calling for a transformation of both Church and society, in keeping with "the spirit of Vatican II." The newly emerging Church leaders seized every opportunity to lead their flock in a new direction. New social-action committees emerged at the parish and diocesan levels. The US Catholic Conference (later restructured to become the US Conference of Catholic Bishops) took on greater authority in Washington, lobbying politicians and generating nationwide support for various public initiatives. Almost without exception, the causes espoused by these Church groups were associated with the political left: disarmament, increased welfare spending, looser restrictions on immigration, an end to US support for the authoritarian regimes that were battling Marxist guerrillas in Latin America.

Bewildered by what they saw as the politicization of their Church, Catholics of more conservative bent questioned how these fashionable political causes were connected with the teachings of faith. If devout Catholics could legitimately take different positions on questions about federal taxation, why was the bishops' conference taking sides? Their questions were sharpened by the observation that the new breed of Catholic social activists seemed uninterested in causes that *were* strongly identified with the Church, most notably the struggle to end abortion.

Political involvement in leftist causes sometimes drew Catholic activists into alliance with groups that worked directly to oppose Church teachings on other issues. Each year, critics pointed to ties between the bishops' anti-poverty program, the Campaign for Human Development, and radical groups that distributed contraceptives, advocated abortion, or endorsed same-sex marriage.

The new Catholic activists were not embarrassed by these associations. For the record, they would patiently remind critics that politics is a pragmatic business, and that a group often forms temporary coalitions with other groups that do not share all of one's beliefs. But in moments of greater candor, some liberal Catholics would concede that they were not troubled by criticism of the Church teaching on issues involving sexuality and gender. The *National Catholic Reporter*, a weekly newspaper that catered to the activist constituency, mixed liberal political commentary with frank criticism of Church teachings.

The high-water market for radical Catholic activism was the Call to Action conference in 1976. Championed by Detroit's Cardinal John Dearden, the Call to Action initiative drew participants from all around the country. Leftist groups were primed and ready for the event, having organized for months to ensure that their groups were amply represented at the conference; conservative Catholics were barely aware that the meeting would take place.

When the meeting opened, Russell Kirk, the author of *The Conservative Mind*, was one of the few conservative Catholics in attendance. Kirk immediately noticed that the Call to Action participants were not representative of the Catholic laity. They were, he remarked, using a memorable image, the "church mice" who scurry through parish and chancery buildings on their own private errands: the self-important activists who had secured minor positions in chancery offices, on diocesan committees, and at Catholic schools and colleges. The Call to Action conference, driven by these individuals—who had few official responsibilities, but sought to enlist the support of the Church for their own causes—loosed a salvo of statements demanding change in Church teaching. To the consternation of the bishops who had given their backing to the event, Call to Action endorsed the ordination of women to the priesthood, called for a change in Church teaching on contraception, and declared that divorced Catholics should be allowed to remarry and continue receiving the Eucharist.

The activists had gone too far; bishops could not endorse the conclusions of a conference that had so boldly and unmistakably rejected Church teaching. Nor were even the more liberal bishops happy with the conference's call for a national review board to reconsider their decisions. The Call to Action initiative ended with a spiral into irrelevancy. Still, the "church mice" who had attended the conference and backed its resolutions remained employed in Catholic institutions. Job notices for positions on diocesan staffs continued to run in the *National Catholic Reporter*, which had given the conference its enthusiastic attention, rather than in its more sober and orthodox weekly competitor, the *National Catholic Register*.

After the Call to Action episode, radical Catholics did not attempt a frontal assault on Church authority. Instead they quietly built up their strength inside Catholic institutions, working for change from within. Soon national organizations representing Catholic theologians, canon lawyers, and university presidents were issuing statements criticizing the Vatican and questioning traditional teachings. In an essay published in the *New York Review of Books* in June 1984, Thomas Sheehan proclaimed a new consensus among Catholic scholars:

> In Roman Catholic seminaries ... it is now common teaching that Jesus of Nazareth did not assert any of the messianic claims that the Gospels attribute to him and that he died without believing that he was Christ or the Son of God.... And it seems that he ordained no priests, consecrated no bishops.... In fact, Jesus had no intention of breaking with Judaism in order to constitute a separate Church.

Conservative Catholic scholars took issue with Sheehan's piece on many other grounds, but did not deny the existence of the consensus he described. Catholic institutions had indeed become hotbeds of theological dissent.

Dissent was especially intense at schools operated by the Society of Jesus. In one flagrant but not atypical sign of the Jesuit contempt for traditional Catholic teaching, Holy Cross College, in Worcester, Massachusetts, announced in 1992 that a young woman had been chosen as the campus chaplain. That woman, Katherine McElaney, told the *Boston Globe* that in her new post she would be "working to change our structures and systems," and in particular she would be working for the ordination of women as priests. Father John Brooks, the president of Holy Cross, told the *Globe* that he was not worried about the new chaplain's stance on women's ordination. "That's not a problem for me," he said. Nor was he concerned that the chaplain planned to emphasize a new approach to the Eucharist, in which "students are taught to preside at a Communion service without a priest."

Early in his pontificate Pope John Paul II showed some inclination to rein in such internal dissent. But apart from a few warnings from the Vatican, the crackdown that liberals feared (and conservatives longed for) never occurred. Theological dissent remained commonplace, particularly at the most prestigious Catholic colleges and universities. Still the most outspoken dissenters complained that they were being muzzled.

Father Richard McBrien—whose regular criticism of the Vatican had not prevented him from holding a tenured position teaching theology at Notre Dame, or writing a nationally syndicated column for diocesan newspapers—compared the Vatican under John Paul II to the Kremlin after an internal coup. At a 1991 conference of Catholic activists he wailed about "the reactionary loss of power, the silencings, the censorship, the loyalty oaths, the search for enemies, the re-imposition of a party line, the promotion of hardliners, the appeal to the glories and the greatness of another time." At the same conference the feminist Mary Jo Weaver decried the influence of Catholic "fundamentalists," defining those dangerous people as "nuns who see the wearing of the habit and pursuing traditional postulates as crucial to their identity ... those who focus on the Mass as a sacrifice; who believe in the devil, who believe in the dreadful reality of personal sin ... who believe that Mary is the Queen of Heaven and the mediatrix of all graces."

In other words the "fundamentalists" were those who believed what *all* Catholics had believed just a generation earlier. Tradition-minded Catholics recognized the contempt that was implicit in such statements, and began to look with suspicion on the institutions that employed and promoted dissenters. But if they complained to their bishops, those complaints went unanswered. The American bishops had more urgent business on their minds, such as approving pastoral letters on divisive political issues.

In 1983, with liberal political activists lobbying intensively for a freeze on the production of nuclear weapons, the US bishops entered the debate, preparing a pastoral letter on the use of nuclear weapons. Early drafts of the statement gave an unambiguous endorsement to the nuclear-freeze movement, and only a forceful intervention by Vatican officials stopped the American bishops from an outright condemnation of nuclear-deterrent strategy in their final document. Soon activists all across the country were citing the bishops' document as support for their disarmament campaigns, while conservative Catholics (including several who were working at that time at the top levels of national-security policy in the Reagan administration) bitterly complained that the bishops had ignored their arguments explaining the moral basis for nuclear deterrence.

Apparently delighted by the publicity that the "peace pastoral" had brought them, the US bishops next embarked on a pastoral letter about economics. Once again the document clearly favored liberal theories and programs; once again conservatives complained that their views had not received adequate attention. Conservative Catholics began to look upon the American bishops collectively as their political enemies.

The bishops' penchant for issuing pastoral letters through their national episcopal conference threatened to become even more contentious with the suggestion that they should prepare a new document on the proper role of women in society and in the Church. Nuclear deterrence and welfare economics had been topics of heated debate in American political circles, but the debate on women's proper role was taking place *within the Church*, with feminists pushing strenuously for the ordination of women as priests. Sure enough, feminists and advocates of women's ordination were well represented at the "listening sessions" conducted by the bishops' drafting committee, and their views were respectfully examined in the early drafts. Meanwhile tens of thousands of women signed a petition circulated by a group called Women for Faith and Family, urging the bishops to reaffirm traditional Catholic teachings on the dignity of marriage and the importance of women as mothers and primary educators; this more conservative group had trouble winning a hearing.

In 1992, when the pastoral on women came up for discussion at a meeting of the American episcopal conference, Bishop Austin Vaughan commented on what he saw as the glaring deficiencies of the latest draft from the perspective of ordinary lay Catholics:

> There's nothing in the document on marriage, at a time when more marriages than ever are breaking up. There's nothing on the bad direction being given out in the Church on birth control. There's nothing on feminism as a problem. There's nothing on the lack of support from the Church for women who are trying to keep families together and to raise teenagers. It's out of touch with the real problems of most of the women I deal with. If it goes out the way it is, no one will read it after a week, and no one will cite it after the first day.

On this issue the American bishops could not find a politically viable compromise. They could not endorse the ordination of women as priests without defying the Vatican; they could not oppose women's ordination without incurring the wrath of feminists within the Church; and they could not ignore the question of ordination without consigning their pastoral letter to irrelevance. After several drafts and countless discussions, the pastoral on women was shelved—but not before another group of conservative Catholics became convinced that their bishops were neither sensitive to their problems nor interested in their opinions.

In Boston the level of dismay over the bishops' public statements was lower than in many other American cities, because the Catholics of the Boston area had been making their own leftward shift, so that the "Coughlinite" stronghold of the 1930s had become a liberal bastion by the 1960s. Remarkably enough, that political shift was *not* caused by a change in the party in power. The same group remained firmly in control: the ethnic Democrats, predominantly Catholic. But the politics of the rising generation were quite different from those of their fathers.

To some extent the change reflected the enormous influence of higher education. Boston is justly famous as a "college town," and as the younger Catholics passed through their universities they fell under the influence of a liberal professorate. (The leftist bias on campus has been thoroughly documented; in 1972, as American voters prepared to give Richard Nixon a landslide victory of unprecedented proportions, a survey of Ivy League professors found that 88 percent favored his doomed opponent, George McGovern.) The situation was not markedly different at the many Catholic colleges and universities in the region. On the contrary, at the Catholic schools political liberalism was typically welded with a "spirit of Vatican II" that encouraged the students to question their parents' outlook on life.

The sheer size of Boston's student population had an effect as well. Thousands of college-age students congregated on Boston Common for protest rallies during the Vietnam era. The youth rebellions of the late 1960s and early 1970s, proclaiming a hip new culture of "sex, drugs, and rock-n-roll," made it unfashionable to profess traditional moral principles on campus. Conservative students were forced to choose between prudent silence or bitter isolation; peer pressure oriented impressionable young people toward the left.

There was one final, powerful factor giving rise to the liberal ascendancy. The Catholic people of Boston, who had arrived as poor immigrants, were rising in socio-economic status, and many young Irish and Italian professionals were anxious to escape the limitations of their parents' sheltered lives in Boston's ethnic Catholic ghettoes. The great migration out of the city, into the leafy suburbs, had begun.

When they left the cities, the upwardly mobile Catholic families left some of the institutions that had shaped their social and political lives: the block parties and informal gatherings on front stoops and porches; the ward bosses and street-corner campaign rallies. As they moved up from blue-collar to white-collar careers, they also left behind the union meetings. And as they joined new communities in the suburbs, they adapted to the new social climate, behaving much the same way as their new neighbors.

Even during the years of conflict between the Boston Brahmins and the Irish immigrant families, some Irish-Catholic families aspired to acceptance by the old Yankee establishment. Crusty Irishmen would speak disparagingly of such "hopers"—who, they said, would go to bed Irish, hoping that they would wake up as Yankees. By the 1950s the "hopers" had become respectable; by the 1970s they had become a majority. Catholics in professional life had learned to tone down the evidence of their ethnic backgrounds and religious beliefs, to gain acceptance in a new, higher social caste.

In many societies, a move upward in social status often presages a more conservative outlook. Not so in Boston. The Yankee elites had clung to their own power and prestige, but their political views had always been colored by a crusading zeal to build a utopia on earth: a rare combination of religious passion and secular politics that could be traced back through Ralph Waldo Emerson to the original Puritan founders of the city.

Now the ambitions of those reformers—the drives to end an unpopular war, to promote racial equality, and to save the environment by curbing human population—gained acceptance among Catholics. Traditional Catholic social teaching, which emphasizes the role of prudence and looks askance at utopian projects, might have inoculated Catholic students against the liberal ideology. But traditional Church social teaching was no longer being offered in the Catholic schools.

On the contrary, during the 1960s and 1970s the Catholics of Boston heard liberal political ideals extolled by their parish priests. Young clerics, affected by the same educational environment as their lay peers, were moving adroitly to the left and bringing their political views into their sermons. Oddly enough, those sermons were not generally heard by their liberal allies, who had stopped attending Mass. Among the faithful Catholics who remained in the pews, liberal ideas were not nearly so popular. But respect for priests remained a cardinal rule for faithful Catholics, so if they were dismayed by the politicization of the pulpit, they suffered in silence. Eventually the steady diet of liberal preaching had its effect, and many Catholics came to assume that to be Catholic naturally entailed embracing the liberal causes. To be conservative, then, seemed to imply resistance against the faith.

Still there *was* resistance, among the individuals who had somehow acquired a better acquaintance with Catholic intellectual history and within the communities that had not joined in the social changes of the 1960s. Older Catholics remembered what they had been taught by the disciplined Jesuits of an earlier generation, and valiantly stuck to those same principles. Unreconstructed conservatives in the enduring ethnic-Catholic enclaves of South Boston and Charlestown sneered at the fashionable liberals in the suburbs and on the campuses.

In South Boston, in fact, a rebellion was brewing.

8

"Southie Won't Go"

Cardinal Humberto Medeiros was never terribly comfortable in Boston. The son of Portuguese immigrants, he felt that he could never be fully accepted in a community so heavily influenced by Irish-American culture. Ethnic tensions had shaped his life, and they would shape his ministry in Boston.

Born in the Azores, Medeiros was a child when his family moved to Fall River, a tough port city in southeastern Massachusetts. Growing up in a poor family, as a member of a despised minority group, he endured more than his share of ethnic taunts; playground bullies were encouraged, no doubt, by the boy's bookish and retiring nature. His intellectual talent was obvious, however, and after entering the priesthood he moved quickly up through the ranks, eventually becoming chancellor of the Fall River diocese.

In 1966 he was named Bishop of Brownsville, Texas. Brownsville is at the southern tip of Texas, bordering the Rio Grande, and the most important social problems that the new bishop faced there involved the treatment of immigrants from Mexico. Evidently his performance impressed his peers and his superiors in Rome, because in 1970 he was summoned to the office of the papal delegate in Washington and informed that he was the Pope's choice to become the next Archbishop of Boston.

In his book *Common Ground*, J. Anthony Lukas recounts how the archbishop-elect reacted to the news of his appointment. After pausing for a few minutes of quiet prayer, he politely asked whether the Pope knew what he was doing. The papal envoy reassured him, but Medeiros persisted:

> "I mean," said the bishop, "does he realize what it's equivalent to?"
> "No," said the puzzled delegate. "What is it equivalent to?"
> "Gethsemane," said the Bishop.

Before he even accepted the assignment, Medeiros had decided that his tenure in Boston would be an arduous trial, comparable to the suffering of Christ in the garden of Gethsemane on the eve of his Crucifixion. He feared that the people would not accept him. If Medeiros had been familiar with the peculiar Boston patois, in which one disdainful term is applied to all unfamiliar ethnic groups, he probably would have anticipated being dismissed as an "Eskimo."

In Boston the appointment caused a sensation—and not a pleasant one. Local Catholics had assumed that their new archbishop would be selected from among the ranks of the current Boston clergy. Since before the Civil War, the Archbishop of Boston had been a native of Boston, of Irish ancestry. Particularly after a quarter-century of Cardinal Cushing's leadership, it seemed just barely possible that an Italian-American priest could succeed him, and utterly unthinkable that his replacement would be a Portuguese immigrant from outside Boston. Some Irish Catholics saw the choice of an outsider as a slight: an indication that the Vatican did not respect the Boston clergy. Their incoming archbishop was right to suspect that he would face resentment.

Cardinal Cushing did nothing to ease the transition. At an introductory press conference, after praising Medeiros, the ailing cardinal almost broke into tears when he was asked about the personal contrast between himself and his successor. Then at the new archbishop's installation ceremony in Holy Cross cathedral, the outgoing prelate upstaged him, and this time the tears were in the eyes of the congregation.

The installation *should* have turned the spotlight onto Cardinal Medeiros, but at the close of the ceremony, when Cardinal Cushing rose to speak, all eyes were on the beloved old native son of Boston. Pale, weak, and shaky, breathing with great difficulty, in a voice cracked by both pain and emotion, he said:

> Whatever time is left for me, whatever pain and suffering, I offer joyfully for the Church that I have loved and tried to serve for three-quarters of a century. Pray for me, as I pray for you. And God bless you all.

With that the cardinal mustered his strength for what everyone knew would be his last procession down the aisle, and the congregation erupted in a standing ovation that pulsated through of the cathedral.

Reaching the door, the old cardinal rasped to his closest aides: "Let's get out of here, so we can be home before the Eskimo gets there." By the time the echoes died down, Cardinal Cushing had left the building. Only then did the people remember that they had come to welcome a *new* archbishop—who now meekly accepted their congratulations, fully realizing that they were thinking about someone else.

Three weeks later Cardinal Cushing died. Only then, reluctantly, did the people of Boston begin to recognize Archbishop Medeiros as the leader of the archdiocese. It might have been a difficult transition under the best of circumstances, because Medeiros was as quiet and careful as his predecessor had been outgoing and impulsive.

But Archbishop Medeiros worked carefully to guide the Church through difficult times. In one respect he was a spectacular success. Cardinal Cushing had a reputation as a champion fundraiser, but the truth is that the old cardinal was even better at spending than at raising money; his non-stop building projects and open-handed generosity to myriad causes had left the Boston archdiocese with a crushing debt. By diligent management, Medeiros whittled down the debt and restored the archdiocese to fiscal solvency. It was a surprising achievement, particularly for a man who was perceived as impractical and other-worldly. Because he was self-effacing, and because the public veneration for his predecessor was so strong, Medeiros never called attention to his own success in this regard. But the Vatican noticed, and while Cushing had been Archbishop of Boston for fourteen years before he received his red hat, in not quite three years the new leader of the Boston archdiocese answered to the title of *Cardinal* Medeiros.

Although he was trusted in Rome, Cardinal Medeiros was viewed with suspicion in Boston, especially in light of the gathering political storm over racial integration of the city's schools. The political resistance to integration was concentrated in South Boston, a neighborhood of working-class families with an unusually strong Irish-Catholic identity.

Liberal editorial columnists at the *Boston Globe* found it easy to write off "Southie" as a racist enclave, and there is no doubt that racism played an important part in the political drama that played out on the streets of that neighborhood during the mid-1970s. But to label the entire community as racist is a gross injustice; there were serious arguments in play, and the doughty residents of Southie were determined to preserve what they saw as their own legal rights.

Southie was a tight-knit community, fiercely proud of its heritage. Young men from the neighborhood went off to serve in Vietnam and returned as heroes, at a time when their counterparts in the suburbs were groping for ways to avoid the military draft. The Catholic parishes were busy, and a remarkable number of young people entered the priesthood or religious life. Life in Southie was friendly (for native residents, at least, if not for outsiders), retaining many of the block parties and ward meetings and neighborhood taverns that had characterized the urban ethnic communities of a previous generation. When tragedy struck local families—when a wage-earner suffered an accident, or a fire destroyed a home—neighbors would regularly host "a time" to collect funds for the victims. Many Southie natives chose to remain in the area, even when they had earned enough money to move into an upscale community; the neighborhood ties were too strong to break.

South Boston was a simple, unsophisticated place, in all respects but one: the neighborhood was justly famous for its political organization. Local elections were fiercely contested, and the winners, having been forced to build a strong campaign team, were well equipped to vie for higher office. The first Catholic Speaker of the US House of Representatives, John McCormack, was a native of South Boston. The young politicians who were formed in the cauldron of the 1970s racial controversies included a future president of the state senate (Bill Bulger), a future mayor (Ray Flynn), and a future president of the city council (Jim Kelly). But the most prominent Southie politician of the era was the woman who would serve three terms on the Boston school committee, three on the city council, and one term as McCormack's successor in the US House of Representatives: Louise Day Hicks.

A distinctly unstylish housewife, with a penchant for wearing outdated white gloves and flowery hats, Louise Day Hicks was an unlikely lightning-rod for controversy. Studiously careful in her manners and her diction, she seemed to be the polished product of some stuffy Catholic finishing school (although in fact she was a public-school graduate). But she was inflexible in her determination to preserve her neighborhood, and at a time of intense political emotions she roused strong reactions. For several years she was accompanied by an armed bodyguard because of persistent death threats. When she delivered her signature campaign slogan—"You know where I stand!"—the crowds in Southie would roar their approval.

Where *did* she stand? Hicks was a champion of neighborhood schools. She strongly believed that young children should be educated in their own communities, under the supervision of their parents. While there was definitely strong racial imbalance in the Boston schools, she insisted that the classroom enrollment only reflected the ethnic composition of the neighborhoods, and children should not be used as pawns in a utopian scheme to transform the city.

Years later, the sociologists who had suggested busing as a means of achieving racial integration in city schools admitted that their plans had been unsuccessful. In their own unsophisticated way, the parents of South Boston anticipated some of the arguments that the sociologists would belatedly concede, after unhappy experience dimmed their initial enthusiasm for busing. Schools in run-down neighborhoods would not magically improve with the importation of students from other areas; students in integrated classrooms would not learn more or achieve higher grades. Busing would damage morale in the schools, threaten educational standards, and drive families out of the public school system altogether. But above all, in South Boston (whose schools were mediocre at best), parents demanded that the schools should reflect the composition the neighborhood. Most Southie residents were prepared for the racial integration of their community, and in fact black families had begun arriving in the housing projects. There were racial incidents—as there were in nearly every neighborhood as integration began—but by and large the people of Southie were prepared to accept black neighbors. They were *not* prepared to accept the forced busing of outsiders into schools that they jealously regarded as their own, nor could they stomach the idea that their children would be sent off into an unfamiliar and unsafe neighborhood to fulfill the vision of an unsympathetic judge.

Hicks and her allies could cite the teachings of the Catholic Church as support for their stance. Parents are the primary educators, they argued, and should have control over the schools where their children are placed. The principle of subsidiarity dictates that social problems should be addressed at the local level whenever possible: in this case, in the neighborhood school rather than the city council, and certainly not in a federal court. In defending their local schools, South Boston residents firmly believed that they were defending the teachings of their Catholic faith. And they could not understand why their efforts were not enthusiastically supported by the archdiocese.

But then again, the archdiocese under Cardinal Medeiros seemed slow to defend Church authority in any area. The changes of Vatican II were ripping through the archdiocese, priests and nuns were deserting, theological dissent was escalating, and still the cardinal was quiet. An angry young priest, Father George Spagnolia, had tested the limits of the prelate's patience, by announcing a hunger strike and setting up a tent on the lawn outside the archbishop's residence to protest when the chancery failed to approve his plan to build a new parish school. The enigmatic Cardinal Medeiros, declining to take disciplinary action against Spagniola, instead praised his resolution. "I wish I had a thousand like him," he said.

But if he admired resolution, why didn't the cardinal support the parents of Southie? In 1972, Medeiros testified at the state legislature in favor of the Racial Balance Act. Understandably sensitive to the needs of racial minorities, he seemed deaf to the concerns of Catholic parents.

The conflict escalated when a federal judge, W. Arthur Garrity, issued a court order requiring a massive program of busing to achieve racial parity in public-school enrolments. During the summer of 1974, Boston school officials, working under the court's exacting supervision, made plans to bus 18,000 children to new schools outside their own neighborhoods.

To the people of South Boston, Judge Garrity—a resident of Wellesley, a suburb favored by socially ambitious Irish professionals—appeared as a perfect villain. In that comfortable bedroom community he would not be personally affected by the chaos his order would unleash on the schools; residents of Wellesley and other affluent suburbs had quickly dismissed suggestions that black students from the inner cities should be bused into *their* schools. The judge's public statements sounded sanctimonious; he seemed determined not only to integrate the schools but also to break the resistance of his opponents. In his court orders he made no real effort to find common ground between two contending parties; he consistently sided with the critics of the Boston school policies, so that his rulings won editorial support from the *Boston Globe*—a newspaper that had vilified Hicks and her allies. The people of South Boston came to believe that the judge was their sworn enemy, and Garrity did nothing to alleviate their fears. As Bill Bulger would later write, in his handling of the busing case Judge Garrity showed "the sensitivity of a chain saw and the foresight of a mackerel."

In the first stage of the busing program, Garrity ordered an exchange of students between South Boston and Roxbury: a mostly black neighborhood with soaring crime rates and abysmal schools. This was no coincidence, the people of South Boston were sure; the judge was punishing them for their resistance. But the order only toughened their resolve. Their children would not be put at risk, they vowed. If necessary they would boycott the public schools. "Southie won't go!" they swore.

As the tension mounted, Cardinal Medeiros appealed for moderation. "Busing might not be the most desirable way to integrate," he said, "but it's all we have right now." He urged the people of Boston to accept the court order calmly. He instructed his priests to do everything possible to keep the peace and urged them to ride the school buses as volunteers on the first days of the busing program, to ensure the safety of the children.

The school year opened, and one-half of all the police officers in Boston were on hand to ensure public order. In South Boston, now at the focus of national attention, only a handful of children showed up for classes. So when the bright yellow buses pulled out of the neighborhood, surrounded by angry demonstrators, their only passengers were policemen and Catholic priests!

The busing controversy continued for months. Angry, bitter, and disillusioned, the people of South Boston saw themselves portrayed as bigots and rednecks. Every sign of intolerance was magnified in the national media, while their reasoned arguments were ignored. Passions flared frequently; Judge Garrity received dozens of death threats (which were given ample media exposure, unlike the threats against Louise Day Hicks). There were reports of gunshots from passing cars into the press room of the *Boston Globe,* whose plant lay on the edge of South Boston.

In the past, the people of South Boston had always been able to look to the Catholic Church for solace and help. Now, sadly, they saw the archdiocese as indifferent if not actually hostile. St. Augustine's parish volunteered to act as a staging area for the police officers who clashed regularly with demonstrators—including, naturally, parishioners from St. Augustine's. At one point, the baton-wielding police waded into a crowd of mothers demonstrating on a public square, and the women ran for shelter to nearby St. Bridget's church, only to find that the doors were locked. The pastor said that the doors had been locked for weeks, because of the threat of crime in the neighborhood; the suspicious women remarked that they had never noticed the closed doors before.

The demonstrators who gathered daily in South Boston to protest the busing program, most of them women and mothers of schoolchildren, thought of themselves as representatives of a Catholic tradition. They often recited the Rosary during their protest vigils. But the archdiocese clearly did not see them in the same terms. Cardinal Medeiros declined to meet with them, or even to visit their parishes. In 1976, when the *Herald American* newspaper questioned him about his reluctance to venture into the neighborhood, the cardinal replied with an unfortunate outburst. "Why should I go?" he asked. "To get stoned?" He continued:

> Is that what they'd like to see? I am not afraid to get stones thrown at me. But I am afraid for Boston. It does not need the opprobrium of national headlines saying that their archbishop was stoned. I've been turned off in South Boston, anyhow. No one there is listening to me.

The cardinal was wrong. The people of South Boston were still listening to him and his words stung, deepening the resentment they already felt. Their archbishop had betrayed them.

No doubt the cardinal had been guided by a genuine desire for racial harmony. But in the pursuit of a political goal, he had been ready to disdain faithful members of his flock and ignore fundamental principles of Church teaching. Cardinal Medeiros did not merely endorse the general principle of racial equality; he endorsed a specific political program designed to achieve that goal, despite the clear indications that many good Catholics found that policy wrongheaded and injurious.

So great was his determination to make the busing experiment successful, that Cardinal Medeiros was ready to sacrifice the health of his own parochial schools. The Catholic schools of Boston had been suffering a serious decline in enrollment, dropping from 151,582 students in 1963 to just 86,469 in 1973, and many of the schools were struggling to survive. But as the 1974 academic year loomed, Boston families saw the parochial schools as a way to escape from the busing. Anxious to close that loophole, city officials asked the cardinal to put a cap on parochial-school enrollment, and he acceded to that request.

In February 1974, therefore, the Archbishop of Boston issued instructions that Catholic schools should stop accepting transfers and refrain from recruiting new students. A handful of pastors later received peremptory letters from the chancery, demanding an explanation of the enrollment increases at their parish schools. It did not matter that many parochial schools had empty seats and desperately needed new tuition revenue. It did not matter that hundreds of black children were studying in the parochial schools, and the freeze on enrollment closed the doors to others at a time when the parochial schools were clearly the best educational option for inner-city families. It did not matter that the Church proclaimed the right of parents to send their children to Catholic schools. The political goal, as set by Judge Garrity, took precedence over the welfare of the Catholic parishes and their children.

Forced busing had a devastating effect on Boston, and especially on the city's public schools. Thousands of families left the city to enroll their children in suburban schools. As neighborhood schools disappeared, the character of the neighborhoods was irreversibly altered. The educational performance of public-school students declined—in part because the most promising students were siphoned off by private schools. Mothers who had stayed at home to raise their families took full-time jobs, placing toddlers in day-care centers, so that they could afford private-school tuition payments.

South Boston, which bore the brunt of the battle, was changed forever. The wounds eventually healed, but the bonds that had united a proud community with the Catholic Church could never be fully restored. Bill Bulger—a young state representative at the time of the controversy, who later emerged as the most powerful politician in Massachusetts—expressed the sense of bewilderment and isolation that hit the community when Cardinal Medeiros closed the doors of the Catholic schools. "If there is no sanctuary in the Church," he asked rhetorically, "then where?"

9

LOST
BATTLES

rriving in Boston early in 1984, Archbishop Bernard Law wasted
no time in announcing that he planned to fight for an end to
legal abortion, which he characterized as "the primordial darkness of our time." Those words were a tonic to conservative Catholics, who
had begun to feel like political orphans in Massachusetts.

Cardinal Medeiros had intervened decisively in public affairs twice
during his stay in Boston, each time with negative results. His strong support of busing had alienated conservatives, while his unwelcome remarks
during Barney Frank's first Congressional race made him a *bête noire* among
liberals. In a city with a large and visible student population, the cardinal
did his best to reach out to young people, but could not reconcile himself to
the campus morality of the 1970s. At a reception for Harvard students, the
cardinal said how he admired the idealism of college students, but . . . and
then he broke off his sentence, shaking his head and repeating, almost
inaudibly, "so much fornication; so much fornication."

A sensitive man by nature, Cardinal Medeiros was stung by the criticism he heard, and frustrated by his inability to make himself understood
even to the people of his own flock. He became more withdrawn, and subject to periods of melancholy that irritated his physical ailments, which
included diabetes and a weak heart. In September 1983 the cardinal was
admitted to St. Elizabeth's Hospital for heart surgery. The cardinal's condition was not considered critical and the procedure was not particularly risky.
The surgery went well, but the patient never recovered; Cardinal Medeiros
died quietly the next day.

Early in January 1984, Pope John Paul II named Law, who had been
heading the little diocese of Cape Girardeaux, Missouri, to lead the Boston
archdiocese. Two weeks later the Pope named a more prominent bishop,

John O'Connor, as Archbishop of New York. Coming so close together, the two appointments in the Catholic strongholds of the American northeast seemed to indicate a trend. Both brimming with self-confidence and unapologetic in their defense of Catholic teaching, Law and O'Connor suggested a bracing trend in the American hierarchy. The two new archbishops—who became close friends and episcopal allies, consulting each other constantly—were recognized from the outset as new leaders in the American Church, yoked in the public imagination as "Law and Order." Together they entered the College of Cardinals in May 1984, barely over a year after having been named archbishops.

As assertive as his predecessor had been diffident, Cardinal Law brought Boston a style of self-confident personal leadership that awakened memories of Cardinal O'Connell. The new archbishop did not have local roots—he was the only child of a military officer who had moved his family frequently—but he had spent four years in the Boston area as a Harvard undergraduate, and felt at ease with the city's culture. Like O'Connell he was equally comfortable in Rome, attuned to the nuances of Vatican politics, and close to a powerful patron (in Law's case, his predecessor in the Cape Girardeaux diocese, Cardinal William Baum) in the Roman Curia. Also like Cardinal O'Connell, Law was clearly ambitious. Soon after his arrival, Boston pundits began to question whether their new cardinal might become—or might at least perceive himself as—a candidate to become the first American ever elected to the papacy. While Cardinal Law dismissed any such speculation, his demurrals were not particularly convincing.

These were exciting times for American Catholics. Pope John Paul II, young and vigorous, had captured the public imagination, commanding a worldwide audience as no Pontiff before him had done. (In October 1979, when he became the first Pope ever to visit the city of Boston, more than one million people waited in the rain to join him for Mass on Boston Common.) Catholicism was on the march, it seemed. And the appointments of "Law and Order" suggested that the American hierarchy might be transformed in his activist image—a prospect that was dreaded by some Catholics and welcomed by others, according to their own predilections.

For Boston's more conservative Catholics, the advent of Cardinal Law promised blessed relief. A decade after *Roe v. Wade*, pro-life activists in Massachusetts were still determined to mobilize the enormous base of Catholic voters to reverse the acceptance of abortion. Cardinal Law looked to be an inspirational new leader for their movement.

Massachusetts had acquired a deserved reputation for liberalism in 1972, when it was the only state in the Union to support George McGovern's doomed presidential candidacy. From that point the leftward drift continued. The "Coughlinite" Boston of the mid-twentieth century was long gone, as were the Democratic politicians who appealed to an ethnic blue-collar base. There were still plenty of Irish- and Italian-Catholic candidates rising through the ranks of the Democratic Party, but their their views were formed by secular ideology rather than Catholic faith.

There was a short break from the trend in 1978, when an Irish Democrat, Edward King, unseated the incumbent governor, Michael Dukakis, in a classic contest between the old and new styles. King was a burly, outgoing man—a former professional football player—with a knack for business dealings and a sympathy for the taxpayer. Dukakis was small, quiet, and serious: the very image of the "policy wonk," determined to use government authority as a force for social change. King won in 1978, running on a platform that promised restraints on soaring taxes.

In office Governor King was modestly successful; his tax policies helped to trigger an economic boom in Massachusetts. But he never won the full support of his own political party. Unflinchingly conservative, he refused to support Senator Ted Kennedy's presidential ambitions in 1980 and developed cordial ties with Ronald Reagan. He was isolated in a Democratic party controlled by the political left. And in what was to become a leitmotif of Boston politics, he was hounded by negative media coverage, led by the powerful *Boston Globe*.

"If God is with you, who can be against you, right? Except the *Boston Globe*." Governor King made that statement playfully in 1981. But the *Globe*'s treatment of his administration was anything but playful. There were complaints of cronyism and hints of corruption; columnists snarled that King was packing the state government with people like himself: Irish, Catholic, conservative, and, in a remarkable number of cases, graduates of Boston College.

A generation or two earlier, the *Globe*'s disdainful remarks about Irish-Catholic politicians would have triggered a backlash of sympathy from a powerful constituency. But the newspaper's editors—many of them Irish now, although few were practicing Catholics—had detected the fault-line in the Catholic community. King was a Catholic of the old school, traditional in his beliefs and practices. He could be criticized safely, as the benighted sort of Catholic to be shunned by those who were infused with the "spirit of Vatican II."

Governor King strongly opposed abortion, but he strongly supported capital punishment, and the latter stance made him anathema to the liberal Catholics who controlled the organs of communication for the Church in Massachusetts. So when the *Globe* attacked, the defense was weak—or rather King's defenders had difficulty making their voices heard, given the bias of the mass media. In a 1982 rematch, Dukakis defeated King to regain his gubernatorial seat. Watching the returns at the studio of a local television station, one Catholic commentator offered a celebratory toast when King's defeat was announced. "We got him!" he cried.

Cardinal Law arrived in Massachusetts too late to save Governor King, even if he had wanted to do so. And Law—who strongly opposed King on the question of capital punishment—would not likely have expended his own political capital on behalf of this Catholic politician. But the new archbishop took an active interest in political affairs, particularly those that touched upon the Church's mission, with abortion at the top of his public agenda.

The cardinal soon had an opportunity to measure the strength of the Catholic political vote. Local activists had managed to put two referendum questions on the ballot for a statewide vote in 1986: one measure that would have allowed the state legislature to regulate abortion, another that would have overturned the draconian state law banning all forms of state aid to private (including parochial) schools. Enthusiastically supporting both efforts, Cardinal Law threw the full political weight of the archdiocese behind them. He encouraged donors to support the referendum campaigns, spoke at rallies, and instructed pastors to speak about the ballot questions and put notices in parish bulletins.

When the ballots were counted in November, the results came as a devastating blow to the archdiocese and to anyone who believed that loyal Catholic voters still constituted a "silent majority" in Massachusetts. The bid to allow protective laws regulating abortion failed by a 54-39 percent vote. The effort to secure public aid for private schools lost by a resounding 65-28 percent. And if those results by themselves were not enough to depress Catholic analysts, the details that emerged from exit polls were bleaker still. On both referendum questions, the majority of voters who identified themselves as Roman Catholics had voted *against* the position favored by the Boston archdiocese.

Catholics still accounted for more than half of the active voters in Massachusetts, but the Catholic vote, as a political force, had vanished.

Fifty years earlier Cardinal O'Connell could kill a popular legislative proposal with a single public statement. Now in 1986, after a long, expensive
campaign, Cardinal Law could not manufacture a voting majority even
among his own people.

Moreover, the two ballot questions provided unmistakable evidence
that most Catholic voters were not indifferent, but actually *hostile* toward the
public stance taken by their own Church leaders. Massachusetts voters had
now clearly endorsed legal abortion. Even more remarkably, the voters—
including the Catholic voters—had endorsed the same overt hostility
toward parochial schools that had been written into state law a century earlier by a frankly anti-Catholic legislature. In the mid-nineteenth century, the
Know-Nothing majority on Beacon Hill had driven through an absolute ban
on any form of public assistance to the private schools that served the
Catholic minority. By the early twentieth century, similar ugly forms of religious discrimination had been erased from the public laws of other American
states. But the absolute ban remained in full effect in Massachusetts, one of
the few states in which Catholics formed a voting majority.

But why would Catholics defend an anti-Catholic tradition? In part
because they had ceased to identify with their faith; by the 1980s, to identify oneself as Catholic in Boston was to give an ethnic rather than a religious description. The voters who identified themselves as Catholics were
telling pollsters something about their backgrounds but not necessarily their
beliefs. The fashionable trend, for well over a generation, had been for
Catholics to leave their religious backgrounds behind. By 1986 a majority
had done so.

The formation of an anti-Catholic majority was effectively promoted
by the local media, which applauded every Catholic who broke with
Church teaching and criticized anyone so retrograde as to uphold Catholic
traditions. The *Boston Globe*, easily the most powerful media voice in New
England, hired and promoted Catholics who criticized the Church, and the
opinions published in the *Globe* shaped the attitudes of other media outlets.
The *Globe*'s distant rival, the *Boston Herald*, used its own meager influence
to boost Republicans, or (since few Republicans had realistic electoral
prospects) simply to snipe at old-fashioned "hack politicians" within the
Democratic majority—more often than not, Catholics.

Catholics have never felt welcome within the Republican Party in
Massachusetts. For generations the GOP was controlled by the old Yankee
establishment: the Cabots and Lodges who were viewed by Irish political

upstarts as tribal foes. By the 1980s that old ethnic antagonism had broken down, while the McGovernite revolution and the liberal advocacy for unrestricted abortion had driven pro-life Catholics out of the Democratic Party. The time was ripe for Republican strategists to capture Catholic voters: to draw the disaffected Irish Catholics of South Boston and the pro-life Catholics of the suburbs into a new conservative coalition, as indeed conservative candidates were doing in other American regions.

But Massachusetts Republican leaders had no interest in making common cause with the voters who, in other states, were known as the "Reagan Democrats." The old Yankee backbone of the Republican establishment had never been conservative, at least not in the sense of that term as it was employed in the 1980s. From the days of the Puritans through the Abolitionists and Transcendentalists, the Boston establishment had always favored the politics of social change. The intellectual heirs of Emerson and Thoreau wanted to *reform* the thinking of their conservative Catholic neighbors, not to accept them as allies.

During the 1980s several Republican politicians made a bid to broaden the party's conservative base, with unhappy results. Ray Shamie, a self-made millionaire, plowed his own resources into a campaign against Senator Ted Kennedy. Predictably enough, Shamie was hammered by the liberal media, who depicted him as a dangerous extremist, dwelling at great length upon his past association with the John Birch Society. More ominously, the state's Republican leaders failed to close ranks behind their candidate, and after a promising start the Shamie campaign sputtered, choked by the incessant negative publicity. An energetic young lawyer, Greg Hyatt, launched a challenge to Governor Dukakis, but was sidetracked by questions about irregular campaign practices. Again the media scrutiny was relentless, and again the candidate had few public defenders; eventually Hyatt withdrew from the race. Paul McCarthy, a candidate for Secretary of State and later for a seat in Congress, had the details of an ugly marital dispute aired in the local media. Frank McNamara, a US attorney with a promising future, saw his secret FBI testimony reproduced in the *Boston Globe*.

Public criticism is a natural consequence of a public life, and each one of these Republican operatives could have foreseen the opposition he would encounter. What is remarkable about their cases is not the criticism that they encountered; in at least some cases the criticism was warranted. What is remarkable is that when the media onslaught came, the Republican Party failed to respond with a vigorous defense.

Shamie, Hyatt, McCarthy, and McNamara had something else in common: they were all pro-life Catholics. And in the Boston of the late 1980s, who would come to the defense of a pro-life Catholic Republican? Neither political party was hospitable. The *Globe* was an implacable enemy, the *Herald* at best an inconstant friend. There were liberal op-ed columnists and talk-show hosts aplenty around the Boston area, whose intellectual hegemony was contested by a few feisty libertarians. There were two tradition-minded Jewish columnists (Don Feder and Jeff Jacoby), and a conservative Baptist (Joe Fitzgerald), but not a single prominent newspaper columnist or talk-show host who could plausibly be described as a Catholic conservative.

In October 1986—just days before the November referendum votes—Cardinal Law made one gesture to break the media monopoly, hiring me to edit the archdiocesan newspaper, the *Pilot*, and encouraging me to take an aggressive Catholic stance on public affairs. That approach yielded some tangible results. In 1987, when the state legislature opened debate on a proposed "gay rights" law, which would have made it illegal to discriminate against homosexuals in employment and housing, the *Pilot* carried a searing editorial opposing the legislation. The editorial drew a strong public response; within hours the state-house switchboard lit up with calls from conservative Catholics voicing their opposition to the bill, and after a few days the bill quietly died. (Similar legislation would be enacted two years later, facing little public resistance.)

The *Pilot* editorial also ignited furious protests by homosexual activists. The newspaper was flooded with letters, the editorial offices were picketed, I had speeches disrupted, and received my first death threats. At one point a man called my office, identified himself as the proprietor of a gay bar in Boston's South End, and threatened to identify the Boston priests who were regular patrons. When I relayed that message to Cardinal Law, to his credit he replied: "He'd be doing me a favor. He'd be helping me identify my problems."

At the time the cardinal's response was reassuring. I was confident that if there were actively homosexual priests in the Boston archdiocese, they were few in number and weak in influence; if they could be identified, they would surely be disciplined. But even at that time, there were reasons to question my confidence. Why were so many priests nervous about my editorial and unhappy about the public response? Why did I detect hostility when I spoke to groups of Boston priests at regional vicariate meetings? Why had the Jesuit Urban Center become a homosexual hangout—

eventually so notorious that *Boston* magazine would designate it the "best place to pick up a mate—gay?"

While I had expected most priests to agree with my editorial on the gay-rights law, I had not been so naïve as to anticipate clerical enthusiasm for another editorial, in which I proudly supported the Church teaching on the immorality of contraception, scolding priests for failing to preach on that topic. Indeed for several years I thought that it was that editorial on birth control that had roused the animosity of the Boston clergy, whose hostility in turn would force my quick departure from the *Pilot*. Dozens of priests had criticized my stand on *Humanae Vitae*, whereas very few had openly questioned my opposition to the gay-rights law.

The most prominent critic of my *Pilot* editorial on birth control was a priest who taught at the Boston archdiocesan seminary. He wrote a long, patronizing letter to the editor, arguing that my position was based on inadequate understanding of the issue. I defended my views energetically in the same column. At a conference shortly after the exchange was published, Cardinal Law pulled me aside to congratulate me for taking a clear stand. Yet just a few months later I was forced to resign as editor of the *Pilot*—with public explanations citing a conflict of editorial vision—while the priest who dissented from Church teaching on contraception remained at his post, teaching moral theology to Boston's seminarians.

Cardinal Law himself was caught up in the quest to appease the liberal media. He had arrived in Boston speaking clearly and openly about the evils of abortion. But by the end of the decade he was taking a more conciliatory approach, reserving his strong pro-life statements for sympathetic audiences, speaking far more cautiously to the general public. When he spoke at major pro-life rallies, he called for strict adherence to non-violent tactics—thereby conceding the rhetorical premise of abortion advocates, who were arguing that pro-life activists were potentially violent. At one major pro-life assembly, the cardinal ignored dozens of pro-abortion counter-demonstrators who were shouting obscenities, but devoted a substantial portion of his address to condemning a single, isolated, unbalanced old man—Jozef Mlot-Mroz, who identified himself as the "Polish-American Freedom Fighter"— who stood at the edge of the crowd holding signs warning of a Jewish-Communist conspiracy. Anyone who regularly attended political events in Boston knew that Mlot-Mroz was a fixture at public rallies, who brought the same anti-Semitic message to every available audience. But somehow Cardinal Law felt it more important to distance himself from this lonely crank than to rally the mainstream workers of the pro-life movement.

Abortion was the most contentious public issue of the 1980s, but not the only one on which the Church took an unpopular position. Boston Catholics became accustomed to angry displays by feminists attacking the Church's teaching that only men can be ordained to the priesthood. Each year, as a new class of young men was ordained to the priesthood, feminists would disrupt the solemn ceremony at Holy Cross cathedral. Rather than risk an ugly public scene, officials of the archdiocese humored the protestors, allowing a few women to make their own unauthorized procession down the aisle of the cathedral and pronounce themselves qualified for priestly ordination. The women would then leave quietly, archdiocesan officials would assure reporters that the story was not worthy of public notice, and after a bit of uneasy throat-clearing the ordination ritual would resume.

No doubt encouraged by the success of the feminist protestors, gay-rights advocates began to join in the demonstrations at ordination ceremonies and each year their participation grew noisier. Pagan groups arrived on the scene, quite literally performing ritual dances around a tree outside the cathedral. Police protection now became a necessity, simply to control the boisterous crowds. But Church officials downplayed the conflict.

Matters came to a head at the ordinations in 1990 when the militant homosexual group Act Up arrived in force, having advertised their plans for a noisy demonstration. Parents and friends had to find their way through a crowd of angry, shouting homosexual protestors. During the ceremony, those inside the cathedral could still hear the shouting of slogans, the obscenities directed at the Church amplified through portable sound systems. Several hundred Boston police stood in formation around the cathedral to cordon off the protestors. From time to time, the Act Up demonstrators rushed across the police barricade, seeking access to the doors of the cathedral. Police calmly picked them up and carried them back outside the barricade; no arrests were made. When one observer saw homosexual activists jumping on top of his car, he asked a nearby officer to stop the destruction; the policeman replied that he was under orders to maintain his defensive position. When the ceremony ended, and the newly ordained priests left the cathedral with their proud parents, the demonstrators moved in, spitting on them and pelting them with condoms.

The Act Up demonstration was a blatant violation of Massachusetts laws prohibiting the disruption of a religious service. Boston's Mayor Ray

Flynn and police commissioner Mickey Roache were both present at the cathedral but issued no orders for arrests. The Boston archdiocese did not press criminal charges against the protestors; on the contrary, Church officials discouraged criminal complaints. One lay group, today known as the Catholic Action League, did press prosecutors to take action. But the local district attorney—Newman Flanagan, who at the time was a ranking official in the national leadership of the Knights of Columbus—did not even answer a letter from the lay activist group. The utter silence from law-enforcement officials, in the face of highly publicized criminal activities, prompted suspicions that archdiocesan officials had asked for a non-confrontational approach.

Those suspicions grew more intense when a later Act Up protest was staged during Easter Sunday Mass at the cathedral in Springfield, Massachusetts. The *Springfield Observer*, the official newspaper of that diocese, praised the homosexual activists for their restraint: on this occasion they had merely dropped condoms into the collection basket, rather than hurling them at priests. The *Observer* went on to comment that Church officials had reacted strongly to previous Act Up demonstrations, and "some might say over-reacted." But serious confrontations had been avoided, the Catholic newspaper concluded, adding: "So far Act Up has wisely chosen the civilized approach."

Thus the pattern continued: an official organ of a nearby Catholic diocese complimented homosexual militants for the "civilized approach" they had taken, when in fact they had sworn, spat, and thrown condoms at priests. The Archbishop of Boston warned against violence within the pro-life movement, but would not condemn the violence of anti-Catholic demonstrators on the streets outside his own cathedral. Church officials were backpedaling furiously to avoid a collision with aggressive adversaries.

When he cautioned pro-lifers against violence, Cardinal Law was obviously referring to the confrontations that occurred outside abortion clinics under the auspices of Operation Rescue, a nationwide movement that used non-violent civil disobedience in an effort to protect unborn children. At strategic intervals, the members of the group would stage blockades by standing or sitting in front of the doors of abortion clinics, forcing police to carry them away one by one, thus prolonging the time before the clinics could open and the destruction of human lives could begin. Leaders of Operation Rescue demanded a commitment to non-violence "in word and deed" from themselves and their followers, but abortion advocates insisted that sidewalk blockades were inherently violent, and those complaints were taken more seriously in the press than the pro-lifers' vows of innocence. Critics of the group tossed in the complaint that Operation Rescue employed violent *rhetoric*—for instance, by brandishing signs that proclaimed, "Abortion kills children." Pro-lifers replied that they were not using inflammatory language but making a straightforward statement of fact. The real violence, they said, took place *inside* abortion clinics.

When Operation Rescue made its first concerted effort to blockade an abortion clinic in Boston, in November 1988, only a handful of people were willing to risk arrest. But the movement quickly won new followers, and by the last day of that calendar year there were over one hundred pro-life activists shivering on the sidewalks, singing hymns and waiting to be jailed. By March 1989, police were forced to arrest 227 pro-lifers in a single day, and the quick expansion of the movement threatened to overwhelm the resources of local law enforcement. Police in Brookline—the town adjacent to Boston where the busiest abortion clinics were located—could barely handle two hundred arrests; what would happen if the movement continued to grow and the next blockade drew five hundred people or more?

Such questions were not merely idle speculation. Operation Rescue was an ecumenical group, with no direct ties to the Catholic Church; but some priests had signaled their approval, and even Cardinal Law had expressed some admiration for the courage of the group's leaders. In New York an auxiliary bishop, Austin Vaughn, had joined the group and been arrested himself, with the approval of Cardinal O'Connor. There was heady speculation among pro-life activists that Cardinal Law himself might join a blockade and submit to arrest. What policeman in Boston would want to see his own picture on the front page of the newspaper, arresting the archbishop? What would happen if the cardinal went a step further, and asked other Catholics to join him—if, for instance, he issued an appeal to the Knights of Columbus to join in acts of civil disobedience? It was easy to imagine a scenario in which public officials simply could not break the blockades, clinics would be closed, and—no matter what the law said—legal abortion would end.

But those scenarios never played out in Boston. Instead Cardinal Law edged away from Operation Rescue. Rather than using the same rhetoric as pro-life activists, he began to use the language of their critics, insisting that the pro-life movement must be non-violent—and thereby confirming the impression that some groups within the movement *could* reasonably be judged guilty of violence.

Neither side of the abortion debate disputed that real violence took place inside the abortion clinics of Brookline on December 30, 1994. John Salvi, a severely disturbed young man who had no previous contact with local pro-life activists, rushed into two of the busy abortion clinics on Brookline's Beacon Street that morning, shooting semi-automatic weapons. Two women—a receptionist at one clinic, a counselor at the other—were killed.

The murders shocked all of Boston and ignited what had been a smoldering political conflict into a full-scale conflagration. Abortion advocates pinned the blame for Salvi's rampage on the pro-life movement and demanded a softening of pro-life rhetoric; a two-page advertisement placed in *The New York Times* carried the headline "Words Can Kill." By now pro-life activists were accustomed to that sort of criticism. But they were not prepared for the statement released by Cardinal Law soon after the shootings in Brookline. After huddling with archdiocesan officials immediately after the murders, the cardinal released a public statement condemning the "reprehensible acts of violence." Then he followed with a sentence that stunned his pro-life flock: "To those in the pro-life movement who express their commitment through prayerful presence at abortion clinics, I would ask that you refrain from such manifestations."

Did Cardinal Law really believe that prayer vigils and peaceful acts of civil disobedience caused violence? Would he renounce his support for pro-life activism? Those questions were soon being asked by the Boston media and repeated by faithful Catholics. Perhaps he had not anticipated the media reaction to his statement, but Cardinal Law was now being cited in support of the argument that pro-life rhetoric had incited the killings in the Brookline clinics. Pro-lifers looked in vain for some clear statement from their archbishop reminding the public that John Salvi had not been a pro-life activist, and—more important—that the two women he had shot were not the only human beings who died in the Brookline abortion clinics that year.

In the week after the shootings, the cardinal met with some pro-life leaders—conspicuously declining to invite representatives of Operation Rescue—and then issued a second statement renewing his call for any demonstrations or prayer vigils at abortion clinics to cease. He explained: "My motive in asking for this moratorium is to avoid anything that might engender anger or some other form of violence." In the same statement the cardinal announced that he would seek meetings with Governor William Weld and with officials of Planned Parenthood, the busiest abortion provider in the region, searching for "common ground." When he did meet with Weld, the cardinal won nothing more than the governor's public support for adoption; Weld, a staunch supporter of unrestricted abortion, yielded no ground at all on that issue. Planned Parenthood officials happily accepted promises that Church representatives would avoid accusatory statements about abortionists, but the abortion advocates did not tone down their own anti-Catholic rhetoric.

From December 1995, Cardinal Law habitually coupled any public condemnation of abortion with a warning to pro-lifers that they must eschew violence. His statements made it easy for editorial writers to depict pro-life activists as extremists; polemicists could—and did—point out that even a notorious foe of legal abortion like Cardinal Law often found it necessary to chastise these people for their behavior. Five months after the shootings in Brookline, the cardinal quietly announced—without a public fanfare, and without even a private explanation—that he was lifting the moratorium on prayer vigils. But by that time the damage had been done; thousands of Catholics were convinced that their archbishop had rendered a negative judgment on the most active wing of the pro-life movement. The devoted Catholics in Operation Rescue, and those who had spent hours on the sidewalks hoping to dissuade young women from having abortions, learned what other activist Catholics had learned in previous years: that the Boston archdiocese was an unreliable ally.

And devout Catholics had another reminder that, in times of intense pressure, their Church leaders were ready to make astonishing concessions for the sake of social concord. Lay Catholics of earlier generations would have taken it for granted that a bishop would *always* recommend sending children to Catholic schools, would *always* say that prayer is appropriate at any time and place, would *always* support efforts to end legal abortion. Yet in the 1970s Cardinal Medeiros had in effect told parents *not* to send their children to Catholic schools, since by doing so they might delay the cause of integration. Now Cardinal Law was explicitly asking pro-lifers *not* to pray at abortion clinics, because their prayers might disturb the search for compromise—compromise on an issue of life and death.

These strategic retreats by Princes of the Church would have shocked public figures of a generation earlier, when Cardinal O'Connell and Mayor Curley might have competed to see who could deliver the most ringing denunciation of legal abortion or the most fervent tribute to parochial schools. But the public figures of that generation were leaving the scene. The younger politicians who replaced them were still predominantly Catholics, but they were Catholics of the post-Vatican II generation, accustomed to the privatization of religious belief and the timidity of Church leadership.

Less than a year after the shootings in Brookline's abortion clinics, on November 28, 1995, two remarkable political careers came to an end. In the morning, Cardinal Law presided at a funeral for John Collins, who had been Mayor of Boston from 1960 to 1968. That afternoon, Senate President Bill Bulger—who had begun his political career in South Boston during the era of conflict over busing—announced that he would not seek re-election to the state senate, after presiding over the oldest legislative body in the Western hemisphere for an unprecedented seventeen years.

Theoretically, Collins had left the world of partisan politics nearly thirty years earlier, after a second successful term as Boston's mayor. But in an unquiet retirement he had been an outspoken and effective advocate for conservative Catholic causes, using his "senior statesman" status in the 1980s to inveigh against abortion and homosexuality. Bulger—who, like Collins, was a practical politician rather than an ideologue—was also a serious thinking Catholic. Time and again, during the 1980s and 1990s, the Church looked to the Senate leader for help in legislative battles on abortion, homosexual rights, and the distribution of condoms. Almost invariably, Bulger had been equal to the task. Even when he did not command enough votes to win a critical contest, he often managed to stall the issue, or adjourn the session, or wield his gavel quickly enough to stave off disaster. At times Bulger had taken the legislative lead even when Church leaders were not ready to follow. When he resigned form the legislature, his greatest regret was his failure, despite persistent efforts, to amend the state constitution and abolish the "Know-Nothing Amendment" barring public assistance to parochial schools.

With Collins dead and Bulger retiring, there was not a single prominent political figure in Massachusetts who could be counted upon to uphold Catholic Church teachings on controversial public issues. As the year 1995 came to an end, ethnic Catholics retained their dominance over the state's political system. The Lieutenant Governor, the Senate president, the Speaker of the House, the Mayor of Boston, the state treasurer, the two US Senators—all were raised as Roman Catholics. But with the single exception of Bill Bulger, every one of those politicians expressed strong public support for legal abortion. When he relinquished the senate presidency, Bulger was replaced by Tom Birmingham: a younger man typical of his generation, a Catholic who supported abortion and homosexual rights.

The rout of old Catholic loyalists was complete. The first early revelations of the sex-abuse scandal were only just beginning to emerge; the full-blown crisis in Boston would not occur for seven more years. But by 1995, the era of Catholic political dominance in Boston was over. Five years before the millennium, the Catholic century had ended.

10

Habits
of Denial

Just a few months after I began editing the archdiocesan newspaper, I reported a personal problem to Cardinal Law.

Moving back to my native Boston to take the job at the *Pilot*, I had found a temporary home for my family in a suburban community. When I signed the lease I was not aware that the local parish was one of the hotbeds of liberalism in the Boston archdiocese. The pastor, an unfailingly friendly man, did his best to make us comfortable. (One memorable evening he invited my wife and me to join him for dinner with members of the parish staff, and we listened in wonder as the director of religious education said that it would be good to incorporate a reading from the *New York Times* into the Mass, to replace "some Old-Testament reading from St. Paul.") But we soon concluded that the liturgical abuses and unorthodox sermons were more than we could stomach, and we decided to make a regular trip to another town, to attend Mass in a more conventional parish.

In case my departure caused comment, I thought that Cardinal Law should be aware of my reasons. But I had another, more serious reason for discussing the matter with him. Just before our meeting, a visiting priest at my local parish had introduced dozens of his own novel prayers and gestures into the Sunday liturgy, altering the form of the ritual so profoundly that I wondered whether the result was a valid Mass.

Among the duties of a Catholic bishop, nothing is more fundamental than to ensure that the faithful have access to the sacraments. And if the liturgical abuses in that parish were so severe that the Mass was not valid, then at least on that Sunday morning the parishioners were not receiving the Eucharist. If my concerns were reasonable, that "Mass" might have been an imposture.

I was raising a very serious charge, and I anticipated a very strong reaction. I would not have been surprised if Cardinal Law had told me that my concerns were absurd and scolded me for being an alarmist. Or if he took my charge seriously, he might have dropped everything, ordered an aide to bring around his car, and headed off immediately to investigate matters for himself—and, if necessary, to replace the pastor immediately with a priest who could be relied upon to provide valid sacraments for the faithful. But I was *not* prepared for the reaction that my report actually received. The cardinal acknowledged by concerns, sighed, and said, "What can I do?" After a moment's reflection he added: "There are never problems when *I'm* there."

On one level the cardinal was absolutely right. Priests were always on their best behavior when he visited a parish, so he never witnessed serious liturgical abuses at first hand. When complaints reached his desk, he could only weigh the worries of the laity against the reassurances he received from their pastors, who would invariably deny any infringement of Church norms. There was never enough evidence to warrant decisive action. So the complaints piled up and the liturgical abuses continued.

A few weeks after my conversation with the cardinal, my family attended a Mass that he celebrated at Holy Cross cathedral. As we were leaving he pulled us aside. "Was that liturgy more to your taste?" he asked. Cardinal Law had apparently downgraded my concerns, at least in his own mind, so that he was not responding not to a question about the *validity* of the Mass, nor even about the observance of concrete liturgical norms, but simply to a question of personal preference. My complaint was no longer a matter of pastoral urgency, on which he was morally obligated to act. It was a question of taste, on which reasonable people might differ.

My experience in this case is in no way unusual. A generation of change had left the Catholic Church scarred by serious internal divisions. But rather than acknowledging those divisions and attempting to address the problems, American bishops had adopted a policy of routine denial. They were acting as administrators of large organizations, doing their best to minimize the friction among their subordinates, rather than as fathers, looking to reconcile fractious children and restore family unity.

If they frankly admitted the severe splits within their flocks the bishops would be obliged to assert their own authority: to intervene, to judge one party right and another wrong, even to take disciplinary action against someone who was flouting Church law or doctrine. That sort of action would be unpopular and it would violate the unspoken rule that in the days after Vatican II, there should be no imposition of hierarchical authority. It was much easier, time and again, for the bishops to deny that a problem existed. If and when it became impossible to deny the problem, he would argue that the scope of that problem had been exaggerated.

So as attendance at Sunday Mass steadily declined, pastors observed that those who *did* attend found the liturgy far more meaningful. As religious orders dwindled in size, superiors claimed that the smaller community was vibrant and active. As teachers in Catholic schools advanced idea that might once have been condemned as rank heresies, bishops saluted the institutions for their willingness to engage in open dialogue. When they did acknowledge negative developments, Church leaders did their best to convey the impression that these were only small clouds in an otherwise sunny sky: unfortunate little accidents of the sort that the faithful should be prepared to accept, in light of the wonderful new developments that were so evident—to the bishop, if not to the laity. Any problems that might exist were minor ones, according to the hierarchy, and probably questions of taste rather than serious issues of Catholic doctrine or discipline. Therefore, laymen who complained too persistently were showing their own regrettable lack of perspective, their inability to adapt to change, their intolerance.

A bishop, Vatican II had taught (*Lumen Gentium* 23), is the "visible source and foundation of unity" in his diocese. American bishops fulfilled this role in a very odd way: not by *restoring* unity, but by *declaring* it. Since the bishop had announced that the local Church was one happy family, anyone who pointed out divisions was offending against that unity, fomenting discord, and subverting the bishop's authority at the same time. The greatest threat to the integrity of the Catholic faith was not someone who denied fundamental Church teachings, but someone who *called attention* to that denial, thereby fracturing the façade of unity. The bishops had found a foolproof way to blame the messenger for bringing bad news.

Dissent from Church teaching was not a new development. What is unique about the period of Vatican II is that doctrinal dissent entered the mainstream, and the vigorous *defense* of Church doctrine was marginalized. Pastors who encouraged married couples to ignore the Catholic teaching on birth control were not disciplined but praised for their "pastoral" approach. Priests who clung to the traditional teaching, exhorting their parishioners to do the same, were declared too "rigid" to handle larger assignments.

In the field of economics, the principle known as Gresham's Law dictates that bad money will drive out good money. When two different currencies are available, one inflated and the other holding its value, people will always choose to pay their bills with the less valuable currency, until the better money gradually disappears from circulation. Since the late 1960s the same general principle has been at work in the Catholic Church: lax pastoral practice has driven out sound spiritual formation. Yes, the Church still bans the use of contraceptives. But for the past forty years, at least, a married Catholic has rarely had difficulty finding a priest who would tell him that in *his* particular case, the use of contraceptives could be morally justified. Similarly, a Catholic who was troubled by the Church's teaching on divorce or on regular Mass attendance has generally been able to find a sympathetic cleric who would salve his conscience. In practice Catholics have found that it is possible to flout Catholic teachings, with the tacit blessing of someone who represents the Church.

This odd dynamic has a demoralizing effect on any priest who honestly wishes to uphold Church teaching. If he demands that an engaged couple live apart until their marriage, they are likely to find another priest who will ignore the fact that they have the same mailing address. If he says that teenagers must attend Sunday Mass regularly in order to receive the sacrament of Confirmation, the youngsters may drop out of his religious-education program. If he preaches unpopular truths in his regular homilies, families may switch to another, "friendlier" parish.

If he refuses to compromise, the stalwart pastor may soon find himself with a smaller congregation to pay the parish bills. He may then acquire a reputation as a poor fundraiser and an inefficient manager to go along with complaints about his harsh and inflexible attitudes. He will never be popular with his fellow priests (since his rigor is an implicit rebuke to their sloth), nor will he be considered for larger assignments. If he *does* compromise, on the other hand—if he ignores the fact that a young woman has already moved in with the man she intends to marry; if he promotes students through the grades of the religious-education program without giving tests that might expose their ignorance—the young priest will reap a harvest of earthly rewards. His own life will be easier, unburdened of the frustrations that come from knowing that his advice has been rejected. He will gain a reputation for flexibility and pastoral judgment. He will be more popular with other priests, and probably with his parishioners as well. He will be considered for plum parish assignments, and might even be considered as a potential future bishop!

In short, the system rewards clerics who learn to dodge controversial issues and paper over serious problems. And watching the system at work, ordinary Americans can conclude, quite reasonably, that the Church is not really serious about those problems. If 80 percent of Catholic married couples are using contraceptives, and bishops do not treat that issue as a matter of urgency, they cannot *really* believe that birth control is gravely sinful, can they? If a pastor can maintain a friendly relationship with a parishioner, yet never admonish him for routinely skipping Sunday Mass, he must not *really* think that the man's eternal soul is in danger.

Watching the clergy at work, observers may lean toward the conclusion that Catholic doctrine is made up of a series of theoretical formulas—that priests may be required to give lip-service to these formulas now and then, but no one takes them very seriously. Indeed a 1998 a study of priestly morale, commissioned by the US bishops' conference, concluded: "Some priests feel that at times they are passing on to parishioners, who clearly disagree, pastoral decisions which they sense their bishops do not fully endorse, and which they themselves personally question."

If this disturbing lack of support for controversial Church teachings had been answered by a clear statement from the hierarchy, endorsing and explaining those teachings, the problem might have been alleviated. But no such endorsement was forthcoming. At a 1990 meeting of the US episcopal conference, Bishop Kenneth Untener—one of the most liberal prelates of his generation—made the observation that the American Catholic Church was like a "dysfunctional family" because no one was willing to speak plainly about dissent from *Humanae Vitae*. Everyone recognized the problem, but in order to preserve a fragile peace, most Catholic leaders pretended that it wasn't there.

Nor was contraception the only question on which the American Catholic hierarchy had lapsed into a dysfunctional silence. Catholic couples were showing an equally cavalier attitude toward Church teaching on the permanence of marriage, and there too their pastors were acting as enablers. The Church has not changed her teaching; a Catholic who had been married and legally divorced cannot remarry. But American tribunals have been so liberal in providing decrees of annulment that the formal doctrine has come to be perceived as a technicality that any parish priest can help the lay Catholic to overcome.

An annulment is a decree that a Christian marriage never took place, that there was some serious impediment preventing a genuine marital commitment. Prior to Vatican II, ecclesiastical courts were reluctant to declare a marriage void and annulment decrees were quite rare; in 1968, there were only six hundred annulments given in the United States. But in the post-conciliar era the tribunals took a more relaxed approach to the process, and began accepting vague psychological theories to explain why one or both spouses may have been emotionally unable to offer full consent to the marital union. The number of annulments granted by US tribunals each year leapt up into the thousands, then the tens of thousands, until Vatican officials began to worry openly about this American form of "Catholic divorce."

Late in the 1980s, during their regular visits to Rome to confer with officials of the Holy See, American bishops were closely questioned about the work of their diocesan marriage tribunals. Pope John Paul II had been urgently demanding a stricter accounting for the dissolution of marriages, and the Pope's remarks on that subject were clearly aimed at American church courts, since by that time the US, with about 6 percent of the world's Catholic population, was accounting for over 80 percent of the world's annulments. But when they returned from their visits, the prelates insisted that the issue was not a cause for concern. Archbishop John Quinn, then the head of the San Francisco archdiocese, told the Catholic News Service, "It wasn't so much that they were telling us we had to make changes; we were able to explain that the situation was not as they perceived it."

Archbishop Quinn went on to say that American prelates had calmed the fears of Vatican officials by explaining that US tribunals were extremely efficient in screening marriage cases and in educating married couples about their canonical rights and duties. He did not explain why a thorough screening of cases would lead to a *rise* in the number of annulments granted; nor did he explain why Pope John Paul continued to voice his concern about that steady increase. Like other American prelates, Quinn had chosen to explain away the problem rather than confront it.

Yet another clear indication of trouble was the decline in sacramental confession. In 1986 a Gallup poll found that only 23 percent of self-identified Catholics had been to confession within the past month, whereas the figure for the early 1960s was about 70 percent. Among younger Catholics aged 18-30—those who had come to maturity in the years after Vatican II—the Gallup survey found that only 14 percent had been to confession within the month. Unless the universal human temptation toward grave sin had disappeared (a hypothesis that does not seem compatible with the facts observable in daily newspaper headlines), the fact that most Catholics were not going to confession, and not being absolved of their sins, indicated that more and more souls were in jeopardy. But again the American hierarchy did not appear to see the question as a matter of pastoral urgency. Bishops occasionally issued statements encouraging more frequent confession, but most of their attention was dedicated to other topics, such as diocesan fundraising or building plans.

Uncertain doctrinal teaching and permissive pastoral practice reinforced each other, so that over the years, ordinary lay Catholics in the pews lost track of what the Church actually taught, what they were required to do, and whether it mattered. In 2003 a *Boston Globe* poll found that among the practicing Catholics in the region—those who said that they attended Mass each week—only 28 percent supported the Church teaching on birth control, and a bare majority (51 percent) supported the Church's unflinching stand against abortion. Most practicing Catholics (66 percent) favored the ordination of women to the priesthood, although Pope John Paul II had already declared that the all-male priesthood belonged to the deposit of the faith, the unalienable patrimony of the Church; and the question was therefore closed. Most (62 percent) believed that homosexual men should be ordained to the priesthood, while only 35 percent accepted the Catholic teaching that homosexual acts are morally wrong. And these poll results, again, were taken from among the Boston area Catholics who did regularly attend Sunday Mass; those who went to church sporadically were even less inclined to support Church teachings.

As few pastors held lay Catholics accountable for *adhering* to Church teaching, it came to seem less important for Catholics to understand those teachings, and the quality of religious-education programs plummeted. The rote question-and-answer approach of the old *Baltimore Catechism* was replaced by lighter programs that encouraged young students to explore their own feelings rather than master truths. The results were predictable: even in Catholic schools, students remained in the dark about fundamental truths of the faith. A survey by the Catholic Press Association found that among Catholics between the ages of fifteen and seventeen, only 37 percent could name the four Gospels; most Catholic teenagers (56 percent) could not name even one.

Faced with such clear evidence of failure in religious instruction, bishops might have begun a thorough overhaul of their educational programs. They might have insisted that henceforth no teenagers would be eligible for Confirmation until they had demonstrated their mastery of rudimentary

Catholic teaching. Instead the American bishops chose the reaction that had now become so familiar to them: they ignored the evidence, proclaimed the educational programs successful, and congratulated Catholic teenagers on their thorough knowledge of the faith.

While they were anxious to avoid placing demands on dissident or apathetic Catholics, the American bishops were remarkably insensitive to the pleas for help that arose from some of the most devout and loyal members of their own flocks. Conservative Catholics had watched in horror as their parish churches were transformed: old statues removed, altar rails torn out, familiar hymns discarded in favor of pop songs, cherished devotional practices discontinued. An entire cultural legacy had been taken from them, and their pastors, who should have defended that heritage, had sided with the vandals. They protested in vain about liturgical abuses or theological novelties; their complaints were ignored. Lay Catholics, and particularly conservative Catholics, grew accustomed to having their protests fall upon deaf ears.

Stymied by their bishops' indifference, and encouraged by another militantly conservative Catholic weekly, the *Wanderer*, hundreds of conservative Catholics began writing to the Vatican to complain about liturgical and pastoral abuses. By the 1980s, these angry letters from the faithful became yet another problem that the bishops found necessary to explain away. After a March 1989 meeting with officials in Rome, Archbishop Daniel Kucera of Dubuque, Iowa, returned to tell reporters: "Unfortunately, some letters addressed to the Apostolic See allege that liturgical abuses are widespread in the United States. In reality, this is not so." In reality it *was* so, and remains so today, unless bishops are prepared to argue that practices repeatedly condemned by the Vatican are not abuses.

A good doctor does not tell patients that they are healthy when in fact they are seriously ill. A corporate executive does not claim success in the face of plummeting sales figures. So why would a pastor of souls deliberately overlook the evidence of spiritual problems? Perhaps the answer lies in the way American bishops perceived their own responsibilities. More and more, the bishops seemed to see their duties as political: to see themselves primarily as community leaders rather than spiritual teachers and guides. Political figures *do* often camouflage dissent within the party ranks, and do their best to distract attention from the weaknesses of their party's programs.

Without question the American bishops as a group were putting more intensive efforts into public issues such as nuclear deterrence, economic welfare, and immigration reform; they were more frequently addressing their formal statements to the general public than to a specifically Catholic audience. Even on an informal basis they were more interested in soliciting the attention of the secular media. Arthur Jones, once the Washington bureau chief for the *National Catholic Reporter*, recalled that in 1985 he had interviewed a number of American bishops for an article that appeared in *Forbes* magazine. All of the bishops were prompt to answer his interview requests, Jones reported, even though the article was for a secular business magazine. So he was taken aback when, a few months later, he called the same bishops in his regular capacity with a Catholic weekly newspaper, and none of them returned his call. But his experience was not unique, nor were the bishops avoiding the *National Catholic Reporter* for ideological reasons. At roughly the same time in the mid-1980s, Charlotte Hayes was a free-lance writer who took occasional assignments for both the *Washington Post* and the *National Catholic Register*—the latter being the conservative competitor to the ultra-liberal *Reporter*. Hayes said that when she called on behalf of the *Post*, a bishop would invariably take the call; when she called for the *Register*, the bishops were too busy to talk.

There is nothing inherently wrong in speaking to *Forbes* rather than the *National Catholic Reporter*, or to the *Washington Post* rather than the *National Catholic Register*. In each case the secular publication has a much larger circulation, and would be a more attractive vehicle for a public figure seeking the maximum exposure. But insofar as they are public figures, bishops acquire their influence not from public exposure but from solidarity among the faithful. A bishop's views on public issues are considered important because they are presumed to reflect the beliefs of the Catholic people—or the beliefs that Catholic people *will* adopt under the bishop's guidance. If that presumption breaks down, then the bishop's opinions no longer carry any particular weight in public discussions. And the presumption might well break down if the bishop fails to hold the loyalty of the laity. When it became evident that the bishops were spending their time and energy cultivating the media rather than instructing the faithful, their public influence waned. When they speak out as prophets, Church leaders carry great moral authority; when they speak as politicians they lose it.

On the American national scene, perhaps the most vivid illustration of how Catholic bishops lost moral authority came with the presidential campaign of 2004. There is no doubt that the bishops were uncomfortable with the fact that the Catholic candidate, Senator John Kerry, endorsed abortion on demand, legal recognition of same-sex unions, and embryonic stem-cell research. Even if most American bishops were Democratic partisans at heart and found Kerry's views on other issues more congenial, there can be no doubt that they would have preferred to see him fall into line with Church teachings on these moral questions. But as much as they might have wanted to see Kerry change his views, they were unable to bring about any such change because of the constraints they had brought upon themselves.

For years the bishops had shied away from public statements denouncing Catholic officials for supporting legal abortion. On paper the matter seemed quite clear: anyone who openly dissented from Catholic teaching on this issue had broken with the Church, and placed himself outside the Catholic community. But in keeping with their usual practice of ignoring problems, the American bishops had declined to make any specific application of that general principle, leaving individual public figures to follow their own consciences.

That unspoken policy was broken in 2004, when Archbishop Raymond Burke of St. Louis announced that he would not administer the Eucharist to a political figure who dissented from Church teachings on the dignity of life and made it quite clear that he was including John Kerry in that category. Several bishops quickly took the opposite position. In Cleveland, Ohio, Bishop Anthony Pilla issued a statement pointing out that "refusing Communion to politicians who support keeping abortion legal is not part of the pastoral tradition of the Church." If by "tradition" he meant to refer to the past thirty years of pastoral practice in the US, his statement was undeniably correct. Since the *Roe v. Wade* decision, no American prelate had ever denied Communion to a pro-abortion politician, although—perhaps not coincidentally—the number of prominent Catholic officials endorsing legal abortion had grown steadily. But now Archbishop Burke was calling upon his brother bishops to take more decisive steps.

From Pensacola, Florida, Bishop John Ricard chimed in: "I do not support those who would want to turn the reception of the Holy Eucharist or the Communion line into a partisan political battleground." Bishop Ricard's statement was remarkable in that his criticism seemed clearly directed at a brother bishop (Burke). Moreover, he seemed to be making the very damaging claim that a brother bishop's policy was guided not by religious zeal or pastoral concern, but by political enthusiasm.

Who was it, after all, who proposed to turn "the Communion line into a partisan political battleground?" Archbishop Burke had explained that he felt *compelled* to deny the Eucharist to dissident politicians, in order to avoid a grave public scandal. And one could argue that it was Kerry who made the question a political issue, when he persisting in coming forward for Communion, even after several prelates had said that he should not do so.

The debate within the American hierarchy continued for weeks, with some bishops supporting Burke and others siding with Pilla and Ricard. Every bishop who spoke out on the issue agreed that Catholic politicians should oppose abortion (although a few pulled their punches by adding that a pro-life stance should include opposition to the death penalty and the war in Iraq as well). Most bishops agreed that public figures who opposed Church teachings on the sanctity of life should not receive Communion. But only a few took the next step, and said that these dissidents should be *denied* the Eucharist. The few who took that stand emphasized that they would withhold Communion only with great reluctance, and only after having given ample warning to the individuals concerned. Those who took the contrary position invariably said that it would *never* be appropriate to withhold Communion. So the argument was not symmetrical. One group of bishops tried carefully to draw a line, arguing that any Catholic who crossed that line should not receive Communion. Their opponents in the public debate did not attempt to argue that the line was being drawn in the wrong location; they contended that no line should ever be drawn at all.

Cardinal Theodore McCarrick of Washington, DC, was appointed to chair a special committee charged with suggesting how the hierarchy should respond to public figures who oppose Church teachings. At a June 2004 meeting of the US hierarchy, the cardinal recommended against denying the Eucharist to dissident politicians. After some heated debate, the American hierarchy reached another compromise, deciding that each bishop should set the policy for his own diocese.

This diocese-by-diocese policy was incoherent on its face. How could someone be a Catholic in good standing in one diocese, but not in another? How could an action be gravely sinful in one geographical area but not so serious elsewhere? The bishops' failure to take a unified stand underlined the weakness of their position. John Kerry could continue to attend Mass in dioceses where he knew he would be welcomed, receiving Communion and allowing photographers to record the event for the next day's newspapers, so that ordinary Catholics received the impression— inaccurate, perhaps, but impossible to ignore—that the Catholic bishops were not ready to condemn Kerry's stand.

Moreover, the bishops' stand was based upon yet another deliberate effort to blur the truth. At the June meeting in Denver, Cardinal McCarrick had said that his recommendation was endorsed by Cardinal Joseph Ratzinger, then the prefect of the Congregation for the Doctrine of the Faith. At best he was stretching the truth. In a letter that later became public, Cardinal Ratzinger had called for a policy nearly opposite to the one McCarrick proposed, saying that if a politician persisted in campaigning for legal abortion despite warnings from his pastor, "the minister of Holy Communion must refuse to distribute it."

By forcing a general discussion of the issue, Archbishop Burke had created an opportunity for the American bishops to undo some of the damage that they had done in previous years and to announce clearly—both to the Catholic faithful and to the public at large—that adherence to Church teachings is not optional. But most of his fellow bishops were not ready to take that step; as Cardinal McCarrick put it, they were not "comfortable" enforcing Church teaching. So they fell back to their usual pattern of behavior: sloughing off responsibility, putting a grossly inaccurate interpretation on instructions from Rome.

After nearly forty years of practice, American Church leaders have growing accustomed to dodging painful issues, using carefully contrived statements, selective amnesia, dissimulation, and outright dishonesty to avoid direct clashes. No doubt the bishops believed that they were justified in denying the prevalence of liturgical abuses, in order to prevent more widespread battles among their parishioners. No doubt they believed that they should avoid confronting dissident politicians so that the liberal media would not accuse the Church of authoritarianism. But notice that the tactics of obfuscation failed to achieve those goals. The liturgical battles *did* continue; the media *did* claim that Catholic bishops were acting as inquisitors. And as we shall see, the habits of denial and obfuscation—patterns of behavior developed in a vain effort to protect the public image of Catholicism—ultimately brought disgrace upon the Church.

In his *Confessions* St. Augustine argued that unswerving fidelity to orthodox doctrine and utter reliance on God's grace are the only reliable ways to ensure the success of the faith. God watches over the Church, the great theologian reasoned, and "God does not need my lie." It is difficult to think of a proposition more radically contrary to the American Church leadership of our time.

PART III

THE COLLAPSE

11

THE
LEARNING CURVE

oday it is commonplace to read that the clerical sex-abuse scandal first erupted in Boston in early 2002. Not so. Church insiders had been aware of the simmering scandal for at least fifteen years. Despite the best efforts of Church officials to keep the story quiet, sensational headlines had begun to appear in the national media by the early 1990s. What came to light in 2002 was the *second* scandal: the public exposure of the American bishops' negligence.

Some observers, anxious to defend the bishops, have suggested that sexual abuse by Catholic priests was rarely known, and still more rarely understood, before the dawn of the twenty-first century. The evidence clearly shows otherwise. But the evidence is equally unkind to another suggestion, often put forward by analysts with an animus against the Church: that priestly sexual abuse has been a constant feature of Catholic history, which has only come to light in our time thanks to the crusading efforts of investigative reporters. The exhaustive studies commissioned by the US bishops since 2002 show a sharp, sudden rise in the incidence of abuse that began in the 1960s, crested in the 1970s, and had already begun to ebb before the phenomenon came to public notice.

Before that alarming spike, clerical abuse had been recognized for centuries as a grievous but fortunately uncommon failing. When the problem did occasionally flare up and capture public attention, Church leaders were inclined to deal with it openly. In 1215, the Fourth Lateran Council reminded bishops of their duty to punish abusers severely. "Prelates who dare support such in their iniquities," the Council declared, "shall be subject to a like punishment."

In 1568 Pope Pius V lamented that the papal states had been "polluted" by sexual abuse. To curtail this "detestable monstrosity," he ruled that any priest found guilty of sexual abuse should be stripped of his clerical status and privilege and handed over to the secular courts. The secular courts were likely to punish their offenses by the death penalty: a prospect that did not worry the Pontiff at all. On the contrary Pius V—today known to Catholics as *Saint* Pius V—said that severe punishment would send a useful message to other clerics who might be tempted to prey on children. He calmly observed that "whoever does not abhor the ruination of the soul, the avenging secular sword of civil law will certainly deter."

That stern approach was long gone by the twentieth century, but the gravity of sexual abuse was still fully recognized. In 1947 a Boston native, Father Gerald Fitzgerald, founded the Servants of the Paraclete to work with priests suffering from a variety of psychological and behavioral problems. Based on his experience with troubled clerics, he was soon warning bishops that pedophile priests, unlike recovering alcoholics and drug addicts, should not be returned to active ministry. "As a class," he wrote, "they expect to bound back like tennis balls on the court of priestly activity." But genuine rehabilitation and reform were unusual, he reported; these predators were likely to molest children again. "Hence, leaving them on duty or wandering from diocese to diocese is contributing to scandal or at least to the approximate danger of scandal."

Father Fitzgerald recognized that bishops would be likely to show paternal concern for the priests accused of molesting children. He argued, however, that "charity to the Mystical Body should take precedence over charity to the individual." A priest who molested children, he said, should be confined to a monastery for the rest of his life, or dismissed from the ranks of the clergy.

The clear-eyed realism of that approach was lost during the 1960s. It was discarded, along with so many other pieces of traditional Catholic wisdom, in the cultural revolution that followed Vatican II. A new generation of Church leaders, impatient with discipline and suspicious of restrictions, could not accept the idea that some human failings are irreformable. Rather than confining pedophile priests to monasteries, bishops began sending them to new treatment centers, where—under the guidance of counselors steeped in secular psychological theories—they would be encouraged to gain a better understanding of their sexual impulses, and then regularly returned to parish work. Even the Servants of the Paraclete adopted this gentler approach, rejecting the advice of their founder.

For generations bishops had been alert for signs of a breakdown in ascetic discipline among their priests. Now they relaxed their vigilance on that score, and concentrated instead on the physical and emotional welfare of their clergy. It is telling that in 1969, when US bishops perceived a growing problem among American priests, the episcopal conference commissioned a study—not of priestly zeal or priestly spirituality, but of priestly *morale*. The author of that study, the ex-priest Eugene Kennedy, concluded in 1972 that American priests were subjected to an *excess* of discipline, which prevented them from achieving full psychological maturity. Kennedy, a trained psychologist, had supervised interviews with hundreds of priests, looking for signs of trouble. Yet although his research was conducted during the years when the incidence of sexual abuse was hitting an all-time high, he did not mention the problem in his final report. Indeed Kennedy wrote: "There is little indication that American priests would exercise freedom in any impulsive or destructive way."

But priests *were* using their new freedoms in destructive ways. The studies commissioned by the US bishops three decades later revealed a three-fold increase in the reports of sexual abuse by priests during the 1960s. That number continued to climb, the studies show, through the 1970s. By the early 1980s, diocesan chanceries were coping with the consequences of this epidemic.

In most cases diocesan officials were successful in keeping complaints quiet. Some aggrieved families were persuaded to keep their complaints private in order to prevent public scandal. Others were silenced just as effectively with out-of-court legal settlements in which all records were sealed and all parties bound to secrecy. But these defensive levees could not hold up forever against a flood of angry complaints.

The first splash of public attention came with the case of Gilbert Gauthe, a Lousiania priest who was convicted in 1985 of molesting eleven boys. A talented journalist, Jason Berry, was living in the region where Gauthe had been assigned, and because he was a Catholic, Berry took a special interest in the case. In May 1985, he published a thorough account in *The Times of Acadiana*. For the first time, the American public had a glimpse into the seedy world of a priest-molester.

Complaints about Gauthe's involvement with children began to arise soon after his priestly ordination in 1971. At first the young priest was able to convince angry parents that he could change his behavior, and the parents agreed to keep his indiscretions hidden from diocesan officials. But by 1974 there were new complaints, and Bishop Gerard Frey of the Lafayette diocese ordered him into therapy. Returning from a leave of absence, Father Gauthe was, unbelievably, appointed diocesan chaplain for the Boy Scouts, and given a new parish assignment, enabling him to resume his pattern of abuse. By 1980, when a new flurry of complaints finally prodded Bishop Frey to suspend him from active ministry, Gauthe had molested dozens of boys; no one knows the exact number, although the disgraced priest himself confessed to abusing thirty-seven youngsters.

Writing about the case in *The Times of Acadiana*, Jason Berry provide a chilling picture of this priest's habits:

> Gauthe committed sodomy in early hours before Mass, introduced oral sex in the confessional, in the sacristy, and he showed his young victims videotaped pornography. He took hundreds of instant snapshots, which he claims to have destroyed, and instigated sex games.

In his ground-breaking coverage of the case Berry noticed several important implications of the scandal. First and foremost, he recognized the devastating effects that sexual abuse had on the young victims. They were permanently scarred by the experience, he reported—particularly because their innocence was violated by someone they had trusted, someone they saw as a figure of moral leadership. Many abuse victims, Berry wrote, were "walking time bombs ticking."

Very early in his research efforts, Berry discovered that Church officials were more interested in guarding their own interests than in helping the victims or in protecting other young people who might become victims in the future. The Lafayette diocese had been slow to respond to the first complaints, but eager to suppress any hint of publicity. Even when the Gauthe case became public knowledge, Bishop Frey declined an interview request, with his lawyer explaining: "A press interview on the matters in litigation could result in the Church and its officials being denied insurance coverage." No doubt that explanation was accurate from a legal perspective, but the words did not quite match what a loyal Catholic might have expected from his spiritual father at a time of crisis within the Church. The bishop's response throughout the crisis was exclusively defensive, never pastoral.

And yet, despite (or because of) that defensive approach, the Lafayette diocese had not been able to avoid heavy financial losses. "Beyond the criminal indictment, the Lafayette diocese and a number of insurance companies have, in out-of-court settlements, already agreed to payments of at least $4.2 million to families of nine of Gauthe's victims in Vermilion parish," Berry wrote. "Eleven additional suits have been filed by other victims for claims of approximately $114 million. But these claims represent only a minority of victims."

As he moved beyond the Gauthe case, expanding his research into clerical abuse for his book *Lead Us Not into Temptation*, Berry slowly uncovered a disturbing pattern in the way Church leaders responded to complaints of sexual abuse. The Gauthe case, he learned, was far from unique. Through most of the 1980s diocesan officials refused to grapple with the root causes of the problem directly, instead treating each incident on an *ad hoc* basis. Time after time, bishops—often following the advice of their lawyers—refused to acknowledge that a problem existed. Priests were shifted from one parish to another and shuttled from treatment centers to new assignments to escape adverse attention.

While the bishops concentrated on damage control, Berry found an oddly mixed triumvirate pressing for a concerted national effort to address the sex-abuse problem. Father Thomas Doyle, OP, was a canon lawyer assigned to the office of the apostolic nuncio in Washington. Ray Mouton was a Louisiana lawyer who had been shocked by what he learned after he naively agreed to defend Gauthe in court. Father Michael Peterson was a psychiatrist, specializing in the treatment of troubled clerics, who was dying of AIDS as the scandal unfolded.

Together the three men pushed the US bishops to recognize the growing problem and set up consistent policies to handle the legal, psychological, and pastoral implications. Encouraged by a few influential prelates, they prepared a hundred-page study of the issue, hoping that it would be discussed at the 1985 meeting of the bishops' conference and adopted as a national policy. The report warned that some new approach was necessary, because, as the three authors wrote: "Recidivism is so high with pedophilia and exhibitionism that all controlled studies have shown that traditional outpatient psychiatric or psychological models alone *do not work*."

Father Doyle later reported that he thought he had enlisted the help of Cardinal Bernard Law, who chaired the bishops' committee on Research and Pastoral Practices, to push for adoption of a national policy. Evidently Doyle was mistaken, because the push for adoption never came; the bishops declined to consider the document. Years later many American bishops defended themselves against charges of negligence by saying that they did not understand the nature of sexual abuse and did not have proper policies to deal with the problem. But in 1985, explaining their decision to shelve the Peterson/Doyle/Mouton proposal, the US bishops' conference was taking a very different line. They did not need the experts' guidance, the bishops said, because they already understood the issue and adequate policies were already in place.

When the trio of activists continued to press for stronger action, they met escalating resistance. In 1987 Bishop A. James Quinn, an auxiliary of the Cleveland, Ohio, diocese, wrote to the apostolic nuncio to protest Father Doyle's public comments on sexual abuse, which he said were inflaming public opinion against the Catholic Church. Other bishops hinted that the three would-be reformers were merely looking for consulting contracts. Mark Chopko, the general counsel to the US bishops' conference, later admitted: "There was a feeling that those guys wanted to set themselves up for work."

In spite of the bishops' lack of interest, the Peterson/Doyle/Mouton proposal came to the fore once again in 1989, when a lay Catholic activist aired a charge which, at that time, seemed almost too sensational to be taken seriously: that an American bishop had repeatedly molested a teenage boy and then tried to pay for his victim's silence.

During the late 1980s, Michael Schwartz managed the Catholic Center for the Washington-based Free Congress Foundation, working to organize groups of conservative Catholics in different areas. He had grown alarmed by the reports that he heard, with disturbing frequency and from cities scattered all across the country, about priests who abused children and bishops who protected them. He did not realize, at first, that others were hearing the same complaints. In Lead Us Not into Temptation, Jason Berry reported: "Between 1983 and 1987, more than two hundred priests and religious brothers were reported to the Vatican embassy for sexually abusing youngsters, in most cases teenage boys—an average of nearly one accusation a week in those four years alone."

After checking into several complaints and finding that the charges were well documented, Schwartz reasoned that if the bishops were deaf to discreet pleas for help from the faithful, maybe they could be forced to respond by the pressure of publicity. Just before a meeting of the US bishops' conference, Schwartz organized a press conference, at which he charged that sexual abuse by Catholic priests was a widespread problem; he pointed particularly to documented reports from Chicago, Illinois; Providence,

Rhode Island; and Milwaukee, Wisconsin. Passing out copies of the Peterson/Doyle/Mouton report, he observed that the bishops had already been informed about the problem and had been given recommendations on how they should handle it, but had chosen to avoid the issue.

The most dramatic moment of the press conference came with the introduction of a young man who spoke from behind a screen to preserve his anonymity, and was identified only as "Damian." (The next day he would overcome his fears and identify himself fully as David Figueroa.) Damian testified that beginning in 1975, when he was fifteen years old, he had been sexually abused by a parish priest in Hawaii who provided him with money in exchange for routine sexual gratification. That priest had risen through the ranks to become Bishop Joseph Ferrario of Honolulu, Damian continued, and had helped his young friend establish residence in San Francisco, where Damian became a homosexual prostitute.

Bishop Ferrario, who firmly denied the charges, retired after undergoing heart surgery in 1993, and died in 2003. The Vatican opened an investigation in 1986, at the prompting of the Figueroa family, but the case was closed after what appeared to be a perfunctory inquiry by another bishop who was friendly with Ferrario. When David Figueroa filed a lawsuit in 1991, the case was dismissed because the statute of limitations had expired. (Figueroa died of AIDS in 1995.) The American bishops ignored the call for action in 1989, just as they had ignored the same exhortation in 1986. Nevertheless a precedent had been set: in 1989 a bishop had been accused of direct involvement in the burgeoning scandal.

During the 1980s, when he began hearing from people who said that they were victims of clerical abuse, Michael Schwartz recalled: "Not one of them wanted money. What they wanted was an apology." But not one of them received an apology and eventually some of the victims turned to the courts. Soon that number began to soar so quickly that a Minnesota attorney named Jeffery Anderson, who won his first award for a sex-abuse victim in 1984, had made a specialty of such cases by 1993 and had two hundred cases pending in the courts of twenty-seven different states.

Many of these lawsuits ended in quiet, out-of-court settlements, with the plaintiffs signing confidentiality agreements to ensure that the charges would never become public. In Lead Us Not into Temptation, published in 1993, Jason Berry estimated that American dioceses had already paid out at least $500 million these settlements, and predicted (far too conservatively, as it turned out) that the legal costs would eventually exceed $1 billion.

In July 2001, Cardinal Bernard Law wrote in the archdiocesan weekly, the *Pilot*, that the Church, like society at large, "has been on a learning curve with regard to the sexual abuse of minors." But he could not plausibly claim to have been surprised as the scandal had begun to erupt with full force in his Boston archdiocese. It was a full decade earlier that Richard Ostling, the dean of American religion reporters, had written in *Time* magazine: "Without doubt it is the worst wave of moral scandals ever to beset Roman Catholicism in North America."

And Ostling wrote that sentence *before* the scandal edged closer to Boston, when the spotlight of the public notoriety fixed on a former priest of the neighboring Fall River diocese.

Born in Boston, James Porter entered St. Mary's Seminary in Emmitsburg, Maryland, and was ordained to the priesthood in Fall River in 1960. By all accounts he was a popular priest with a special knack for establishing friendships with young people. But within a few months after he took his first parish assignments, ugly reports began to reach his superiors. When these reports came to the attention of the diocesan chancellor, Monsignor Humberto Medeiros, Father Porter was quietly transferred to another parish assignment. There were soon new accusations and another transfer. Finally in 1963, Medeiros confronted Porter openly about the stories of child abuse. But the future Archbishop of Boston did not remove this dangerous priest from ministry, nor did he alert Fall River's Bishop James Connolly until March 1964. By that time the evidence against Porter was compelling, and he was sent away for counseling.

After thirteen months he was back on parish assignment, molesting children again. In 1966 Father Porter was again removed from ministry; parishioners were told that he was on sick leave. Soon he was back again and through the late 1960s he continued to shuttle between parish assignments and treatment centers, until finally in 1970, on the recommendation of counselors at the Paraclete Center in New Mexico, the Fall River diocese began the long canonical process that resulted, in 1974, with Porter's formal removal from the priesthood.

Meanwhile one of Porter's earlier victims, Frank Fitzpatrick, had grown into adulthood and opened a business as a private investigator. Troubled by his own past, Fitzpatrick used his professional skills to locate other victims of the former priest and quickly found dozens. Pressing forward with his investigation and hiring a lawyer to file a lawsuit on behalf of the victims, Fitzpatrick was stunned to learn that each time Porter had been transferred, he had arrived at his new parish assignment with a clean slate; diocesan authorities never warned the pastors who would supervise him—to say nothing of the parishioners whose children he would befriend—that Porter was a serial molester.

Fitzpatrick received no help at all from the Fall River diocese during his investigation, but Massachusetts prosecutors recognized the strength of his case, and in 1992 the former priest—now married and living with his wife and children in Minnesota, where new abuse charges were cropping up—was brought back to Massachusetts to face criminal charges. In October 1992, Porter was formally charged with forty-six counts of sodomy and indecent assault, and entered a guilty plea, with his lawyer explaining that his client "needs to get on with his life."

The Porter case was the first to receive saturation coverage in the mass media. During the summer before Porter entered his guilty plea, the *Boston Globe* ran seventeen front-page stories about his predatory behavior and his superiors' attempts to cover up the evidence of his crimes. For the first time American Catholics—and certainly those in Boston, close to the epicenter of this tremor—were learning that their bishops had betrayed their trust and endangered their children.

A few years later, the eyes of the public were opened to another dimension of the scandal: the enormous financial risk to Catholic institutions. In 1997, a Texas jury awarded $120 million in damages to the victims of Rudy Kos, a former priest of the Dallas diocese. (To avoid protracted appeals and a possible bankruptcy filing by the diocese, the plaintiffs later settled for a $31 million payment and a formal apology from Bishop Charles Grahmann.) Kos had a history of trouble even before he entered the Dallas seminary. He had served a year in juvenile detention at the age of seventeen for molesting a young boy. He married, but the union was annulled after five years, with his wife reporting that the marriage was never consummated and that Kos "has problems with boys." Yet even with those facts on the record he was admitted to the Dallas seminary. Reports of his assaults on altar boys had begun to arrive at the chancery, but like Porter he was switched from one parish to another, and then from parish to treatment center and back, until he had abused dozens of young men. The Texas jurors were persuaded that Church officials had been grossly negligent in supervising Kos.

There was one final warning for Boston's Catholics before the tsunami struck the archdiocese. In June 2000 police arrested Christopher Reardon, a layman working as a youth minister in a parish in suburban Middleton,

Massachusetts, and charged him with 130 counts of abuse; at the time it was the largest sex-abuse case in the state's history, surpassing even the charges against Porter. Reardon pleaded guilty, but before the case was resolved, colleagues at the parish would testify that they had been urged by officials of the Boston archdiocese not to cooperate with an investigation for fear that unwanted scrutiny might fall upon the pastor, who had been accused of lax supervision over Reardon. Father Jon Martin, it seems, had reasons for turning a blind eye to his subordinate's misbehavior. The parish staff revealed that the pastor frequently entertained male guests overnight in his bedroom. These guests included inmates on furlough from a nearby prison.

By now those who were following the story realized that the headlines about clerical abuse were not going to go away. It was becoming steadily more obvious that the cases of Gauthe and Porter and Kos were not isolated examples of individual depravity, and that the American bishops—unlike the stunned lay members of their flocks—had *not* been caught off guard by the revelations of priestly abuse. The reports of a systematic campaign to cover up these crimes, which had sounded so outlandish in the late 1980s, no longer seemed so implausible. Accusations against the clergy were still shocking, but they were not longer unbelievable. Informed Catholics were bracing themselves for further revelations of corruption within the Church. But no one was prepared for what was coming.

12

NOT ENOUGH
MILLSTONES

When the barrage of stories about clerical abuse swept across America in 2002, Boston was the primary target of attention because of one individual. Not John Geoghan, the defrocked priest whose obsessive pursuit of children was the first focus of media attention. Not Cardinal Bernard Law, whose inept handling of the crisis led eventually to his resignation. Not even one of the investigative reporters of the "Spotlight team" for the *Boston Globe*, whose coverage drove the story for months. The eyes of the nation were fixed on Boston because of Constance Sweeney.

In 2001 the *Globe* had decided to focus on Geoghan as the subject of a Spotlight team investigation. At the time the former priest faced two criminal charges and dozens of lawsuits for sexual abuse of children. The *Globe* learned that other suits against the priest had already been settled quietly by the archdiocese, and the editors sued for access to the court records, arguing that the public had a right to be informed about the misconduct of a deviant priest and about any archdiocesan efforts to conceal that misconduct.

Massachusetts Superior Court Judge Constance Sweeney agreed with the *Globe*. Refusing to be swayed by the bitter, protracted arguments and appeals of lawyers for the Boston archdiocese, Judge Sweeney ordered the records opened, and gave the *Globe* access to thousands of previously confidential documents which showed, in vivid detail, how the Boston archdiocese had sought to camouflage a cancer growing within the clergy.

When they first planned out their investigative effort, the *Globe* reporters had anticipated writing a final report on the secret settlements that had kept Geoghan's misbehavior out of the headlines for years. Then as they perused the records and realized how severely the priest had

damaged many young lives, the Spotlight team began to focus on the victims. But as they read more documents, growing more familiar with the
case, the reporters found that they could not pry their attention away from
questions about Cardinal Law's involvement: what did he know about
Geoghan's abuse, and when did he know it?

A shy, elfin man, John Geoghan had encountered trouble in St. John's
Seminary in the 1950s; the rector found him "a little feminine in his speech
and approach" and complained of his "very pronounced immaturity." He
was temporarily dismissed, but an uncle who was an influential monsignor
in the Boston archdiocese arranged his return to the seminary in 1957 and
he was ordained as a priest in 1962.

The first pastor to supervise young Father Geoghan recalled in 2002
that the new priest had sometimes brought boys into his bedroom. After
telling reporters that he had brought this behavior to the attention of
chancery officials, the pastor—who by now had been warned that he could
face charges and was represented by an archdiocesan lawyer—said that his
earlier remarks had been misinterpreted and he had *not* notified archdiocesan officials. Later Geoghan would admit to abusing four boys during that
first assignment.

The Boston archdiocese definitely heard complaints against Geoghan
beginning in the late 1960s and continuing through the 1970s. In 1980 he
admitting molesting boys and was placed on sick leave. But once he was
returned to duty in 1982, he almost immediately began seeking out boys—
including some he had violated on his previous assignment. By now there
were scores of complaints against him, yet in 1984 he received a new assignment to St. Julia's parish in the affluent suburb of Weston.

In March 1989, Geoghan was sent to the St. Luke's Institute in Maryland, where he was diagnosed as a homosexual pedophile. He was placed on
sick leave and treated for three months at the Institute of Living in Connecticut. Upon his discharge, the Boston vicar general, Bishop Robert
Banks, asked for and received a professional evaluation of Geoghan that
stated: "The probability he would act out again is quite low. However, we
could not guarantee that it would not re-occur." He was returned to St.
Julia's parish. Less than a year later, new accusations arose.

In 1993 Father Geoghan was finally removed from parish ministry and
assigned to a residence for retired priests. But his movements were not
supervised, and the complaints that he was preying on young boys continued to reach the chancery. He was placed on sick leave again in September

1996. In December of that year Cardinal Law granted his request for early retirement. Two years later, as the lawsuits against him multiplied, Geoghan was dismissed from the priesthood.

Digesting all this information and much more, the Spotlight team prepared a story that was splashed across the front page of the *Boston Globe* on January 6, 2002, leaving readers aghast. Geoghan had been accused of molesting 130 boys, the *Globe* reported. The archdiocese had already reached out-of-court settlements in fifty cases, at a total cost of about $10 million. Most shocking of all, the *Globe* had clear documentary evidence that the priest had remained on active parish assignment for at least fifteen years after the archdiocese recognized his problem.

The 1984 transfer to St. Julia's in Weston drew special scrutiny. That assignment had been approved by then-Archbishop Law, and although Law had only recently arrived in Boston, there was indisputable proof that he had been informed about Geoghan's history. Bishop John D'Arcy, then serving as an auxiliary in the Boston archdiocese, wrote to his new superior strongly criticizing the assignment of a priest with a "history of homosexual involvement with young boys" to active parish ministry. But Bishop D'Arcy was a lonely force in the circles of archdiocesan leadership, and he—perhaps not coincidentally—had left Boston soon after lodging that protest; he was appointed by the Vatican to head a diocese in Indiana.

The *Globe* Spotlight team depicted the leaders of the Boston archdiocese—D'Arcy aside—as utterly insensitive toward Geoghan's victims, driven only by their desire to keep his crimes quiet. It was an ugly portrait, and it was not difficult to detect a note of glee in the work of journalists from a newspaper that had locked horns with Cardinal Law on many political issues. Many Catholic readers, mindful of the *Globe*'s long history of hostility toward the Church, saw the sensational story as one more attack on their faith. The misdeeds of a few clerics were being exaggerated, they felt sure; if the archdiocese had not taken action, it was probably because there was not enough evidence to prove serious misconduct.

But the *Globe* report could not be dismissed; the documentary evidence was far too damning. There *was* ample evidence of Geoghan's abuse, and his superiors had seen it. There was evidence that other priests were abusing children, and now the general public had seen that as well. Even if the reports were sensationalized, the facts were stunning. Writing for the secular audience of *National Review Online*, John O'Sullivan refused to accept the loyalists' protests about a media conspiracy. Noting that some reporters had predicted that fifty Boston priests would face charges, O'Sullivan wrote: "That is almost certainly a large exaggeration. But suppose the true figure is five. Would that not be shocking enough?" The predictions were not exaggerated; the number of accused priests would soar far above fifty. But O'Sullivan's point remains true. If the archdiocese had knowingly harbored just *one* pedophile priest, that would have been unforgivable.

The crime of sexual abuse is repugnant to any normal sensibility. To a believing Christian it is even more abhorrent because it threatens the very souls of the victims, introducing them to degrading acts and twisting their outlook on sexuality. Jesus had a clear message regarding the man who corrupts youth: "It would be better for him if a millstone were hung round his neck and he were cast into the sea, than that he should cause one of these little ones to sin."

The little children who were victimized by depraved priests cannot be held responsible for actions that they neither chose nor comprehended. Even the older victims of priestly abuse, who may have understood exactly what they were doing, cannot be judged culpable if they acted under pressure from a much older seducer. These young people were being lured into acts which, the Church teaches, are gravely sinful. Worse, they were being lured by men they trusted, men who represented the spiritual authority of the Church.

Even if they were not morally responsible for their actions—even if they were unwilling participants in the perverse fantasies of an older man— victims could not escape the psychological consequences of abuse. The victims of sexual abuse are prone to self-loathing, depression, and drug abuse; their suicide rate is notoriously high. Pushed into sexual activity before they are emotionally prepared, they often have difficulty achieving sexual maturity and maintaining normal relations with the opposite sex. A disproportionate number of victims become active homosexuals, and a frightening number go on to become abusers themselves.

If the leaders of the Boston archdiocese were not familiar with these facts when they shuffled John Geoghan from one parish to another, it was only because they did not look into the consequences of sexual abuse for the victims. Their focus was exclusively on the consequences for the archdiocese—and for the public *image* of the archdiocese rather than its spiritual health.

Even in their solicitous attitude toward the priests committing the abuse, Church leaders showed no particular concern about the obvious spiritual problems of these twisted men. One treatment center, returning John Geoghan to Boston after an interval of counseling, included a "spiritual assessment" that read: "there are no particular recommendations concerning [Geoghan's] spiritual life since he is involved in spiritual direction and seems to have a good prayer life." How could one possibly combine a "good prayer life" with the routine molestation of children? Geoghan was a man in very deep moral trouble, and his superiors were not calling him to account.

When he at last accepted Geoghan's resignation from active priestly ministry, Cardinal Law wrote a letter that contained this breathtaking sentence: "Yours has been an effective ministry, sadly marred by illness." The cardinal's sympathetic attitude toward a serial rapist and his blithe dismissal of abuse as an "illness" were staggering.

"Christ himself would have spoken far more harshly to John Geoghan and the other priests who destroyed the innocence of those in their care," wrote John O'Sullivan. "Yet in speaking harshly he would have loved them more. For he might have turned them away from the sins that corrupted their souls and attacked the bodies of children in their charge." The *National Review* writer summed up his analysis with the trenchant observation that "there was apparently a shortage of millstones in Boston over the last three decades."

The shortage of millstones, really, translates into a lack of interest in the *spiritual* welfare of the archdiocese and its faithful. Boston's Catholic leaders had grown accustomed to looking upon the Church as an important civic and cultural institution. Now in a time of moral crisis they neglected the supernatural dimension of the faith. Archdiocesan officials went into the parishes where abuse had occurred and offered profound apologies. But they did not question whether the pastors who had preyed on children had also preached unsound doctrine or offered misleading advice in the confessional. It was taken as axiomatic that a priest's misconduct was an aberration, which would not affect his ability as a pastor of souls. (Thus Cardinal Law could *assume* that Geoghan's priestly career had been marked by "effective ministry.") The cardinal and his subordinates set out to restore confidence rather than to restore souls.

Confidence would not be easy to restore, because archdiocesan leaders were not giving the laity any reasons to trust them, beyond blind faith. Jack Connors, a prominent Boston advertising executive, told the Spotlight team that Cardinal Law had called to ask for his advice just before the story broke on January 6. When the cardinal told him that the *Globe* would expose a pedophile priest, Connors asked if other priests could be vulnerable to charges. The cardinal replied that "there may be one or two."

There were dozens. That January 6 story was just the first salvo in a steady bombardment of media coverage that pounded the Boston archdiocese all through 2002. The *Globe* alone published over three hundred stories about priestly sexual abuse in the first six months of the year. Church leaders were constantly on the defensive, forced to respond to new revelations after assuring the public that the worst had already come to light.

Time after time, a reassuring statement by Cardinal Law was contradicted by new headline reports. The cardinal told reporters that the archdiocese was not aware of any priest currently engaged in parish ministry who faced sex-abuse allegations. Within a week, a young priest was arrested and charged with rape; later reports indicated that the archdiocese had prior knowledge of the impending arrest. The cardinal pledged that the archdiocese would cooperate fully with prosecutors; within hours local district attorneys were loudly complaining that the chancery would not surrender needed documents. The cardinal promised that victims of sexual abuse would receive prompt payment on any reasonable financial claims; the next day lawyers for several victims disclosed that they had been warned the coffers were already empty.

Pouncing on an opportunity, the public enemies of Catholicism seized the offensive. Radio talk shows included hour after hour of leering criticism of Catholic priests and bishops. The *Globe* featured a parade of "expert" witnesses who suggested that the problem of priestly pedophilia was caused by the discipline of celibacy, helpfully suggesting that the Church might restore her credibility by abandoning traditional Catholic teachings on contraception, homosexuality, abortion, and the ordination of women. It did not matter that such arguments were non sequiturs; rapacious critics of Catholicism had overrun the rhetorical field. The media had no time to listen to Catholic apologists.

For his part Cardinal Law acknowledged responsibility for the crisis facing his flock, but he did so in a curiously detached, lawyerly statement, peppered with phrases that diminished his guilt. He wrote: "*In retrospect*, I acknowledge that, *albeit unintentionally*, I have failed in that responsibility. The judgments, which I made, *while made in good faith*, were tragically wrong" [emphasis added]. The problem had persisted, he said, because he had not properly understood the nature of sexual abuse. Now the cardinal unveiled a series of new policies designed to deter clerical abuse; he empaneled a blue-ribbon committee of health-care professionals to recommend further policy changes. In what sounded like a desperate attempt to extract some positive message from the uniformly grim news, he argued that society had a better understanding of the problem, and the Boston archdiocese could learn from its mistakes. Sweeping aside the suggestions that he might resign, Cardinal Law boldly announced: "I want the archdiocese to become a model for how this issue should be handled."

The cardinal was showing his bulletproof self-confidence in saying that *he* would lead a model program to correct the problem. His critics were saying that he was a major *cause* of the problem. Any real solution required his removal. The arguments that he had been following the advice of experts, and that no one recognized the dangers posed by pedophilia, were persuasive only to his friends. It requires no special expertise to recognize that molesting children is wrong, or that a man who molests children on dozens of different occasions can never be trusted with children again. Even the cardinal's own statements in defense of his actions (or inactions) relied more and more on the unflattering argument that he had not known what he was doing.

Most seasoned journalists snickered when the cardinal explained that he had not seen a memo about an abusive priest or carefully read a letter before signing it. But I was inclined to credit the excuses. Those who had worked closely with Cardinal Law knew that his reputation as a hands-on administrator was a myth. He was notoriously sloppy with paperwork and inattentive to details. It was quite possible that Cardinal Law was only vaguely aware of these priests' misconduct, I thought. Although that ignorance did not excuse him—he was ultimately responsible, even if he had delegated his authority—it did attenuate his guilt. It was possible to believe that Cardinal Law might survive the scandal. His shell-shocked supporters (and I counted myself among them) could still argue that the cardinal was suffering for his subordinates' mistakes. Then came a new explosion, and the cardinal's last credible defense was blown away.

In the weeks after the revelations about John Geoghan, the *Globe*—now joined by other media outlets in mining the archdiocesan files—had unearthed stories about other priest-molesters. The cases of Joseph Birmingham, Ronald Paquin, and Eugene O'Sullivan were all depressingly similar. The priests had been accused again and again; the archdiocese had first ignored the complaints, then chastised the accusers, and then finally—

when the emerging evidence made it impossible to temporize any longer—
pulled the accused priest out of his assignment and transferred him to
another parish, where the same pattern was repeated. The case of Paul
Shanley was quite a different story.

Most of the other priests accused of molesting children had camouflaged their activities, functioning as ordinary priests in parish assignments,
doing nothing to call attention to themselves. Father Paul Shanley, on the
other hand, had been a flamboyant rebel from the time of his ordination in
1960. He cultivated an image as a "street priest," and in the 1970s he persuaded Cardinal Medeiros to assign him a special, unconventional ministry
to "alienated youth." Prowling through Boston's seedy Combat Zone with
his long flowing hair and tight jeans, in daily contact with runaways and
drug addicts and teenage prostitutes, he soon became recognized as a
"player" in the city's homosexual subculture.

Working without supervision, Shanley became a sort of Pied Piper for
young homosexuals, holding parties in a rented apartment at which illegal
drugs and sexual favors were readily available. When troubled youngsters
worried about these activities, he reassured them, putting a spiritual gloss on
his own lust. "It is better for you to come to me for this," he told one young
sex partner, "than it is to be down on your knees in some dirty alley for a
stranger." The parties might have continued indefinitely if Rome had not
intervened.

Shanley, who now claimed a special ministry to homosexuals, began to
speak out regularly at gatherings of homosexual activists, assuring them of
his support. He suggested—at first obliquely, then openly—that homosexual activities can be healthy and desirable. He even spoke favorably of
affairs involving mature men with young boys and delivered that message to
the first organizing meeting of a group that was to become known as the
North American Man-Boy Love Association.

Cardinal Medeiros wrote to Shanley in 1973, urging him to be more
prudent in his public statements about sexuality. The renegade priest shot
back a belligerent reply, saying that he would not change his tune. Shanley
added that if the cardinal dared to take disciplinary action, he would take
his story to mass media, darkly hinting that he had damaging information
to disclose.

Outraged lay Catholics complained about Shanley's speeches, saying
that he was giving an improper understanding of Church teaching to many
highly impressionable people. Those complaints were, as usual, ignored.

When one woman wrote to Cardinal Medeiros in November 1977, she received this response from his auxiliary, Bishop Thomas Daily: "The position of the Archdiocese of Boston is that while Father Shanley enjoys the faculties of the Archdiocese of Boston, he alone must be held responsible for any statements regarding homosexuality." So concerned lay people brought their concerns to the Vatican.

In November 1978 the prefect of the Vatican's Congregation for the Doctrine of the Faith, Cardinal Franjo Seper wrote to Cardinal Medeiros, calling his attention to Shanley's public statements. His letter closed with a request for action: "May I ask you to inform this Congregation of any steps you have already taken or intend to take in regard to the spread of these erroneous ideas and regard to the position of Father Shanley?" In a long, anguished reply, Cardinal Medeiros showed an overwhelming anxiety about the damage that could be done if Shanley went to the media. (Cardinal Medeiros also portrayed himself as the hero in a valiant, lonely campaign to prevent public acceptance of homosexuality, a portrait that Boston Catholics would have recognized as almost entirely fictional.) But he did promise to relieve Shanley of his special ministry and place him in a more conventional assignment. Later Medeiros reported back to assure Cardinal Seper that Shanley had accepted his new post at a suburban parish, "but not without going to the newspapers."

At St. Jean's parish in Newton, Father Shanley soon became the focus of complaints. But the complaints were deflected by chancery officials, and in 1985 Shanley was promoted to the pastor of St. Jean's. That promotion—for a priest with a long history of sexual misconduct and open dissent from Church teaching, a priest whose public statements had drawn scrutiny from a ranking official at the Vatican—was approved by the newly arrived Archbishop Law. And of course the complaints kept coming, prompting the standard demurrals from the chancery.

In 1990 this wretched priest traveled to California on sick leave. Bishop Robert Banks, the vicar general of the Boston archdiocese, wrote to the Bishop of San Bernardino, California, to notify him about Father Shanley's arrival. Banks wrote that Shanley was "a priest in good standing," and asked for help in finding appropriate pastoral assignments that Shanley could fill during his time there. "I can assure you," Banks wrote, "that Father Shanley has no problem that would be a concern to your diocese."

In 1996, Cardinal Law accepted Shanley's retirement from active ministry, in a letter that repeated the same themes that he had expressed in his retirement letter to Geoghan. "This letter provides me with an opportunity to thank you in my name and in the name of the people of the archdiocese," he wrote. Praising the record of pastoral care that Shanley had compiled "despite some limitations," the cardinal said, "That is an impressive record and all of us are truly grateful."

Just one year later, Shanley had managed to find a new position as acting executive director of Leo House, a home for troubled youngsters in New York City. Shanley sought a permanent appointment as executive director, and Cardinal Law prepared and signed a letter to his counterpart, New York's Cardinal O'Connor, saying: "If you decided to allow Father Shanley to accept this position, I would not object." The letter acknowledged that Shanley would come with "some controversy from his past," and warned that this controversy "could draw publicity to him, to Leo House, and to the Church." The letter was never actually mailed, because a subordinate told Cardinal Law that the New York archdiocese had already decided against hiring Shanley, because of "the publicity which might arise." But in the letter that Cardinal Law had planned to send—and for that matter, in the preemptive announcement from the New York archdiocese—the focus of attention was not the likelihood that Shanley would molest young men, but the possibility of adverse media attention.

In the Geoghan case Cardinal Law had obviously been guilty of negligence and of accepting bad advice, but the more serious charges against him were supported only by circumstantial evidence. The cardinal could still say that he gave a wayward priest a new assignment because he was convinced that Geoghan had reformed. That argument was painfully weak—the benefits of Geoghan's possible rehabilitation were massively outweighed by the costs of his far more likely relapses—but it was still an argument. In the Shanley case there was not even the fig-leaf of that sort of argument. Here the cardinal had not only failed to discipline a priest who molested young men, but had actually endorsed him for pastoral assignments in Boston and in two other dioceses. This time the cardinal's involvement was quite simply indefensible.

Now the people of Boston had no reason *not* to believe that the archdiocese was sheltering abusers. With more reporters joining in the hunt for evidence and courts opening access to more documents, there were new revelations nearly every day. The evidence all pointed to the same inescapable conclusion: many priests had abused children and the archdiocese had protected the abusers.

As the documentary evidence emerged, it soon became impossible to believe that the archdiocese had taken complaints about abuse seriously. Cardinal Law's lieutenant dealing with clerical personnel, Father John McCormack (later to be named the Bishop of Manchester, New Hampshire) was responsible for dealings with troubled clerics. His light-hearted approach to the charges that he was assigned to investigate became evident when he was called to give testimony—for example, in the case of the accused serial molester Joseph Birmingham:

> The only step I remember taking is saying to Father Birmingham one time ... that, you know, I know about your—about some complaints about you in Salem, and, I said, "I'm wondering, you know, how you're handling that." And he said that "I'm clean."

McCormack testified that he saw no reason to question Birmingham any further: "Because I considered him to be an honest person."

Or take the case of another accused molester, Ronald Paquin:

> I spoke with Father Paquin. He assured me there was no sexual contact, that this was a boy he had known, that he was trying to be helpful to. So I took him at his word.

McCormack testified that he saw Paul Shanley as "an honest guy, who was always trying to help the Church reach out to the alienated, the marginalized." Pressed to explain why he was not alarmed by Shanley's public statements on man-boy relations, he offered a halting incoherent explanation:

> No, my understanding was ... that he wasn't endorsing man/boy relationships but that he, at the time, was explaining that some boys seduce men and that they—by prostituting themselves and that some people—and some of these people think that, you know, that they're always the ones. And he was saying that sometimes these boys need help; they're the ones who really have a problem.

Clearly the officials of the Boston archdiocese had reached out to embrace any explanation, however strained, for the conduct of their priests. Just as clearly they had rejected any complaints—however plaintive, however well documented—from the laity.

During testimony about his dealings with abusive priests in Boston, Bishop McCormack admitted that in order to protect children, he should have alerted parishioners about the allegations against their parish priests.

But he decided not to do so, he recalled, after discussion with other archdiocesan officials. Asked how the policy of silence was established, McCormack said that "it was a matter of discussion among some of us."

By treating allegations of abuse confidentially, McCormack testified,
his goal was to avoid the publicity that "would raise it to the level of a scandal." Even in retrospect, he seemed unable to recognize that the violation
of children was *already* a scandal, whether or not it was known to the public. He showed only a passing interest in the suffering of innocent children,
but a mortal fear of media coverage. His policy was based on fear of publicity, not fear of God.

Thus when one young man arranged a meeting with McCormack to
report that he had been abused by Father Paquin, the victim was distressed
by the priest's lack of concern. The young man recalled that he told
McCormack about Paquin's habit of taking boys on camping trips in New
Hampshire, plying them with liquor, and then molesting them. On one
such trip, the young man reported, after a night of heavy drinking, Father
Paquin had fallen asleep at the wheel of his car on the return trip. The car
crashed, and the boy who had shared Paquin's sleeping bag the previous
night was killed.

The victim claimed that McCormack had shown no special interest as
he told this tragic story. When he finished his presentation and pleaded for
Paquin to be removed from ministry, the young man said that McCormack
asked a businesslike question: "How much are you looking for?"

Next the young man then told McCormack that if the archdiocese did
not take action against Paquin, he would tell his story to the media. That
threat at last drew the archdiocesan official's attention. "Consider it done,"
McCormack told him.

Silence was not the only tactic that the archdiocese used to avoid public disclosure of clerical abuse. When necessary, Church officials told outright falsehoods. In his 2002 testimony McCormack was questioned about
a letter he had written in 1987, to a man who was worried about the influence of Father Joseph Birmingham over his young son. The boy's father
asked whether there was any truth to the rumors that Birmingham had been
transferred from previous parish assignments because of sex-abuse complaints. Father McCormack told him: "There is absolutely no factual basis
to your concern." Asked why he had written such a clearly dishonest letter,
McCormack answered: "I can't explain that." It was easy to explain, actually. The future bishop had lied.

Among all the documents made public during 2002, none were more heartrending than the letters that a simple Catholic woman wrote to two different Boston archbishops, pleading for action against a priest who had molested seven of her nephews. In 1982, after learning about the molestation of her nephews, Margaret Gallant met with Bishop Thomas Daily and received assurances that Geoghan would be removed. A few weeks later the priest was still working at the same parish, and she wrote a respectful but angry letter to Cardinal Medeiros. "Am I to assume now that we were patronized?" she asked.

Margaret Gallant's letter, loaded with common sense and righteous anger and honest Catholic piety, packs enough emotional punch to justify quotation at length:

> Our family is deeply rooted in the Catholic Church, our great-grandparents and parents suffered hardship and persecution for love of the Church. Our desire is to protect the dignity of the Holy Orders, even in the midst of our tears and agony over the seven boys in our family who have been violated. We cannot undo that, but we are obligated to protect others from this abuse to the Mystical Body of Jesus Christ.
>
> It was suggested that we keep silent to protect the boys—that is absurd since minors are protected under law, and I do not wish to hear that remark again, since it is insulting to our intelligence. . . .
>
> While it is true that a layman in the same situation would only be confined for observation for a limited time—he would also be exposed. Parents would know then not to allow children near this type person. In this case, not only do they not know, but by virtue of his office he gains access quite easily, which compounds our responsibility! His actions are not only destructive to the emotional well-being of the children, but hits the very core of our being in our love for the church—he would not gain access to homes of fallen-away Catholics.
>
> Regardless of what he says, or the doctor who treated him, I do not believe he is cured; his actions strongly suggest that he is not, and there is no guarantee that persons with these obsessions are ever cured.
>
> Truly, my heart aches for him and I pray for him, because I know this must tear him apart too; but I cannot allow my compassion for him to cloud my judgment on acting for the people of God, and the children in the church. . . .

We did not question the Authority of the Church two years ago, but left it entirely in your hands. Now, we will not settle for this, but must insist on knowing what action is taken—where he is sent, etc. I will not allow this Temple of God to be overshadowed by a sin of omission. . . .

My heart is broken over this whole mess—and to address my Cardinal in this manner has taken its toll on me too. May Almighty God, Father, Son and Holy Spirit have mercy on all of us.

It is instructive to notice that Margaret Gallant seemed to grasp the spiritual and psychological dimensions of John Geoghan's crimes quite accurately, twenty years before Cardinal Law spoke of the "learning curve" along which the hierarchy was slowly progressing. But her simple wisdom was ignored. Her pleas went unanswered. Two years later, after hearing fresh reports that Geoghan was molesting boys, Gallant wrote to the newly installed Archbishop Law. She received a curt reply: "The matter of your concern is being investigated and appropriate pastoral decisions will be made both for the priests and God's people." A few weeks after writing that note to Gallant, the cardinal gave Geoghan his new parish assignment in Weston. The record would show that archdiocesan officials accepted Geoghan's claim that he was "cured" of his problems on the basis of a scribbled note from a doctor who was not a specialist in pedophilia, nor even a psychiatrist, but Geoghan's family physician.

In 2002 Margaret Gallant, whose devotion to the Church was so evident in her plea to Cardinal Medeiros, reported that she was no longer an active Catholic. Her faith had been shattered. She was another victim of the sex-abuse scandal.

If Gallant was the most memorable whistle-blower in the Geoghan case, Jackie Gauvreau filled that role for Paul Shanley. Brassy and aggressive where Gallant had been deferential, Gauvreau hounded the chancery with her complaints, asking why a known child-molester was serving at her parish in Newton. Bishop Daily grew tired of making excuses, and left instructions that her phone calls were never to reach him. Confronted by Gauvreau at various public functions, Cardinal Law first assured her that he would investigate her complaints, then suggested that she speak to his auxiliary bishops—who, of course, were dodging her phone calls. For fifteen years she persisted with her accusations; never did an archdiocesan official admit that they were accurate.

Dozens of other witnesses came forward with evidence against Geoghan and Shanley and other priests. Invariably they were told to keep their suspicions private. Usually they were told that those suspicions were unjustified. Often they were scolded for harboring uncharitable attitudes. In several cases they were charged with spreading false accusations—even when chancery officials knew quite well that the accusations were true.

In January 2002 Cardinal Law made the first in a serious of apologies to the victims of sexual abuse. But he did not apologize to the witnesses who were ignored and patronized and misled and even calumniated. Even as I write now, five years after the public records vindicated them, these witnesses have never been acknowledged by the archdiocese. And that omission is significant, because whereas the victims testify to the first scandal—the abuse itself—the witnesses are reminders of the second scandal—the clerical cover-up—which the hierarchy has still not acknowledged.

13

LOST
IN DALLAS

From the day that the first *Globe* revelations appeared—January 6, 2002—it was open season on the Catholic Church in America, and very few dioceses were spared from the furor. Day after day brought new reports of clerical abuse. New victims came forward, encouraged by the public outcry against the Church, demanding restitution from dioceses that had allowed abusers to remain in ministry. Lawyers for these victims were no longer content with quiet financial settlements and confidentiality agreements; following the pattern that had worked so effectively in Boston, they demanded the opening of diocesan files.

As a group, the American bishops responded much as Cardinal Law had responded. They fought to prevent disclosure of confidential files, affecting outrage that anyone would question their integrity. They denied the problem until public revelations made denial impossible. Then they offered familiar explanations: that they had received assurances from experts that the priests were reformed, or that they had not fully understood the nature of sexual abuse.

The bishops seemed determined *not* to recognize some aspects of the crisis that struck other observers as obvious. For instance, they did not seriously question the effectiveness of the treatment centers that had sent so many abusive priests back into parish work with clean bills of health; they continued to call upon the same experts for advice. Although the vast majority of abuse victims were adolescents rather than younger children, and roughly 90 percent of these victims were boys, the bishops shrank from any discussion of the possibility that homosexuality was a more widespread problem than classic pedophilia.

Wherever and whenever new cases arose, the facts that emerged through court proceedings conformed to the pattern established by the first revelations in Boston. Scores of priests were exposed as serial molesters. Bishops in one diocese after another were shown to have ignored warnings and kept known predators in parish assignments, switching them from one town to another to avoid public exposure. Each new story provoked a media frenzy in the city where it broke, and editorial writers thundered their denunciation of the Catholic hierarchy. Dozens of prelates were facing demands for their resignation.

By April the crisis was severe enough to prompt a rare Vatican intervention in the affairs of the American hierarchy. Early in the month the president and vice-president of the US Conference of Catholic Bishops (USCCB) met privately with Pope John Paul II, and although the agenda for that meeting was not made public, there is no doubt that the burgeoning scandal was discussed. Briefing reporters before his return to the US, the USCCB president, Bishop Wilton Gregory, said that the Pope was confident that the American bishops could solve the problem by themselves. But within thirty-six hours, the Pope summoned the USCCB leaders back to Rome, asking all the American cardinals to join them to confer with Vatican leaders about the crisis.

In the days leading up to the "Vatican summit," Bishop Gregory and other American prelates told reporters that the main purpose of this extraordinary meeting would be to brief the Pope on their activities. Some prelates, speaking more expansively, suggested that the American delegation might call for an end to priestly celibacy. One cardinal, who spoke to the *Los Angeles Times* anonymously, said that the US cardinals would make a forceful argument for the resignation or removal of Boston's Cardinal Law.

As soon as the meetings opened in Rome, all such discussion ceased. Issues such as priestly celibacy were not on the agenda, the cardinals now told reporters. Cardinal Roger Mahony—widely believed to be the "anonymous" prelate who spoke to the *Los Angeles Times*—informed the media that there was no discussion of Cardinal Law's status. The American bishops no longer made any effort to suggest that they were in Rome to give the Pope the benefit of their opinion.

Clearly something had happened at the Vatican. The American bishops realized that they had been summoned to account for themselves. The focus of the meeting was not on Catholic teachings, but on the moral leadership of the American hierarchy.

When Pope John Paul addressed the Vatican meeting, his message was plain:

It must be absolutely clear to the Catholic faithful, and to the wider community, that bishops and superiors are concerned, above all else, with the spiritual good of souls. People need to know that there is no place in the priesthood and religious life for those who would harm the young. They must know that bishops and priests are totally committed to the fullness of Catholic truth on matters of sexual morality, a truth as essential to the renewal of the priesthood and the episcopate as it is to the renewal of marriage and family life.

Before their departure for Rome, the American bishops had devoted most of their energy to a discussion of a "zero tolerance" policy, calling for the immediate suspension of any priest found guilty of sexual abuse. This proposal sounded like an aggressive response to the misdeeds of wayward priests. But the "zero-tolerance" policy by itself could not restore confidence among the laity, particularly if it was implemented by the same bishops who had already tolerated so much abuse. The Pope was looking for something more than a new way to respond to priestly misconduct. He was asking for clear moral leadership from the American bishops.

If the "zero tolerance" approach was discussed during the closed-door meetings with the Roman Curia, it was not mentioned in a final public statement, signed by both Vatican officials and American prelates at the conclusion of the meeting. That statement read in part:

Given the doctrinal issues underlying the deplorable behavior in question, certain lines of response have been proposed:

a) the pastors of the Church need clearly to promote the correct moral teaching of the Church and publicly to reprimand individuals who spread dissent and groups which advance ambiguous approaches to pastoral care.

b) a new and serious apostolic visitation of seminaries and other institutes of formation must be made without delay, with particular emphasis on the need for fidelity to the Church's teaching, especially in the area of morality, and the need for a deeper study of the criteria of suitability of candidates to the priesthood.

An "apostolic visitation" is essentially an investigation. Although the reason for such an inquiry was not explicitly mentioned in the statement, it was tacitly understood that Church leaders were concerned about reports of homosexual influence in the seminaries. The Vatican—with the acquiescence of the US prelates—was indicating that the reports were credible enough to warrant an in-depth investigation.

Thus the Vatican meeting concluded with a call for more forthright moral teaching, more vigilant enforcement of Church discipline, and more careful oversight of Catholic seminaries. By implication, the final statement pointed to a failure of leadership among the US bishops, who hold the responsibility in all these areas.

Writing in the *National Catholic Reporter* soon after the Vatican summit, John Allen disclosed that some American participants were not overly enthusiastic about the statement that they had endorsed. One bishop, speaking to Allen on condition of anonymity, said that language in the statement criticizing "dissent" and "ambiguous pastoral practices" had been written by Vatican officials. The Americans thought that they had reached a general agreement to drop some of that verbiage, the anonymous bishop recalled, but after a last-minute flurry of activity in preparation for a final press conference, they realized that the disputed phrases remained intact in the document that was distributed to the media.

With the Vatican meeting behind them, the leaders of the American episcopate now turned their attention to a meeting of the entire USCCB membership, which would take place in Dallas in June, with the topic of sexual abuse foremost on every bishop's mind. This would be an opportunity for the American bishops to inaugurate the sort of reforms they had discussed in Rome. But a curious thing happened as the date of the Dallas meeting approached. The leaders of the American hierarchy rapidly lost interest in discussing the moral leadership that had been demanded of them in Rome. They resumed talking about technical proposals that they could enact immediately, such as a "zero-tolerance" policy.

The logic of the "zero-tolerance" approach was based on the American bishops' newfound understanding that a priest who molested young people could not be trusted to amend his ways. In the past, bishops had been convinced that a priest could learn to master his sexual impulses through prayer, penance, and ascetical struggle. More recently therapists had persuaded the bishops that a regimen of counseling and treatment would make the offender safe for a new pastoral assignment. Now the American hierarchy had learned, in the most painful way possible, that any such assurances were mistaken. A priest who committed sexual abuse would always be a threat to commit sexual abuse again and his bishop would be liable for the consequences.

Those consequences, the US bishops had belatedly realized, could potentially include criminal prosecution. Many American Catholics were bemused to hear their bishops announce, as if it were a new revelation, that molesting children is illegal. "The law rightly makes it clear that sexual abuse of minors is a crime," wrote Bishop Gregory in an unforgettable column for *USA Today*. "We have all been enlightened."

If sexual abuse was a crime, then the bishops who had allowed abusers to continue soliciting young victims were involved in a criminal enterprise. That realization cast a pall over the American hierarchy. Abusive priests were not the only clerics who were villains in the drama being played out in American newspapers; bishops were suspects as well.

The Dallas meeting was conducted under suffocating media scrutiny. Reporters took over nearly the entire first floor of the Fairmount Hotel, with television crews taping interviews in suites on one side of the lobby while about a thousand print journalists converged on the "media center" set up in the grand ballroom. On the streets outside the hotel there were sound trucks from the major networks. Demonstrators clustered on the sidewalk across from the main entrance, carrying placards and chanting slogans, anxious for attention. In the lobby and the coffee shop, spokesmen for various victims' groups buttonholed reporters and held impromptu news conferences. At any such mass-media event, the heat of publicity tends to reduce complex questions to simple ones, and the simple question reporters were asking was: Would the bishops approve that zero-tolerance policy?

When the meeting began, the very first event highlighted an interesting difference in approaches to the scandal. At an introductory press briefing, members of the bishops' ad hoc committee on sexual abuse shared the platform with representatives of victims' groups. The bishops' spokesmen emphasized their determination to create a policy that would put an end to priestly sexual abuse. The victims, on the other hand, observed that no policy would be effective unless the bishops were diligent in carrying out their own responsibilities.

That difference of perspectives was evident throughout the discussions in Dallas. The bishops looked for a policy that would solve the problem; their critics waited for the bishops to shoulder their own responsibility for the scandal. Time and again the bishops edged toward an acknowledgment of their failures—as, for instance, when Bishop Gregory, in his opening address at the first plenary session, noted "a profound loss of confidence by the faithful in our leadership as shepherd." But each time a speaker raised that issue, the next speaker would switch attention back to the merits of a "zero-tolerance" policy.

Unwilling to discuss their own culpability for the scandal, the bishops were also unready to discuss the lack of clear moral leadership that the Vatican had detected at the root of the crisis. Late in the debate, Bishop Fabian Bruskewitz of Lincoln, Nebraska, rose to suggest that a commission be formed to explore the roots of the sex-abuse scandal. That commission, he added, should be sure to study the connection between theological dissent and sexual immorality. The Bruskewitz proposal was obviously based on the insights of the Vatican summit meeting. But the proposal received no support at all from the body of bishops; it was rejected without a debate.

Bishop Bruskewitz, the most outspoken conservative in the American hierarchy, was a lonely figure at the Dallas meeting. The USCCB leadership had not structured the sessions to encourage discussion of moral leadership; their goal was the fastest possible approval of a comprehensive set of policies and procedures. Nor had the organizers bothered to ensure that the speakers invited to address the bishops would represent a wide variety of viewpoints. To give the bishops a general perspective on the problem, the USCCB had invited a liberal professor, Scott Appleby of Notre Dame, and a liberal journalist, Peggy Steinfels of *Commonweal.* No conservative voices would be heard.

The experts who briefed the USCCB meeting were also drawn from the short list of psychiatrists and counselors who had been providing the bishops with advice during the years that scandal developed. Father Stephen Rossetti was the head of the St. Luke Institute in Maryland— which at the time of the Dallas meeting was under investigation by state licensing authorities. Father Canice Connors was the counselor who had seen no particular need to worry about the spiritual life of John Geoghan. It was on the advice of these men, in many cases, that abusive priests had been sent back into parish assignments with disastrous results. Still the USCCB continued to solicit their advice rather than to seek other opinions.

The bishops began their deliberations about a nationwide policy on Thursday morning, June 13. By that night it was clear that a "zero tolerance" policy would be approved. And when the "Dallas Charter" won initial approval the following day, it did call for the suspension of any priest credibly accused of abusing a child under the age of eighteen. The question that had been asked so many times during the week had been quickly resolved.

But in the course of the discussions, another question had become prominent in the minds of the reporters who were following the discussion. Would the bishops recognize that *they* were an important cause of the scandal? On the eve of the bishops' meeting, the *Dallas Morning News* had published a front-page story showing that about two-thirds of all American bishops had been guilty of covering up sexual abuse. If priests who abused children were to be subjected to prompt and severe discipline, what about bishops who neglected their duties?

Only once in the course of the US bishops' meeting did a prelate raise that question directly. Bishop Joseph Sullivan, a Brooklyn auxiliary, rose to say that the proposed "Dallas Charter" seemed to deflect attention from the grave failures of the hierarchy. If some clerics were to be dismissed from priestly ministry, he said, some bishops should be asked to resign because of their own failures. The statement by Bishop Sullivan prompted a hush in the media center, where dozens of reporters looked up from their laptops and muttered that at long last, one bishop seemed to "get it." When he concluded his remarks, Bishop Sullivan even drew a smattering of applause from among his fellow bishops. But his suggestion was ignored.

Before the meeting ended, Bishop Gregory did suggest that if any bishops had *themselves* been guilty of abusing children, they should resign. (No one accepted his suggestion—although subsequently several bishops have stepped down *after* their misconduct became public knowledge.) But this impotent suggestion was directed only to those bishops who had personally engaged in sexual abuse, not to those who condoned abuse by other clerics.

After agreeing to the "zero-tolerance" approach in principle, the bishops had a lengthy debate over the details of their policy. They worried, for example, about the question of whether every allegation of sexual abuse should be reported to local law-enforcement officials. (Even at this late date, many bishops seemed unaware of the laws in most states *requiring* them to report suspected abuse.) Some allegations would obviously be false—perhaps even demonstrably so. The bishops had no desire to risk a priest's reputation on the basis of a complaint that had no merit. But then again, if the bishops had the discretion to judge for themselves whether or not a complaint was credible, then they might be accused of ignoring valid complaints. The bishops eventually decided to protect themselves from such accusations, even at the cost of endangering their priests; all accusations would be reported.

As the debate wore on, some bishops began hinting that a draconian policy, banning any priest who was accused of abuse, would be a policy induced by panic. They urged their colleagues carefully to consider the long-term implications of their choices, rather than becoming fixated on how the policy would be play in the media. Any glimmer of an exception to the "zero-tolerance" rule would surely be seized upon by reporters as a sign that the bishops were backing away from their commitment. But the policy must be carefully crafted, these concerned bishops argued, to respect the rights of accused priests and the requirements of canon law.

On the final day of debate, Cardinal Avery Dulles made a powerful argument against the sweeping policy that had been presented to the bishops for approval. The respected Jesuit theologian complained that the definition of "sexual abuse" was far too broad; it could include touches or even looks that the priest himself intended as harmless. An innocent priest could be removed from ministry on the basis of a single false charge, the cardinal observed; and months or even years might pass before that priest could restore his reputation and vindicate his rights. A priest would not be able to confide in his bishops or mention his failings—perhaps even his thoughts—without running the risk of dismissal. This lucid and balanced critique by Cardinal Dulles left reporters in the press room wondering for the first time whether the USCCB proposal would be accepted by the body of bishops. But any worries on that score were unnecessary. When the votes were counted, the "Dallas Charter" won easy approval.

Approval from Rome was not so easy to obtain. The Dallas Charter set new canonical norms for the Church in the United States, and Vatican approval was required before this canonical legislation could go into effect. In October the Holy See declined to grant its approval—the canonical *recognitio*—for the American norms. But in a rapid sequence of events that contradicted reports of a deep rift between Rome and the American hierarchy, a joint Vatican-US commission quickly amended the proposed policy to satisfy the Vatican's concerns, and the revised norms were approved by the USCCB at its regular meeting in November.

Victims of sexual abuse complained at first that the Vatican objections were designed to scuttle the "zero tolerance" policy approved by the USCCB in Dallas. But in fact the Vatican gave every indication of support for the overall thrust of the American bishops' policy. The problem, Vatican officials patiently explained, was that the US proposal conflicted with the Code of Canon Law.

Specifically, officials in Rome cited the lack of "due process" safeguards to protect priests from wrongful accusations of sexual abuse, to ensure that every accused cleric would be able to defend himself against the charges. The Vatican also looked askance at the vague definition of sexual abuse contained in the Dallas norms, and the equally vague responsibilities assigned to lay review boards. Some canon-law experts also wondered whether the USCCB, by setting up a mandatory nationwide policy, was undermining the authority of individual bishops to govern their own dioceses. With a few strategic amendments crafted to answer the Vatican's concerns, the Dallas Charter was adopted, essentially intact.

Apart from the zero-tolerance policy, the most striking aspect of the Dallas Charter was the creation of a National Review Board, composed of prominent laymen and authorized to investigate and make judgments on the bishops' implementation of their own plans. By its nature the Review Board was designed to make criticisms of American bishops. Within a matter of months it became clear that the bishops' willingness to accept such criticism had definite limits.

Less than a year after he was appointed to chair the Review Board, the former Oklahoma Governor Frank Keating became embroiled in a dispute with Cardinal Roger Mahony. Frustrated by the cardinal's reluctance to disclose information about abusive priests in the Los Angeles archdiocese, an angry Keating remarked that some bishops were following the same code of silence that protected criminals in the Cosa Nostra. That comparison understandably outraged many bishops, and Keating was soon pressured to resign from the Review Board. But before he left the scene, the Oklahoma politician explained his outrage in a *New York Times* op-ed, shining the spotlight directly on the American bishops. "Obstructing justice, excusing and concealing those who victimize innocent children: these are not the actions of holy men," he wrote. "God may hold them accountable in the next world, but we will certainly hold them accountable in this one."

In February 2004 the Review Board issued its first comprehensive report. The fundamental causes of the scandal, the Board said, were:

(i) a failure to grasp the gravity of the problem of sexual abuse of minors by priests; (ii) deficiencies in the response to victims; (iii) unwarranted presumptions in favor of accused priests; (iv) reliance on secrecy and an undue emphasis on the avoidance of scandal; (v) excessive reliance on the therapeutic model in dealing with priest offenders; (vi) undue reliance upon legal advice that placed a premium on adversarial defense tactics at the expense of concern for victims of abuse; and (vii) a failure to hold themselves and other bishops accountable for mistakes, including a failure to make use of lay consultative bodies and other governance structures.

By removing scores of accused priests from active ministry, the American norms have certainly eliminated any basis for complaint about "unwarranted presumptions in favor of accused priests." But even today the bishops could be judged guilty of "excessive reliance on the therapeutic model" and "undue reliance upon legal advice."

The National Review Board explicitly recognized that the scandal was created not only by a small minority of priests who engaged in unspeakable crimes, but also by the passive reaction of bishops who failed to make an appropriate response. In a particularly poignant, understated passage of their report, the Board said:

> The lack of expressions of outrage by bishops—both at the time they first learned of the abhorrent acts of some priests and in dealing with the crisis publicly—is troubling. The Board has seen no letters condemning the men who have engaged in such conduct.

Moreover, the National Review Board confirmed suspicions that predatory priests have been protected by a homosexual network in seminaries and diocesan chanceries:

> In the 1970s and 1980s, in particular, there developed at certain seminaries a "gay subculture," and at these seminaries, according to several witnesses, homosexual liaisons occurred among students or between students and teachers. Such subcultures existed or exist in certain dioceses or orders as well. The Board believes that the failure to take disciplinary action against such conduct contributed to an atmosphere in which sexual abuse of adolescent boys by priests was more likely.

That initial report from the National Review Board was calling attention yet again to the bishops' moral leadership: the topic that had *not* been discussed in Dallas. But the Board's criticism did not elicit a response from the hierarchy. Since adopting the Dallas Charter, the bishops have confined their attention to regular revenues and "audits" of their compliance with the policies they established. In 2007, the latest audit of American dioceses showed a high level of compliance with the terms of the Dallas Charter. But that compliance does not mean that the sex-abuse scandal has been resolved.

The first such audit, in 2003, bestowed two separate commendations on the Diocese of Manchester, New Hampshire—where Bishop John McCormack was forced to enter into a plea-bargaining agreement with the attorney general to avoid prosecution. Just a few months before receiving the audit commendations, the bishop had signed a statement in which "the diocese acknowledges that the state has evidence likely to sustain a conviction" for the failure of diocesan officials to report sexual abuse of minors. A few months thereafter, an editorial in the *Manchester Union Leader* charged: "Even now the leadership of this diocese continues to damage the reputation of the church by offering the public more lies and deception."

If it is possible for a diocese to be fully compliant with the Dallas Charter yet guilty of criminal activities, lies, and deception, then the medicine prescribed by the bishops at their Dallas meeting has not cured the disease.

In 2006, as she delivered the audit results for that year, Teresa Kettelkamp—the USCCB official charged with oversight of child-protection efforts—made a remarkable comment. After measuring diocesan compliance for several years, she said, "It is now time to shift to examining effectiveness."

For five years the American bishops had been grading themselves on their faithful observance of the Dallas Charter. Five years later, for the first time, the USCCB showed a willingness to question whether the policies contained in that Charter would actually solve the problem.

14

THE
DEATH WATCH

ngry Catholics had planned a massive demonstration for Sunday, December 8, 2002, outside Boston's Cathedral of the Holy Cross. When Cardinal Bernard Law arrived to celebrate Mass, the protest organizers planned to confront him, demanding his resignation. Hundreds of people were expected to participate, expressing their outrage over the cardinal's handling of sex-abuse complaints. These demonstrations had become regular events at the cathedral over the course of the year. By December the protestors were openly incredulous that the cardinal was still in office so many months after he had lost all public credibility.

On the day before that scheduled December protest, however, the organizers' plans hit a snag. The Boston archdiocese announced that Cardinal Law would not be celebrating Mass at the cathedral that Sunday. Donna Morrissey, the public spokesman for the archdiocese, offered no further details about the cardinal's schedule.

A full day passed quietly by. The protest outside the cathedral took place on schedule, but the crowd was not nearly as large as expected, and the participants seemed to have some difficulty mustering their sense of outrage against a man who was nowhere to be seen.

Then on Sunday afternoon, Cardinal Law *was* seen—not at his residence in Brighton, but in Rome. He was spotted by John Allen, the Vatican correspondent for the *National Catholic Reporter*, having dinner with Bishop James Harvey, the American-born prefect of the Pontifical Household.

So the people of Boston learned that their archbishop had quietly slipped out of town, for the second time in less than a year, to speak with Vatican officials about his future. In April, after a flurry of rumors that he would resign, Cardinal Law had dropped out of sight, traveled unannounced to Rome, and returned to say that he had been "encouraged" by a meeting with Pope John Paul II. He had resolved to stay at the helm of the Boston archdiocese "as long as God gives me the opportunity." But this time, the cardinal's trip would have a different outcome.

The cardinal's sudden flight to Rome occurred at the end of a week that can only be described as catastrophic. Throughout the year the Church in Boston had been buffeted by a stream of revelations about the clerics who had abused children and the archdiocesan officials who had covered up their crimes. But not even a full year of adverse publicity had prepared local Catholics for the stories that hit the headlines, one after another, during the first week in December.

- On Monday, the media reported that the Boston archdiocese might file for bankruptcy protection in the face of potential legal damages of approximately $100 million stemming from sex-abuse lawsuits.
- On Tuesday, lawyers representing sex-abuse victims released a new series of personnel files from the archdiocesan archives, showing that the pattern of quietly shifting predator priests from one parish to another had been more widespread than previously realized and had apparently continued through 1999.
- On Wednesday, Cardinal Law met with the members of the archdiocesan finance council and received their approval to proceed with a bankruptcy filing.
- On Thursday, the cardinal fueled the wrath of liberal clerics when he announced that the archdiocese would not sponsor any meetings at a particular parish in suburban Newton—a parish that had become closely identified with the cardinal's critics, where a group of dissident priests planned to meet the following day.
- On Friday, state troopers arrived at the cardinal's residence to deliver a subpoena requiring his testimony before a grand jury convened by the attorney general of Massachusetts, who was probing the possibility of criminal charges against officials who had concealed evidence of sexual abuse.

On Friday, Cardinal Law left town.

To this day, no one outside the cardinal's tight circle of confidants knows exactly when Law slipped out of the city. Father Christopher Coyne, a Boston priest who frequently acted as the cardinal's spokesman during the year of troubles, later told reporters that the cardinal had reached the conclusion by Thursday night, December 5, that he should offer his resignation.

But another tumultuous week would pass before the people of the Boston archdiocese knew of that decision.

As late as Thursday afternoon, Cardinal Law was still keeping to his announced schedule. That evening he had planned to attend a fundraising dinner for the Catholic Action League, a conservative activist group. Just two hours before the event, the cardinal's secretary called the organizers with a few last-minute questions about the program, explaining that he was help-ing Cardinal Law to prepare his remarks. Then the secretary called back again, explaining that the cardinal had been detained by an important con-ference call. Cardinal Law did not attend the dinner; his secretary arrived to tell the disappointed crowd that Law had been called into "urgent" meetings, related to the events that were dominating the headlines.

At that point, the embattled Archbishop of Boston slipped out of pub-lic view. His office was silent on Friday. He failed to appear at another fundraising event, for Catholic Charities, on Friday night. Even on Saturday, when his office revealed that the cardinal would not celebrate Sunday Mass at the cathedral, there was no indication that he was out of town. He was still expected to travel to Washington on Sunday night, for an annual meeting of the board of directors of Catholic University, of which he was chairman.

By Sunday night, however, the news of his trip to Rome had broken, and it was clear that Cardinal Law had more pressing concerns than the Catholic University board meeting. (On December 10—during the second day of the board meeting, while he was still in Rome—the cardinal resigned his position as the chairman of the university's board.)

When she was told that Cardinal Law had been spotted in Rome, Donna Morrissey confirmed that he had made the trip to consult with Vat-ican officials, but offered no further information about his plans. On Mon-day the Vatican press office, hounded by American reporters for details about the cardinal's status, released a remarkably bland statement, which could have applied with equal accuracy to any of the dozens of bishops who travel to Rome on routine business in a given week: "Cardinal Law has come to Rome to inform the Holy See about the different aspects of the sit-uation in Boston."

Still, while the media continued to pester official Church spokesmen on both sides of the Atlantic, there was really no mystery about the reasons for the cardinal's unexpected trip. After all, this had happened once before.

Early in April, Cardinal Law's credibility was irreparably damaged by the release of archdiocesan files relating to the treatment of Father Paul

Shanley. From the earlier Geoghan case the Catholics of Boston had learned that their cardinal had covered the tracks of an abusive priest. But until April it was still possible for the cardinal's defenders to believe that his errors in handling abusive priests had been caused by ignorance and/or negligence: serious problems, certainly, but not proof that he was unfit for his office. The Shanley case exposed a much broader, unmistakable pattern of corruption within the archdiocese. The revelations provoked howls of shock and out-rage, and drew the first chorus of public calls for the cardinal's resignation. An opinion poll by the *Boston Globe* found that 65 percent of the people of Boston wanted a change in the leadership of the archdiocese. In response to the furor, Cardinal Law disappeared from public view for a full week, leav-ing Donna Morrissey to tell reporters that he was "in meetings and prayer."

As the days passed and the cardinal remained incommunicado, reporters began to hear rumors that he would soon announce his resigna-tion. On April 11 those rumors reached a crescendo. One reporter, citing a reliable source within the archdiocesan bureaucracy, insisted that the car-dinal would fax his resignation to the apostolic nuncio in Washington at exactly 11 that morning. Television sound trucks pulled up in a line beside the cardinal's Lake Street residence, waiting for the formal announcement, in an exercise that grim journalists likened to a "death watch."

But the following day, Cardinal Law—who was still in seclusion—sent a letter to the priests of Boston indicating that he planned to stay. "My desire is to serve this archdiocese and this whole Church with every fiber of my being," he wrote. "This I will continue to do as long as God makes it possible."

Only several days later—on April 17—did the cardinal disclose that he had traveled secretly to Rome that week "to seek counsel and advice." In a fresh public statement, he reported that Vatican officials were now "very conscious of the gravity of the situation," and he explained that he had explicitly discussed the calls for his retirement. After meeting with the Pope, he said that he had returned home "encouraged in my efforts to pro-vide the strongest possible leadership in ensuring, as far as is humanly pos-sible, that no child is ever abused again by a priest of this archdiocese."

That April statement was not incompatible with rumors that although Cardinal Law had offered to resign, Pope John Paul II had asked him to remain in Boston. In December, when he traveled to the Vatican once again, sources in Rome confirmed that Cardinal Law had indeed submitted his resignation in April, and the Pope had rejected it.

In May, Law became the first American cardinal ever compelled to testify under oath in a lawsuit in which he was a named defendant. He would testify several times over the course of the year. Each time excerpts from his testimony found their way into the press, new questions were raised about the accuracy of the cardinal's sworn statements. He claimed that he did not know about certain instances of abuse, although other witnesses testified that they had informed him. He said that he was unfamiliar with documents that had crossed his desk and even bore his signature. He testified that he had not been aware of sexual abuse during his early years as a priest in Mississippi, but a witness emerged to report that Law had been directly involved in handling the case of an abusive cleric there.

The cardinal's testimony was always defensible. Certainly there was no clear evidence that he was deliberately misleading the court. But at a minimum his testimony was self-serving; his supporters found it difficult to persuade skeptics that he was being entirely truthful and forthcoming. Cardinal Law frequently testified that he could not recall events that put him in a bad light. His memory was much sharper about exculpatory details.

My own suspicions about the reliability of the cardinal's sworn testimony were awakened by an odd detail. In April, a man who had been molested by Father Joseph Birmingham revealed that he had spoken about it personally to Cardinal Law in 1989. The cardinal, he told reporters, had ordered him to remain silent about the abuse, under "the seal of confession." During a deposition in August 2002, Cardinal Law was questioned about that encounter. He testified that he could not remember the conversation. But he did say: "I cannot imagine ever saying to anyone, 'I bind you by the power of the confessional.'"

I could imagine it very easily, because Cardinal Law had once said something very similar to me. In 1987, while I was working at the archdiocesan newspaper, I asked the cardinal a question about what I thought was a routine personnel issue. He answered me, but only after saying, "I'm putting you under the seal." I was so thoroughly taken aback that the meeting was etched clearly on my memory. In sacramental confession, the *priest* is bound by an absolute seal of secrecy. The penitent is not; he is free to discuss the matter of his confession with others if he chooses to do so. The priest cannot impose the seal on a layman.

Nor was my discussion with Cardinal Law on that occasion a sacramental confession. It was a routine business meeting. The information that he disclosed to me was mundane: not potentially damaging or even particularly interesting. A simple request to "keep it confidential" would have been adequate; invoking a sacramental seal was grossly unnecessary. Yet the cardinal had done it without any hesitation, as if it were something he did routinely. In April, when Father Birmingham's witness said that the cardinal had placed him under the seal, his report rang true to me. (It was not, in any case, the sort of detail that someone was likely to fabricate.) When Cardinal Law testified that he could not *imagine* saying such a thing, I could not choke down my suspicions.

Others were suspicious about other details of Law's testimony, and his credibility was in tatters. Still the cardinal remained at his post, apparently determined to ride out the storm. As the months passed he remained in office, preserving a low profile, but gradually he began to resume his public leadership role. He attended World Youth Day festivities in Toronto with a friendly delegation of teenagers from Boston. He participated in the ribbon-cutting ceremonies for a bridge dedicated to the memory of a Jewish community activist with whom he had been particularly friendly. He voiced his support for janitors who were engaged in a labor dispute with the City of Boston. He participated in an annual pro-life rally on Boston Common.

On November 4, standing before the altar of Holy Cross cathedral, he delivered what seemed to be designed as a definitive apology for his role in the sex-abuse scandal. "I want to acknowledge publicly my responsibility for decisions that I now see as clearly wrong," the cardinal said, his voice cracking as he spoke. "The forgiving love of God gives me the courage to beg forgiveness of those who have suffered because of what I did."

Barely a week later, the cardinal was in the headlines again—and for the first time in 2002, the topic was something other than sexual abuse. Cardinal Law served as the principal spokesman for the US bishops' conference in questioning the wisdom of US policy toward Iraq. He made an appearance at a mosque in Boston and bowed to venerate the Qu'ran along with the Muslim believers. His prominence in these new roles drew sharp criticism—from defenders of US foreign policy in the former instance, and critics of religious indifferentism in the latter—but they signaled the cardinal's return to the limelight.

Still the sex-abuse scandal would not go away. All through the year the Boston archdiocese had been battling—in most cases, unsuccessfully—to prevent new disclosures. Full transcripts of Cardinal Law's depositions in the Shanley case had been made public, along with similar testimony from auxiliary Boston bishops; critical analysts quickly pointed out discrepancies between the prelates' sworn testimony and previous public statements from the archdiocese. A steady trickle of fresh allegations and new revelations had eroded the cardinal's public standing.

Meanwhile Judge Constance Sweeney, who had been assigned to preside over all the cases associated with the Boston sex-abuse scandal, had become increasingly impatient with the efforts by archdiocesan lawyers to slow the proceedings.

Late in November, Judge Sweeney ruled against the archdiocese yet again, authorizing the public release of new files in connection with the Shanley case. In doing so, the judge made it clear that she was losing her patience with the desultory legal tactics employed by the archdiocesan lawyers. And she raised some doubts about the accuracy of statements made by Church leaders. Judge Sweeney wrote:

> The actual discovery material before the court includes statements from Cardinal Law that between 1984 and 1989 some offending priests were returned to active ministry when, after treatment, archdiocesan personnel and the cardinal determined they did not present risks of harm to children. Despite this assertion, other archdiocesan records obtained through discovery reveal that some offending priests may well have been assigned to parishes, youth groups and the like, even though the cardinal or other archdiocesan personnel knew that the priests in question were at the least suspected of engaging in continuing sexual encounters with children.

The negative publicity was compounded by complaints from some priests who insisted that they had been falsely accused of sexual abuse. Dozens of clerics had been suspended from priestly ministry under a sweeping new archdiocesan policy. Some priests complained that they had never been informed of the charges against them or given an opportunity to respond to the accusations.

The most bizarre of these cases involved Monsignor Michael Smith Foster, a highly placed canon lawyer and official on the archdiocesan tribunal. In August, Monsignor Foster was suspended from ministry after being accused of molesting a young man nearly twenty years earlier. Almost immediately the accusations against Monsignor Foster were questioned—at first by other witnesses, later by the accuser's own lawyer. On September 4 a lawsuit against Monsignor Foster was withdrawn, and on September 10 the priest was told that his suspension had been revoked.

Archdiocesan officials, however, still had not met the accuser, and when they did, on September 12, he repeated his charges. The investigation of the prominent cleric was immediately re-opened, and once again he was suspended. Monsignor Foster remained in ecclesiastical limbo until October 30, when—without apology or explanation—Cardinal Law informed him that the investigation had concluded, and he could return to active ministry. In December the *Boston Herald* added a new wrinkle to the complicated story, discovering gaping holes in the archdiocesan investigation of the case and concluding that Church officials had exonerated Foster on the basis of patently inaccurate information—presumably because the accused priest had many friends both in the media and in the chancery, pressing for his exoneration.

For some priests, Monsignor Foster now became the symbol of fears that they could expect summary judgment if they were accused—accurately or inaccurately—of child abuse. For others his case caused resentment because Foster, an influential figure in the archdiocese and a favorite of local reporters, had been given the sort of quick, favorable treatment that other priests in regular parish assignments could only long for. Monsignor Foster himself said that he was "angry at the treatment I have received." He wondered aloud why the archdiocese had not come to his defense even sooner and more decisively, pointing out to the *Boston Globe* that "we have put a lot of resources into helping the cardinal with reputational issues."

By now unhappy priests were joining sex-abuse victims in their open criticism of Cardinal Law. Lay activists, too, joined the chorus. The group known as Voice of the Faithful took root in Boston, and although the organization had national ambitions it gained particular strength in the Boston archdiocese by calling Church leaders to accountability. Voice of the Faithful (VOTF) was viewed with open suspicion by archdiocesan officials, and Cardinal Law resisted efforts to meet with the group's leaders. More conservative Catholic laymen were also suspicious of the new group, wondering why VOTF—whose leaders insisted that it was a "moderate" organization—was so reluctant to stake out a clear position on controversial issues such as homosexuality or the ordination of women. But VOTF enjoyed a cozy relationship with the editorial staff of the *Boston Globe*, a newspaper with enormous power in the local market and a relentless hostility toward the teachings of the Catholic Church.

In the fall of 2002, VOTF was joined on the scene by the Boston Priests' Forum, which claimed a membership of two hundred among the roughly one thousand priests active in the archdiocese. The most visible leaders of the Priests' Forum were two outspoken liberal priests, Father Walter Cuenin and Father Robert Bullock.

The case of Father Cuenin, like that of Monsignor Foster, deserves a bit of special notice. Years before, while he was teaching Jesuit seminarians at the Weston School of Theology, Father Cuenin had decided to abandon the priesthood. But after several months living as a layman, he returned to the archdiocese, was reinstated as a priest—and was re-assigned to teach young prospective priests at St. John's Seminary. Over the years Cuenin has been one of the most voluble theological dissidents among Boston's priests, yet he had been appointed by Cardinal Law to head one of the most attractive parishes in the archdiocese: Our Lady, Help of Christians, in the affluent suburb of Newton. From that highly visible post, Father Cuenin began to issue statements to friendly media outlets, until reporters developed the habit of calling his Newton parish for a reaction whenever Cardinal Law issued a statement on the sex-abuse scandal. Father Cuenin also became a leading spokesman for VOTF, and his parish became the de facto headquarters of the activist group.

By early December, then, Cardinal Law was facing a variety of serious challenges. VOTF and the Priests' Forum were directly challenging his authority. Judge Sweeney was questioning his credibility. An archdiocesan fundraising campaign was foundering. Mass attendance was dropping. Sex-abuse accusations—and the lawsuits that inevitably followed—were proliferating. Thus the stage was set for that disastrous first week in December.

For several weeks knowledgeable lawyers had whispered that the Boston archdiocese was investigating the implications of filing for bankruptcy, in anticipation of $100 million in damages from sex-abuse lawsuits. At first the rumors had been dismissed as mere speculation; cynics suggested that the archdiocesan lawyers were trying to frighten the plaintiffs into a quick settlement. But by December 2 it was clear that the discussion of bankruptcy was not merely an idle gambit; the option was being seriously considered by archdiocesan officials.

The active discussion of bankruptcy was condemned by Father Robert Bullock as "blasphemous." Speaking as a representative of the Priests' Forum, he said that the move "would be outrageous and unbearable—pastorally and theologically and spiritually disastrous." When the archdiocesan finance council gave Cardinal Law the green light to proceed with a bankruptcy filing, Father Bullock was one of several commentators who remarked that financial bankruptcy might be an appropriate symbol, since the Boston archdiocese was already spiritually bankrupt.

Next came the release of a new set of personnel files, confirming the pattern—now depressingly familiar—in which archdiocesan officials had sloughed off complaints about clerical sex-abuse, shuffled the guilty clerics from one parish to another, concealed evidence of wrongdoing from the public, and provided the offending clerics with glowing recommendations even after they confessed their misdeeds.

The details of the new revelations were stunning, even to readers who had been hardened by the previous disclosures of the Geoghan and Shanley cases:

- Father Robert Meffan had routinely molested naïve young girls who were planning to enter the convent, telling them that by performing sexual favors for him they were showing their love for Christ. When he was finally approved for retirement, Cardinal Law wrote to tell him: "We are truly grateful for your priestly care and ministry to all whom you have served." The cardinal's letter gave absolutely no indication of any misbehavior.

- Father Peter Frost confessed that he was a homosexual "sex addict" who had molested boys for twenty years. Cardinal Law wrote to him: "It is my hope that some day in the future you will return to an appropriate ministry, bringing with you the wisdom which emerges from difficult experience."

- Father James Foley had been involved with a troubled woman who died of a drug overdose in the 1960s; he was present when she lost consciousness, but did not call for help because he was in a compromising position. Over the years he had fathered two children and carried on relationships with three married women. He was still assigned to active parish ministry in December 2002 when these stories surfaced.

Even before these new stories came to light, the pressure on Cardinal Law had been enormous. Now it became overwhelming. James Post, the president of Voice of the Faithful, said that the cardinal could no longer function as a pastoral leader. "We are a diocese without a bishop," he said. Speaking in more measured tones, Robert Bennett, a member of the National Review Board set up by the USCCB in Dallas, told *The New York Times*: "The board is very troubled about the most recent revelations that show that the abuse and its handling was more aggravated than we thought before." The most vituperative reaction came from Adrian Walker, a regular columnist for the *Boston Globe:* "How can any sane person worship at an altar presided over by a cleric who provided the support—I refuse to call it moral support—to sick, depraved priests that Cardinal Bernard F. Law did?"

Some fifty-eight members of the Priests' Forum quickly attached their signatures to an open letter urging Cardinal Law to resign. "While this is obviously a difficult request, we believe in our hearts that this is a necessary step," the priests wrote, explaining that "your position as our bishop is already so compromised that it is no longer possible for you to exercise the spiritual leadership required for the Church in Boston." But by the time that letter was hand-delivered to the cardinal's residence, Law was already in Rome.

Neither the Boston archdiocese nor the Holy See would comment on the cardinal's reasons for traveling to Rome or even divulge his schedule of meetings with Vatican officials. But Church officials did concede that there were two topics on the agenda: the prospect of a bankruptcy filing by the Boston archdiocese—which would have to be approved in advance by the Holy See—and the future of Cardinal Law.

American bankruptcy law offered several attractive possibilities for the archdiocese. A bankruptcy filing could bring an end to the exhausting sequence of new sex-abuse lawsuits, new depositions, and new revelations. The bankruptcy would consolidate all existing complaints, shut the door (after a firm deadline) to all new lawsuits, and stop the release of new testimony. The agonizing public trial of the Boston archdiocese, which had been conducted primarily through the media for eleven months, could be brought to a merciful end.

A bankruptcy filing would also put heavy pressure on other parties to cooperate in a quick settlement. Insurance carriers for the Boston archdiocese had been expressing a reluctance to pay off sex-abuse claims, reasoning that Church officials had been negligent in their duties. But American bankruptcy courts are notoriously unsympathetic toward insurance companies; their payments—amounting to as much as $90 million, from a total settlement estimated at $100 million—would almost surely be forthcoming. Plaintiffs' lawyers had been aggressively pushing for a higher settlement price, but bankruptcy courts are also notorious for pruning lawyers' fees.

If archdiocesan officials had introduced the discussion of bankruptcy as a bargaining ploy—to push plaintiffs' lawyers toward a speedy settlement—

the gambit was successful. When they learned that Cardinal Law was in Rome and realized that he could return with the authority to initiate bankruptcy proceedings immediately, lawyers for the sex-abuse victims showed a keen interest in reaching a quick out-of-court settlement for their claims.

But Vatican officials were far less enthusiastic about the bankruptcy option. After all, they reasoned, the Archdiocese of Boston *could* manage even $100 million in settlement costs, if necessary. Under the circumstances, a plea of bankruptcy might be interpreted as an effort to deprive the victims of the full compensation to which they were legally entitled. And while the niceties of US bankruptcy law might be attractive to American lawyers, the Vatican had to consider the implications of the move for Catholics in other countries. The stigma attached to a bankruptcy filing—especially by an affluent American see—would have serious repercussions for the universal Church. By all indications, Vatican officials took a dim view of the bankruptcy option, and the discussion in Rome turned toward the future of Boston's archbishop.

As Cardinal Law's visit to Rome continued, stories of his impending resignation were circulating widely through the American media. On Thursday, December 12, several media outlets reported that he had already formally submitted his resignation. The Vatican promptly denied that story, but disclosed that the American cardinal would meet privately with Pope John Paul II on the following day.

By now, American media outlets were buzzing with speculation. Dozens of reporters were working their contacts in Rome, and even if they could only draw responses from minor Vatican officials, the second-hand reports all pointed in the same direction: If Cardinal Law had not yet submitted his resignation, he would do so when he met with the Pope.

When the news finally broke, on Friday the 13th of December, it was anti-climactic. Cardinal Law had met with the Pope. He had offered his resignation. The Pontiff had accepted it. Bishop Richard Lennon, a Boston auxiliary, had been appointed as apostolic administrator to head the archdiocese until a new archbishop could be named.

When he was appointed Archbishop of Boston in 1984, Bernard Law had been seen as a rising star in the ecclesiastical firmament. He was a comparatively young prelate, with obvious talent and ambition. Elevated to the College of Cardinals in 1985, by 2002 he was the senior figure in the US hierarchy. He had displayed his influence repeatedly, as his former auxiliary bishops were assigned to head their own dioceses: Archbishops Alfred

Hughes of New Orleans, Louisiana, and Roberto Gonzalez of San Juan, Puerto Rico; Bishops Thomas Daily of Brooklyn, New York; John D'Arcy of Fort Wayne, Indiana; Robert Banks of Green Bay, Wisconsin; John McCormack of Manchester, New Hampshire; William Murphy of Rockville Centre, New York; and Daniel Hart of Norwich, Connecticut.

But now several of those former Boston auxiliaries—Bishops Daily, McCormack, Murphy, and Banks—faced questions about their own conduct in Boston's sex-abuse scandal. Like Cardinal Law, each of these bishops had been involved in the cover-up of priestly sexual abuse. And if a powerful prelate like Cardinal Law could fall, could less prominent bishops survive?

PART IV

RUIN

15

GENERATIONS
BETRAYED

A bit more than six months passed between the resignation of Cardinal Law and the naming of his successor, Archbishop (soon to be Cardinal) Sean O'Malley. In the interim the Boston archdiocese, along with every other diocese in the country, began the implementation of the Dallas Charter.

A genuine reform of the Catholic Church in America might have begun in Dallas with a frank admission of the corruption that had allowed the sex-abuse scandal to fester. Instead, by instituting a series of policy norms, the bishops had sought to deflect attention from their own appalling failures. Only a small minority of American priests—2-3 percent, by most calculations—were ever accused of sexual abuse, whereas the vast majority of bishops were involved in the cover-up effort. Nevertheless all priests were now treated like members of a suspect class, while bishops preserved all their dignity and privileges.

All across America, priests were required to submit to fingerprinting and criminal background checks. They were ordered to attend programs on recognizing and reporting sexual abuse. They were told that all members of their parish staffs—all schoolteachers, all janitors, all Sunday-school volunteers—should be expected to go through the same tests and training. One of the priests who resented this treatment, Father Jerry Pokorsky, wrote in *Catholic World Report* in August 2005: "If Martin Luther taught 'salvation by faith alone,' it might be said that the bishops' approach is 'salvation by policies, procedures, and protocols alone.'"

If these new policies had been in place ten or twenty years earlier, would they have stopped the sexual abuse that led the USCCB to produce the Dallas Charter? Obviously not. The Boston archdiocese did not need background checks to identify John Geoghan and Paul Shanley as abusers;

the evidence in the priests' personnel files was more than enough to warn the hierarchy. Parents and parishioners did not need much instruction in reporting sexual abuse. They *had* reported it, and their reports had been brushed aside.

Before the Dallas meeting American bishops had ample authority to discipline priests who were guilty of sexual abuse. They could have suspending misbehaving priests, limited their assignments, turned them over to the police for prosecution, required them to spend time in seclusion and penance, or even recommended their removal from the priesthood. They chose not to use that authority. Now, rather than resolving to carry out their duties conscientiously, the bishops had voluntarily stripped themselves of their own individual prerogative and bound themselves with absolute and unswerving rules. With the Charter in place, the bishops could and did answer all questions by saying that they were following the policies set by the USCCB. The Dallas norms were designed not so much to deter abuse of children as to deflect criticism from bishops.

For ordinary priests the Dallas norms created nightmarish uncertainties. At any time, a priest could be suspended without notice on the basis of a single accusation. There was no statute of limitations on accusations. A middle-aged priest could look back to his high-school days and realize that a former girlfriend, if she harbored a grudge against him, could end his priestly ministry by mentioning some liberty that he had taken prior to her eighteenth birthday. The accusation might even be false; if it was plausible, that was enough.

Bishops began listing the names of priests accused of abuse, exposing them to public humiliation whether or not they were guilty. Hundreds of accused priests protested their innocence, but they were forced to wait weeks, months, or even years for an opportunity to present their case. Many priests complained that they were not even informed about the allegations against them. Elderly priests, living in retirement, were curtly informed that their faculties had been removed and they could not celebrate Mass or wear clerical garb. Some priests, having grown forgetful with old age, were unable to understand the reason for their suspension; a few died, disconsolate, before receiving any explanation. Priests became convinced—not without reason—that their bishops would readily trample on their rights if necessary to preserve themselves from embarrassing questions. It was a reign of terror—and it still is.

If the Dallas norms caused heartache and anxiety for parish priests, they also imposed new burdens even on the children for whose benefit the

Dallas Charter had (at least theoretically) been written. Each diocese was expected to adopt a "personal safety" course approved by the USCCB, to be become a standard part of the curriculum for all students in Catholic schools or religious-education programs. Beginning in kindergarten and continuing through high school, all Catholic students were to be instructed about the dangers of sexual abuse and trained in proper reporting of any adult misconduct.

The arrogance of the USCCB in presuming to instruct students about sexual abuse was breathtaking. For years, trusting parents had sent their children into Catholic parishes and schools, confidently assuming that Church leaders would protect them. Now the same church leaders who had betrayed that trust presumed to instruct the parents and their innocent children about the dangers that children might face. Rather than ensuring the innocence of young students, these programs were designed to put the burden of reporting on the children, making them more effective witnesses if and when they were molested.

Still worse, these programs themselves deprived little children of their innocence, leading them into explicit and uncomfortable discussions of sexual topics. In Boston, archdiocesan officials chose a program called "Talking about Touching." In this curriculum, first-grade students practice giving the proper names to male and female genitalia. The second grade brings classroom discussion of various types of abuse; children are asked how they would respond if a relative suggested a "touching game." When they heard about the curriculum, some outraged parents charged that the program *itself* was a form of sexual abuse.

In Norwood, Massachusetts, a group of young parents formed in opposition to the Talking about Touching curriculum. They argued that the program violated their rights and the rights of their children, citing authoritative Vatican documents to back up their arguments. First, the parents argued, the curriculum was a form of sex education. In his 1981 apostolic exhortation *Familiaris Consortio*, Pope John Paul II had written: "Sex education, which is a basic right and duty of parents, must always be carried out under their attentive guidance. . . ." In this case the parents had no control over the instruction.

Next the parents noted that Talking about Touching discussed sexuality without giving children any clear moral framework for that discussion. "The Church is firmly opposed to an often widespread form of imparting sex information disassociated from moral principles," noted a 1995 document from the Pontifical Council for the Family. And that same document said that even parents should educate children about sexuality "without going into details and particulars that might upset or frighten them." The Talking about Touching program, with its repeated warnings to children about the potential danger posed by relatives and neighbors, violated that principle as well.

But when the Norwood parents brought these concerns to the attention of the Boston archdiocese, they ran into a stone wall. Deacon Anthony Rizzuto, the official responsible for implementing this "personal safety" curriculum, admitted that he had not read the Vatican documents that the parents cited. (Rizzuto actually had no background at all in education or family affairs. A retired Air Force officer, he had supervised the archdiocesan cemeteries before being appointed head of the newly created Office of Child Advocacy, Implementation, and Oversight.) Deacon Rizzuto asked the parents why they would not trust the archdiocese to educate their children properly.

Recent history had given parents ample reason to mistrust the archdiocese. But as they investigated the origins of the Talking about Touching curriculum, the Norwood parents found entirely new reasons for suspicion. The program had been developed in Seattle, by the Committee for Children. That group was an offshoot of an organization originally known as COYOTE (an acronym for "Call Off Your Old Tired Ethics"), which was founded by a self-described Wiccan priestess to work for the repeal of laws banning prostitution. To be sure, the organization had changed radically since its inception in the early 1970s. But the bizarre history of the Committee for Children certainly gave Catholic parents no reason to assume that the Talking about Touching program would reflect Christian moral principles.

A few Boston pastors joined the Norwood parents in opposition to Talking about Touching. Arguing that the program violated the innocence of children and the rights of parents, Father David Mullen informed the newly installed Archbishop O'Malley that he could not in conscience allow Talking about Touching in his parish. Rejecting the criticism, archdiocesan officials plowed ahead with their plans, announcing that Talking about Touching was to be a required part of the curriculum for every Catholic school and religious-education program. Father Mullen continued to lead public protests for a few weeks, until a rumor circulated that he had received orders from the chancery to be silent on the issue. When I called to check that rumor, Father Mullen replied simply: "I can't talk to you."

Talking about Touching has now been implemented in hundreds of American parishes. If they do not use that particular curriculum, bishops must choose from a short list of similar "safe environment" programs approved by the USCCB, and require their use in every Catholic school. A bishop who fails to carry out this mandate will be identified as "not in compliance" with the Dallas Charter. Bishop Robert Vasa of Baker, Oregon, opted to accept that designation, explaining in October 2005 that he had a number of serious questions about the approved curricula:

> Are such programs effective? Do such programs impose an unduly burdensome responsibility on very young children to protect themselves rather than insisting that parents take such training and take on the primary responsibility for protecting their children? Where do these programs come from? Is it true that Planned Parenthood has a hand or at least huge influence on many of them? Is it true that other groups, actively promoting early sexual activity for children, promote these programs in association with their own perverse agendas? Do such programs involve, even tangentially, the sexualization of children, which is precisely a part of the societal evil we are striving to combat? Does such a program invade the Church-guaranteed right of parents over the education of their children in sexual matters? Do I have the right to mandate such programs and demand that parents sign a document proving that they choose to exercise their right not to have their child involved? Do such programs introduce children to sex-related issues at age-inappropriate times? Would such programs generate a fruitful spiritual harvest? Would unsatisfactory answers to any of the questions above give sufficient reason to resist such programs?

In May 2007, Bishop Vasa revealed that he had not yet received answers to all of those questions. On some points he had found a clear answer, and that answer redoubled his suspicions about the USCCB-approved curricula. In October 2006, the Catholic Medical Association released a fifty-five-page report on the "safe environment" programs, finding them all defective. The group said that the curricula were ineffective, inconsistent with the best contemporary work on the emotional and moral development of children, and in conflict with Church teaching on education in sexuality. Bishop Vasa—still carrying the dreaded "not in compliance" label—announced that he planned to develop a new curriculum, guided by the moral principles that the existing programs ignore.

Back in Boston, Archbishop O'Malley evinced no interest in preparing a new curriculum or replacing Talking about Touching. The new archdiocesan leader—who assumed the title of Cardinal in March 2006, less than three years after his installation in Boston—was far too busy coping with lawsuits. When he first arrived, O'Malley's top priority was to reach an out-of-court settlement with the victims of sexual abuse, bringing an end to the litigation that had virtually paralyzed the archdiocese. The negotiations were contentious, but within a few months a deal had been struck, with the archdiocese pledging payment of $85 million. Some of the payments would be covered by insurance policies that the archdiocese carried. But even the insurance companies were ready to haggle, arguing that they should not be forced to pay for damages incurred through the culpable negligence of archdiocesan officials. So there was another round of tough negotiation and legal maneuvering before the issue could be resolved. Then the new challenge for the archdiocese was to find a way to pay the bills.

An ambitious drive to raise a capital endowment for the Boston archdiocese, begun under Cardinal Law, had staggered and collapsed under the pressure of the sex-abuse scandal. Wealthy Catholics were reluctant to make major gifts, fearing that their donations could be soaked up immediately in lawsuit settlements. The annual archdiocesan fundraising campaign had lagged for the same reason. Spokesmen for the archdiocese did their best to reassure donors, saying that the funds for sex-abuse settlements would not be taken out of the regular operating budget of the archdiocese. But few laymen found that claim convincing. Money is fungible, after all; the damages paid to victims might not have been drawn from separate bank accounts, but ultimately the money came from the faithful Catholics of Boston. The funds that were paid to abuse victims would not be available to pay for the heating bills for needy parishes.

Parish heating bills had become a source of real concern for the archdiocese, as a matter of fact. Many parishes had been unable to meet their own costs even before the scandal erupted. Now, with the archdiocese facing huge legal expenses, these struggling parishes could not expect a regular subsidy from the central administration. Church leaders concluded that some serious belt-tightening was necessary.

Archbishop O'Malley arrived in his new see in July 2003 and immediately began studying plans for "reconfiguration." In December 2003, the archbishop announced that serious changes were needed to respond to several factors: the changing demographics of the region, which saw Catholics moving out of the cities and into the suburbs; a decline in the number of available priests; and cash-starved parishes, mostly in urban areas, some of them nearly side by side. The only practical option, the archbishop said, was to close parishes and sell the properties. Since 1998, a series of parish mergers and quiet transfers had subtracted forty-two parishes, but the new archbishop saw the need for more. He said that some closings would be announced as early as July 1, 2004—just six months later. After the press conference, analysts speculated that the final reconfiguration plan would call for fifty to sixty Boston parishes to be closed down and sold off.

That figure would prove to be an underestimate. After several months of uncertainty, with priests and lay people pleading for the lives of their parishes, in May 2004 the archdiocese unveiled a list of seventy parishes chosen for pruning, with some of them expected to close their doors within weeks. The announcements provoked wails of protests from hundreds of Catholics who wondered why *their* parishes were slated for destruction.

Countless arguments can be made, and were made, about the practical considerations involved in closing one parish rather than another. (In a few cases, parishioners sued in secular or canonical courts, arguing that the archdiocese had overstepped its legal authority. No such suit was successful in stopping a parish from closing.) Angry parishioners staged sit-ins and prayer vigils in some parishes, vowing that they would not allow the doors to be closed. Tense stand-offs occurred, with lay people defying their pastors. In a few cases police were called in to maintain order, and in one particularly unfortunate incident at Sacred Heart parish in Natick, a Catholic layman was arrested for refusing to leave the church on Christmas Eve.

These disputes between the laity and the hierarchy gave the media regular opportunities to characterize Church leaders as arrogant and insensitive. For many years officials of the Boston archdiocese had been nearly exempt from criticism; now their every move was scrutinized. Reporters kept finding new reasons to mistrust the archdiocesan leadership. First the *Globe* revealed that archdiocesan managers had diverted $4.5 million from the funds collected for the priests' retirement fund, using those monies for other purposes and leaving the retirement fund critically low. Then another exposé showed that the archdiocesan cemeteries were failing to honor commitments for perpetual care of burial plots. Through it all the archdiocese persisted in ham-handed attempts to squelch the stories, thus compounding the impact of each public-relations debacle. Perhaps the most vivid example of this maladroit approach to crisis management—and certainly the most comical—came when archdiocesan officials learned that parents were likely to demonstrate against the closing of a parish grammar school, so the administrators ended the academic year a few days early, thinking that they would thereby avoid the negative publicity attendant on an organized public protest. The result was an impromptu "graduation" ceremony staged by parents at a traffic circle near the school, with lavish media coverage. Eager reporters coaxed tearful children to worry about the health of a goldfish left unattended in their classroom. This incident occurred, again, because archdiocesan officials thought they had found a way to *avoid* negative publicity.

As I write now, three years after the reconfiguration plans were first announced, the fights continue over parish closings. Bowing to the public outcry, Cardinal O'Malley instituted an appeal process, and some of the parishes scheduled for closing have won a reprieve. Others are still fighting for survival. Driving around Boston, one can see makeshift billboards on the front of church buildings, boasting of how long the parishes have remained open since they first received the directive to close. During the summer of 2007, protesting parishioners at several of these parishes called public attention to the fact that their vigils had lasted for 1,000 days or more. At a few churches the protestors had set up cots and even installed amenities such as televisions and refrigerators to ease the monotony of their round-the-clock vigils. At the parish of Our Lady of Mt. Carmel in East Boston, they had taken the precaution of changing the locks to discourage any sudden moves by archdiocesan officials.

Several especially rebellious parishes have broken off all communication with the Boston archdiocese, organizing their own lay-run prayer services. At a few of these hotbeds of resistance, like St. Albert the Great parish in Weymouth, the activists hold unauthorized "communion services." If the hosts that they distribute have been consecrated by sympathetic priests, those priests are acting in open defiance of their superiors. If the hosts are *not* validly consecrated, then the participants in these services are making a mockery of the Eucharist and risking the penalty of excommunication. Either way, these services illustrate how close a few Catholics have come to breaking entirely with the Church and setting up their own independent religious denominations.

"Closing parishes is the hardest thing I have ever had to do in forty years of religious life," then-Archbishop O'Malley wrote in a memorable column for the *Pilot*. He went on:

I never imagined I would have to be involved in anything so painful or so personally repulsive to me as this. At times I ask God to call me home and let someone else finish this job, but I keep waking up in the morning to face another day of reconfiguration.

No doubt the archbishop's anguish was genuine. But in an important sense the painful process that he began was the logical result of policies that the Boston archdiocese had followed for several decades. When they argued that the parish closings were unrelated to the sex-abuse scandal, archdiocesan spokesmen were at least partially correct. The cost of settling lawsuits might have sharpened the crisis, making it impossible to delay a financial reckoning. But sooner or later the archdiocese would have been forced to slash spending and sell assets. As an institution the archdiocese had been living beyond its means for years, with no practical plans for balancing the budget. Indeed in July 2007, a leaked report from an archdiocesan pastoral-planning committee noted that under Cardinal O'Malley's leadership the archdiocese had now closed more than sixty parishes, leaving 295 open, but "even this number cannot be sustained for long."

The fundamental problem, however, was not economic; it was pastoral. Catholics had stopped going to church, stopped donating to their parishes, stopping feeling a commitment to the Catholic faith. The census figures showed that the Catholic population of Boston was still growing, but for all practical purposes the figures had been in a steep decline for at least a generation. Only one in six registered Catholics was attending Mass on a weekly basis at the end of 2003. (That number had dipped only modestly—from one in five—since the onset of the scandal.) Those who did go to Mass were, as a group, less generous than their Catholic ancestors. At parishes that had been built with the nickels and dimes contributed by hard-pressed manual laborers, located in communities that were now populated by affluent professionals, the weekly collection was barely enough to cover the fuel bill. And even if the financial problems could somehow be resolved, the archdiocese soon would not have enough priests to cover all its parishes. The ranks of the clergy were thinning; there were not nearly enough young men entering the seminary to replace the many elderly priests headed into retirement. The pastoral-planning committee, in its July 2007 report, predicted that within seven years the number of active priests in the Boston archdiocese would dip under three hundred, and of these, dozens would be unavailable for parish work because of ill health or conflicting duties. So unless more Boston churches closed, there would not be enough priests to provide a full-time pastor for every parish.

In his plaintive appeal for understanding, O'Malley likened the sale of parishes to the example set in the Acts of the Apostles: "Those who had properties sold them and gave the proceeds to the Apostles who distributed to each one according to his needs." But that comparison only underlined how different the situation in Boston was. The Acts of the Apostles recount the growth of the young Church; in Boston the Catholic community was contracting. In the Acts, the early Christians sold their goods for the welfare of the Church. In Boston the Church was selling property to individuals or to non-Catholic institutions.

After fighting for years to gain equal standing in Boston, Catholics had grown complacent during the twentieth century and ceased to think of the Church as a missionary enterprise. Rather than planning to make new converts and open new parishes, Church leaders were content to serve the existing Catholic population. For a while Catholicism had shaped the culture of Boston. Now the culture was shaping Catholicism. The engines of evangelization were running in reverse.

If money were the only major issue, Church leaders might have preferred to invest $85 million on a program to revive parish life and restore the missionary impulse, rather than spending that amount to pay the costs of moral corruption. But no one was proposing any such program of revival around the year 2003, and the archdiocese did not have that amount of money to spend. It is fitting that in order to fund that payment to abuse victims, the archdiocese sold a large piece of valuable property—in fashionable Chestnut Hill, around the grounds of the chancery, the seminary, and the palatial residence of the archbishop—to neighboring Boston College. That Jesuit-run university, having long ago made its peace with secular liberalism, had been enormously successful in wooing new major donors. Flush with cash, the school was looking for new ways to expand its influence. So in a suitably symbolic exchange, Boston College advanced where the Boston archdiocese receded. The increased prominence of the Jesuit school would testify to a new model of Catholicism: sleek, confident, and disdainful of tradition.

Once sold, an asset can rarely be recovered. Cardinal O'Malley moved into a modest apartment near Boston's cathedral; no future Archbishop of Boston will live in the mansion that Cardinal O'Connell had built. In May 2007 the archdiocese announced another sale of property to Boston

College, yielding another needed infusion of cash. The rector of St. John's Seminary, Father John Farren, OP, had argued vigorously against the sale, pointed out that the archdiocese was whittling away at the resources of the archdiocesan seminary, making the institution less effective and less attractive to potential students and teachers. (At the same time, the Dominican rector observed, the sale would provide valuable new resources for Boston College, an institution whose indifference to Catholic doctrine compounded the problems facing the archdiocese.) In an angry letter of resignation after the sale was announced, Father Farren predicted that within five years the seminary would close.

As for the parishes that have closed, and will close in future years, the sale of property—or "alienation," to use the canonical term—represents something more than a loss of memories for fond parishioners. It is sad that Catholic couples will be unable to visit the church where they were married or where their children were baptized, because the building has been torn down and replaced by condominiums. It is sadder still that by selling that outpost of the Catholic faith, the Church has ceded even the realistic *possibility* of having a parish in that neighborhood sometime in the future. The sacraments will no longer be available at that address; the Catholic faith will not be proclaimed there. The sale of parish properties is not just a reconfiguration of the archdiocese; it is a retreat.

A military commander might order a prudent retreat in order to gain some new strategic advantage. But the Boston archdiocese, in its retreat from dozens of parishes, has gained nothing more than temporary financial relief. The fundamental problems that caused the retreat—the decline in Mass attendance and financial contributions, the shortage of priestly vocations—have been exacerbated, not alleviated, by the parish closings. The archdiocesan budget is still imbalanced. Barring some unforeseen change in existing trends, Church leaders face the prospect of selling *more* parish properties to ease a cash shortage in a few years, and then selling more again a few years after that.

The Archdiocese of Boston is facing a real financial crisis; that much is clear. But by any economic measurement, the Church in Boston today has far more material resources than the Church of one century earlier. In the early twentieth century, Catholicism in Boston was poised for a dizzying period of growth; now we anticipate nothing but steady retrenchment.

The problem, again, is not economic but pastoral and spiritual. One hundred years ago, Church leaders took it for granted that their policies should be guided toward steady expansion of the faith: more Catholic parishes, more Catholic schools, more Catholic families and children, more Catholic converts, more Catholic priests and religious, more Catholic influence in secular society. Today those assumptions are gone, and Church leaders seem to be satisfied if they can cling to their dignity while conducting what is, in effect, a going-out-of-business sale.

16

THE BEACON HILL
MASSACRE

Political foes of the Church in Massachusetts could scarcely contain their glee as they watched Catholic leaders squirm through the revelations that continued through 2002 and 2003. The bishops were too busy with their own internal crisis to pay much attention to the public affairs of the Commonwealth. Moreover, the nature of the Church scandal made it particularly difficult for Catholic leaders to speak out on the most contentious public issues of the day, the questions of sexual morality.

Could someone who had been implicated in the sexual abuse of children survive as a public leader? That question had already been answered affirmatively in Massachusetts. In 1983 Congressman Gerry Studds, a Massachusetts Democrat, was censured by the US House of Representatives for his sexual involvement with a teenage boy. Although badly embarrassed by the episode, Studds won re-election even after his censure, and continued serving in Congress until he freely chose to retire in 1995.

The political survival of Gerry Studds demonstrated the power of the Democratic party in Massachusetts. In sending him back to Congress, the voters were not endorsing his sexual escapade but concluding that they could tolerate a flawed moral character for the sake of effective representation in Washington. Fortunately for Studds, the issues most important to the voters of his southeastern Massachusetts district, such as the health of maritime industry, were completely unrelated to the question of sexual abuse.

The situation was quite different for the Catholic hierarchy twenty years later. Homosexual activists in Massachusetts were pushing for legal recognition of same-sex unions. If Catholic bishops dared to say that these unions were unnatural, they could expect sneering replies that the Church had been protecting quite a few unnatural unions. If Catholic activists argued that young children should be raised by a mother and father, their adversaries would immediately reply that Church leaders had not shown much interest in the welfare of children when priests were molesting them. The sex-abuse crisis had compromised the moral leadership of the Catholic Church, with the most pronounced effects in precisely those areas where society needed the witness of traditional Christian teaching to balance the growing power of secular liberalism.

The bishops' plight differed from that of Congressman Studds in another critical respect as well. Democrats supported the incumbent lawmaker on the basis of party discipline; they reasoned that the re-election of a loyal Democrat would maintain the strength of their party and advance its ideology. In Massachusetts, for the past forty years Catholics had been discouraged from thinking that the faith had any distinctive position on public issues. There were Catholics on both sides of every conceivable political debate. With the hierarchy now retreating into silence, there was no simple way to determine which side represented the authentically Catholic public stand—if such a stand existed.

In May 2003 the state legislature held hearings on a bill that would have defined marriage as a bond between a man and a woman. Introduced by pro-family activists, the legislation was a pre-emptive move to halt the drive toward legal recognition of same-sex marriage. A parade of witnesses came to testify at the legislative hearings: representatives of pro-family organizations and gay-rights lobbies, ministers from Evangelical Christian parishes and liberal Unitarian churches. No witness appeared on behalf of the Boston archdiocese or the Catholic dioceses of Worcester, Fall River, and Springfield. There were, however, four Catholic priests on the list of witnesses. All four of those priests testified against the legislative proposal, arguing in effect that same-sex couples should be allowed the legal privileges of marriage.

The proposal to safeguard male-female marriage died quickly in that legislative session. Presumably no lawmakers were swayed by the arguments of four priests whose views were unmistakably at odds with Church teaching. But the appearance of those four men on Beacon Hill, wearing their Roman collars, offered protective cover for any legislators who wanted to mollify unhappy Catholic constituents. The lawmaker could explain that while *some* Catholics supported the bill, others, like these respected clerics, had recognized the problems that caused him to oppose the measure.

One of the four priests who testified against the pro-family initiative has been such a prominent dissenter from Church teaching for such a long time that his case merits special attention. Father Walter Cuenin has appeared previously in this narrative. He once abandoned the priesthood, but on his return he was assigned to teach at the archdiocesan seminary. He championed radical theological causes, yet won sympathetic treatment from Cardinal Law, who appointed him to head a flourishing suburban parish. He was a leader among the priests calling for Cardinal Law's resignation in 2002. His parish in Newton became the rallying point for the cardinal's critics. Law made an impotent show of his frustration with Cuenin by announcing that the archdiocese would no longer host events at his parish. But he did not remove Cuenin from his position as pastor.

In September 2002 the *Boston Pilot*, Cardinal Law's own newspaper, ran an editorial criticizing Voice of the Faithful, arguing that the group encouraged dissent from Church teachings. As evidence for that argument, the *Pilot* editorial cited the views of Father Cuenin, "an early and enthusiastic promoter of the group." The editorial, entitled "You Are Known by the Company You Keep," cited Cuenin's public questioning of Church teachings on birth control, divorce, remarriage, the ordination of women, celibacy, and homosexuality. Voice of the Faithful had generally avoided clear statements on those issues, but Father Cuenin had not. So the official newspaper of the Boston archdiocese advanced the bizarre argument that a Catholic group was tainted by association with a priest who remained a pastor in good standing for the same archdiocese! If Father Cuenin's influence was so malign that it discredited a lay initiative, why was he still considered qualified to act as a pastor of souls?

The arrival of Archbishop O'Malley did little to change Cuenin's behavior. In December 2003, with Massachusetts caught up in a heated debate about same-sex marriage, Father Cuenin told his parishioners: "We should never think that there is a single Biblical model of family life." In his parish bulletin Cuenin argued that the traditional model—Jesus, Mary, and Joseph in their home in Nazareth—is no longer realistic. Society, he said, should welcome homosexual couples, as well as divorced and remarried couples. What made Father Cuenin's argument especially noteworthy is the fact that it appeared just before Archbishop O'Malley was scheduled to visit the parish—as if the pastor felt an unshakable confidence that the new archbishop either would not or could not discipline him.

Finally, after two more years, O'Malley did remove Cuenin from this pastoral assignment. But even then the story had a strange twist. In September 2005 an audit by archdiocesan officials uncovered financial irregularities in the Newton parish, and Father Cuenin was asked to resign. Yet as the leading dissident in Boston left his post as pastor, archdiocesan officials took great pains to say that Cuenin was *not* being disciplined for his heterodox views. He was removed because he accepted special stipends from parishioners, in a violation of archdiocesan policy. But was that fiscal policy more important than the Church teachings on sexuality and marriage, which Father Cuenin had questioned for years?

Nine months after leaving the Newton parish, Father Cuenin was preaching at an ecumenical "gay pride" ceremony in Boston. Now assigned as chaplain at Brandeis University, he remains to this day a priest in good standing in the Boston archdiocese. Proponents of same-sex marriage can still answer campaign opponents by saying that their position obviously must not put them outside the scope of what is acceptable for a Catholic, since a prominent Boston priest agrees with them.

Politicians who followed the long public career of Walter Cuenin drew another lesson from his story. They realized that Catholics—even Catholic priests—could flout the teachings of the Church without paying any political price. The hierarchy obviously would not take action against a lay politician if it would not discipline a priest who holds the same views. Catholic politicians could ignore or even openly reject the teachings of their Church. They would still be invited to speak at Catholic schools, accorded honors by Catholic institutions, and asked to sit on the boards of Catholic charities.

When the sex-abuse scandal reached its zenith, politicians had yet another insight: that public criticism of Catholic leaders was a sure way to generate favorable media coverage. The attorney general of Massachusetts, Tom Reilly, announced in 2002 that he was considering criminal charges against Church officials who covered up evidence of sexual abuse. After a lengthy investigation Reilly released a report that severely chastised the leadership of the Boston archdiocese. The attorney general uncovered very little new information and found no cause for criminal prosecution. But his strongly worded denunciation of Church leaders put him in the headlines, confirming the political benefits of confronting the Church.

At the State House on Boston's Beacon Hill, legislators found other opportunities to capitalize on the surge of public indignation against the Church. In the state legislature, too, the rout was complete. Lawmakers hastily approved a bill requiring clergymen to report all credible accusations of child abuse. After initially opposing the bill, the Catholic bishops recognized that argument was futile and withdrew their objection. Brushing aside complaints by Catholic lobbyists, the legislators gave their overwhelming approval to a bill requiring contraceptive coverage in health-insurance policies. A proposed amendment exempting religious institutions was roundly defeated. The contraception bill passed through the state senate without a single negative vote. (Adding insult to injury, the *New Bedford Standard Times* published a follow-up analysis arguing that the Catholic Church had exerted too much control over the legislation.) Next, the legislature passed a bill requiring hospitals to furnish the abortifacient "morning-after" pill on request to women who reported having been raped. Again the legislation was enacted quickly, without any opposition in the state senate.

Lobbyists for the Catholic Church could still exert some influence on legislators when the subject was capital punishment or welfare reform. On those questions—not coincidentally, issues on which the archdiocese took a stand alongside the liberal Democratic majority—lawmakers enjoyed claiming the backing of the Catholic hierarchy. But on issues closer to the core teachings of the Christian faith, issues on which the Catholic Church was the most prominent public voice for traditional morality, the archdiocese was now effectively powerless.

The most humiliating display of Catholic political impotence came in 2005 when a new legislative proposal arrived on Beacon Hill requiring all religious organizations to disclose their financial affairs to Massachusetts public officials. The proposal was intended to pry open the accounting books of the Boston archdiocese, giving critics a more effective way to protest parish closings. For weeks Catholic lobbyists argued that the bill was an infringement on religious freedom. Those arguments fell on deaf ears. Then in November, as the legislative year moved toward a close, a coalition of Protestant church representatives met with Democratic leaders and persuaded them to drop the proposal. The Protestant lobbyists advanced the same arguments that their Catholic counterparts had used, saying that financial scrutiny was a form of government intrusion into the affairs of religious bodies. But politicians in Massachusetts—where the Catholic Church had been the dominant cultural force for so many years, where the majority of legislators were self-identified Catholics—were no longer listening to representatives of the Catholic Church.

Of all the issues on the political agenda in Massachusetts, the most important by far from the perspective of Catholic teaching was the preservation of marriage. Recognizing the advantage that they enjoyed because of the decline in Catholic influence, gay-rights activists were pushing for legal acceptance of homosexual unions. In the early months of 2003 the top priority for the gay-rights movement was a legislative proposal to recognize "civil unions" giving unmarried couples (heterosexual or homosexual) most of the same legal rights and privileges that married couples enjoyed. By the end of the year that goal seemed overly modest, since a state court decision had overthrown centuries of tradition, ruling that same-sex couples could contract legal marriages.

For Catholics—or at least for those Catholics who listened to the teachings of the Church—the stakes of this political battle were raised in July 2003, when the Vatican released a document reiterating the Church's firm opposition to legal recognition of same-sex unions and reminding Catholic politicians of their solemn obligation to oppose any such measures.

The ten-point document, entitled *Considerations Regarding Proposals to Give Legal Recognition to Unions Between Homosexual Persons*, was released by the Congregation for the Doctrine of the Faith. The document had been signed by Cardinal Joseph Ratzinger, the prefect of that Congregation, and approved by Pope John Paul II. In a short but forceful presentation, the Vatican document rebutted popular arguments in favor of same-sex marriage and other forms of legal recognition for homosexual partnerships. The document warned politicians that voting in favor of legislation that recognized homosexual unions would be "gravely immoral."

The document did not present any new theological arguments regarding homosexuality, but advanced clear logical arguments against the legal acceptance of same-sex unions. The Vatican noted that these arguments were "drawn from reason" rather than revealed truth, and should therefore be accessible to all public figures, whether or not they were Catholic or Christian. The Vatican statement was clearly aimed at politicians and other public figures, providing them with "rational argumentation" against various initiatives toward same-sex "marriage," and urging them to make their own "clear and emphatic" arguments against such proposals. The Congregation for the Doctrine of the Faith also pointed out that bishops in individual countries could advance the cause of Catholic teaching by making "more specific interventions" on the issue.

The introduction to *Considerations* described homosexuality as a "troubling moral and social phenomenon," especially in those countries where activists have launched drives for "legal recognition to homosexual unions, which may include the possibility of adopting children." While reiterating the teaching of the *Catechism of the Catholic Church* that people with homosexual inclinations should be treated with respect, the document also noted the unswerving Church teaching that the homosexual inclination is "objectively disordered," and that homosexual acts are grave sins against chastity. The Catholic understanding of marriage, the CDF observed, is not merely the policy of the Church; it is "evident to right reason and recognized as such by all the major cultures of the world." The document flatly stated: "No ideology can erase from the human spirit the certainty that marriage exists solely between a man and a woman."

When that document first appeared it seemed likely that Catholic leaders could successfully hold the line against legal recognition of same-sex unions in Massachusetts. For more than a decade, gay-rights activists had brought legislative proposals to the Massachusetts legislature every year, seeking various forms of legal recognition for same-sex unions. From 1991 through 2002, those proposals had been unsuccessful. Although the homosexual lobby was steadily attracting more support for its legislative efforts, pro-family activists still confidently expected to beat back any proposal for civil unions (let alone same-sex "marriage") in the 2003 legislative session.

Then quite suddenly the opposition to same-sex unions crumbled. The political tides turned on October 23, when Bishop Daniel Reilly of Worcester, representing all the bishops of Massachusetts, testified before a legislative committee. Bishop Reilly told the public hearing that the Catholic bishops of Massachusetts would continue to oppose any move to grant legal recognition for same-sex "marriage." But he added: "If the goal is to look at individual benefits and determine who should be eligible beyond spouses, then we will join the discussion."

Although he stopped short of an explicit endorsement for proposals that would grant legal and financial benefits to "domestic partners," the bishop lent strong support to the arguments advanced by homosexual activists, by conceding that these benefits should be seen as matters of "distributive justice."

In 1991, when Massachusetts legislators first discussed providing "domestic partnership" benefits to homosexual couples, Monsignor William Murphy—then the vicar general of the Boston archdiocese, later to become the Bishop of Rockville Center, New York—referred to the proposal as "the farthest shore of madness." Now Bishop Reilly, speaking for all the bishops of Massachusetts, had endorsed a similar proposal, identifying it as a matter of "distributive justice."

"Whatever rights a citizen has in the United States should not be denied to another citizen," the bishop told reporters after his formal testimony. Asked specifically about the benefits sought by homosexual couples, Bishop Reilly replied: "There should be a way for the state to provide the benefits they have a right to, like other citizens." One reporter pressed still further, asking the bishop about state policies that denied benefits to homosexual couples. "That's wrong, and that's too bad," he said. "We have to find a way to give civil benefits to gay partners."

The political impact of Bishop Reilly's testimony—and his subsequent off-the-cuff statements to the press—was enormous. Mass-media outlets in Boston announced that the Catholic bishops had withdrawn their opposition to legislation that would recognize "domestic partnerships" and "civil unions." Homosexual activists welcomed that development, voicing their delight with the new position of the Catholic hierarchy. Prominent political leaders who had been avoiding any clear statement on the issue announced that they, too, would support the more "moderate" proposals for recognition of same-sex unions.

More ominously, the legislators who had previously been at the forefront of the opposition to the proposals of the homosexual lobby grew quiet. No politician wanted to be seen as "more conservative than the Catholic bishops." John Rodgers, a state representative who had been honored by conservative groups for his steadfast commitment to the pro-family cause, announced that he was preparing a legislative proposal for the recognition of "civil unions."

On October 30—a full week after Bishop Reilly's fateful testimony—the Massachusetts Catholic Conference (which represents all the bishops of the state) issued a public statement denying that the bishops had changed their position regarding same-sex unions. Skipping lightly past the bishop's actual words, the Conference insisted that Bishop Reilly's testimony had been misinterpreted and that he had intended only to indicate his support for the provision of medical benefits to the adopted children of same-sex couples.

But that strained disclaimer came too late to alter the new political realities that had emerged in the aftermath of the bishop's testimony. In the week after Bishop Reilly's appearance on Beacon Hill, one legislator after another shifted his stance on same-sex unions. By the end of October, the opposition to same-sex unions had virtually disappeared, and astute political analysts predicted that the legislature would approve a "civil-union" bill—even before the state's highest court weighed in.

When the Supreme Judicial Court of Massachusetts finally issued its ruling in the case of *Goodridge v. Dept. of Public Health* on November 18, that decision was long overdue in more ways than one. The top court in Massachusetts had delayed for months, postponing the publication of a ruling that had been heavily anticipated since the spring. Court-watchers suspected that the justices were wrestling with the case, wondering how far they should go to accommodate the homosexuals' demands. Perhaps they were emboldened by the political shift that became evident after Bishop Reilly delivered his testimony. Gay-rights activists had always felt their case in Massachusetts, arguably the most liberal state in the US, presented their best chance for outright judicial approval of their bid for legal recognition of same-sex marriage.

Those activists were not disappointed. In a 4-3 decision, the Supreme Judicial Court ruled that Massachusetts engaged in unconstitutional discrimination by refusing marriage licenses to same-sex couples. The Court gave the Massachusetts legislation 180 days in which to correct that alleged discrimination.

"Marriage is a vital social institution. The exclusive commitment of two individuals to each other nurtures love and mutual support. It brings stability to our society," Chief Justice Margaret Marshall wrote in the ruling. "For those who choose to marry, and for their children, marriage provides an abundance of legal, financial and social benefits." The four-member majority of the Supreme Judicial Court simply swept aside all arguments—historical, sociological, religious, or legislative—that defined "marriage" as a union between one man and one woman. In effect they ruled that the legal meaning of the word "marriage" must be changed to accommodate homosexual couples.

This brash assertion of judicial power outraged pro-family activists all across America. But although conservatives in Massachusetts hoped somehow to block the legal recognition of same-sex unions, the Court's ruling left them with very few options.

- The decision could not be appealed, since the Supreme Judicial Court was the highest authority on the interpretation of the state's constitution—on which the ruling is allegedly based.

- The Massachusetts constitution could be amended to include an explicit definition of marriage as a union of man and woman. In fact a proposed amendment was already on the legislative agenda when the Court's ruling was announced. But the process of changing the constitution is a lengthy one; an amendment could not take effect until November 2006 at the earliest. By then, under the terms of the *Goodridge* decision, many homosexual couples would already be legally married. At that point, defenders of traditional marriage would be forced to argue in favor of rescinding legal recognition of these unions: an unattractive argument to make in a notoriously liberal state.
- The state legislature could simply ignore the Court's mandate. But after the 180-day period provided by the *Goodridge* ruling, some adventurous town clerks would no doubt begin issuing marriage licenses to homosexual couples, bringing about the same practical result as a statutory change.

There was another, more radical alternative. The Massachusetts legislature could impeach the justices who formed the majority in the *Goodridge* case, arguing (quite accurately) that the judges had engaged in a blatant abuse of their power and usurpation of the legislature's proper function. But not a single member of the legislature raised that possibility in the days immediately following the court's decision. The political leaders of Massachusetts had no desire for a pitched battle on the issue. So Massachusetts become the only state in the Union to recognize homosexual "marriage."

The Massachusetts constitution allows for amendments by citizen initiative. Even before the *Goodridge* decision, pro-family activists had anticipated the need for an amendment that would explicitly define marriage as a union between one man and one woman—an amendment that would have made the *Goodridge* decision impossible. A petition was circulated in 2002 and was signed by over 70,000 qualified voters. Under the provisions of the Massachusetts constitution, the next step for that measure was to be brought before the state legislature, meeting in constitutional convention. If the proposed amendment received support from at least fifty legislators in two consecutive sessions, it would go on the ballot at the next statewide election, and a simple majority of the voters could ratify the amendment.

The state constitution is clear; the state legislature is *required* to take a vote on a qualified petition to amend the constitution. But in July 2002, the Democratic leaders of the Massachusetts legislature defied the constitution; they recessed a constitutional convention without voting on the marriage amendment, and declined to schedule another convention before the legislative session ended. Supporters of the initiative brought their protest to court, and the Supreme Judicial Court—the same body that produced *Goodridge*—ruled unanimously that the legislators had shirked their legal responsibility. But the court had no power to compel legislative action, and the marriage amendment died.

The voters of Massachusetts had an obvious remedy for their legislators' blatant violation of the constitution; they could have voted the offending lawmakers out of office in the next statewide elections in November 2004. But they did not. The Democratic juggernaut rolled to another sweeping victory; most incumbents were returned to office. Although the campaign season did produce a groundswell of pro-family activism, the most noteworthy story of the 2004 election was the complacency with which Massachusetts voters accepted the imposition of same-sex marriage by a court decision. An activist minority protested bitterly, but the majority passively accepted this revolutionary social change—and accepted, too, the legislature's refusal to let voters decide the issue for themselves.

Determined pro-family activists regrouped after the election and decided to launch another petition drive to amend the constitution. This time the signature-gathering process broke all records; 66,000 signatures were needed to put the measure before the legislature, and by November 2005 there were over 120,000 signatures on the petitions.

After a heated debate, the legislature did bring the measure up for a vote this time, on the very last day before the legislature adjourned. (Homosexual activists, with support from incoming Governor Deval Patrick, had urged the legislators not to vote on the measure, in spite of a fresh ruling from the Supreme Judicial Court reminding the lawmakers that the constitution obliged them to do so.) The proposed amendment won just enough votes to advance to a second test in the following session of the legislature.

One aspect of that signature-gathering drive is noteworthy here. Although the political establishment in Massachusetts is thoroughly dominated by Irish and Italian Catholics, the process of collecting signatures was driven by Evangelical Protestants. The Catholic bishops gave their full support to the effort, but individual Catholic pastors were much less supportive. Some priests discouraged or even forbade the collection of signatures outside their parish churches, and relatively few priests signed the documents themselves. At the local level most Catholic pastors ignored the petition drive. The *Springfield Republican* studied the completed petitions and found that only 20 percent of the priests in the Springfield diocese—31 out of 154—had signed the petition to restore traditional marriage.

With the signatures duly certified, the new marriage amendment now faced the legislature. Once again there were signs that the Democratic leadership would seek to avoid a vote. Some representatives did not want to be forced to put their support for same-sex marriage on the record; they preferred to duck the issue entirely. Others feared that the pro-family movement had enough support to meet the 25 percent standard and wanted to kill the proposal by procedural means.

As the legislature stalled, pro-family activists made their move. Joined by Governor Romney they filed suit, asking the court to force a legislative vote. The Supreme Judicial Court refused to take action, but did issue a strong advisory opinion saying that the legislators would be violating their duties if they failed to vote on the petition.

Despite that judicial mandate, legislators continued to dawdle through the end of the 2006 calendar year. A constitutional convention was finally scheduled for January 2: the last day before the final adjournment of that legislature. Homosexual activists openly encouraged the legislators to adjourn without voting, and Governor-elect Deval Patrick joined in that plea. Nevertheless a vote was taken and the initiative petition won sixty-two votes—twelve more than the fifty needed to meet the 25 percent requirement. The marriage petition had survived to face another second legislative test.

Immediately after that tense session, a new legislature was sworn into office. Governor Patrick assumed office as well, and at an interfaith prayer service on his inauguration day, Cardinal Sean Patrick O'Malley of Boston led the prayers for the new governor—who, just hours earlier, had been advising lawmakers to violate their oaths of office in order to protect homosexual marriage.

The legislative session of 2007 brought new tactical considerations to the state house. Pro-family activists resumed their efforts to force a vote on the proposed amendment, worrying that legislators would continue their pattern of stalling. But the emboldened Democratic leadership had a different plan in mind this year. With a stronger majority than ever and a sympathetic governor to back their plans, they began plotting a strategy to defeat the amendment in an open vote.

As late as mid-May, pro-family lobbyists were still confidently assuring their allies that they had more than fifty solid votes in favor of the initiative petition. But gay-rights activists were claiming new gains. The conservative lawmakers who had backed the marriage amendment in the 2006 session were facing new pressures and new promises. Governor Patrick was dropping unsubtle hints that legislators who voted against the amendment might be in line for desirable executive positions in his administration. Democratic Party leaders from Washington were calling recalcitrant lawmakers, urging them to vote with the liberal majority. The Republican leadership on Beacon Hill was neutral, and former Governor Romney—now a full-time candidate for the US presidency—took no part in the lobbying effort. But another former Republican governor, Bill Weld, was working the phones in support of same-sex marriage.

In the last few days before the June 14 vote, the lobbying became frenetic, and some legislators were apparently demanding exorbitant rewards for their votes. Arline Isaacson, the leading representative for gay-rights activists on Beacon Hill, complained to the *Boston Globe:* "It's very frustrating because legislators keep upping the ante on what they want to get for their votes."

Cardinal O'Malley was reportedly making phone calls, too, at the eleventh hour, urging the legislators to hold firm in their support for the marriage amendment. But he might have spent his time more productively by talking to his pastors some months earlier, ensuring that Catholic voters were rallied on the grassroots level.

By June 2007, veteran legislators knew that they did not need to fear the clout of the Catholic Church, and a phone call from the Archbishop of Boston failed to convey the powerful impact it once held. Writing after the fact, the editor of the Fall River diocesan newspaper, Father Roger Landry, made the observation that the votes cast by Catholic legislators at the constitutional convention provided "a clear indication that they did not think that their Catholic constituents would care about their vote as much as the gay lobby would in the next election."

So the vote was taken at that constitutional convention on June 14, and supporters of the marriage amendment found, to their consternation, that the attrition of support had been much worse than they realized. The amendment was killed. Even assuming that a third effort to amend the state constitution could overcome the hurdles that have thwarted the first two efforts—a very large assumption, since the political trends are clearly adverse—a new petition initiative could not become part of the state constitution until 2011 at the earliest. In Massachusetts, same-sex marriage is here to stay. In a strongly worded statement released after the vote, the Catholic bishops of Massachusetts said: "Today, the common good has been sacrificed by the extreme individualism that subordinates what is best for children, families, and society."

In their sharp criticism of the legislature, the bishops asked a rhetorical question: "Do we live in a country where people are free to vote their conscience or are we controlled by what is viewed as politically correct and by powerful special interest groups?" Following the same game-plan that had governed their efforts throughout the controversy, they complained that the June 14 vote on Beacon Hill had the effect of "blocking the people from exercising their right to vote" on the definition of marriage.

While it is certainly true that a democratic society should give voters the opportunity to express their opinion on an issue as important as the definition of marriage, the bishops' argument failed to grasp the essential facts of the case. The people of Massachusetts *were* given a chance to vote in 2004 and again in 2006, when they elected the representatives who would kill the marriage amendment. And when they voted against the initiative petition those lawmakers were not violating the constitutional process; they were acting as a check on the popular trend, and the amendment process clearly anticipated that they should.

And where had the visible leadership of the Catholic Church stood during the long campaign to stop same-sex marriage? The bishops of Massachusetts issued several statements in 2005 and 2006 endorsing the petition drive and urging the legislature to vote on the measure. Diocesan newspapers chimed in with a few supportive editorials. But it was difficult to detect any sense of urgency in these statements. Except when they were pressed for a statement on the issue, Church leaders rarely raised the question in their public talks and never denounced the legislators who had stalled the amendment process by shirking their constitutional duties. The impetus for the amendment drive came as much from small Evangelical Protestant groups as from the powerful Catholic Church.

In November 2005, as the signature-gathering campaign reached its successful conclusion, there was a good reason for the Boston archdiocese to keep a low profile. Yet again the archdiocese had been caught up in a scandal—not just *any* scandal, but one that deprived the Church of the ability to speak out persuasively on a key moral issue.

In their arguments for the proposed constitutional amendment, pro-family advocates were emphasizing the needs of young children. Every child, they argued, should be nurtured by a mother and a father; same-sex couples cannot supply that necessary care. Then in October 2005 reports emerged that, even before the *Goodridge* decision, the Boston office of Catholic Charities had been arranging adoptions by same-sex couples.

That revelation was deeply embarrassing to the Boston archdiocese, and not only because Catholic Charities was undercutting the argument for the marriage amendment. Church teaching—reaffirmed by the Vatican statement on homosexual unions that had been released just a few months earlier—was quite clear in condemning homosexual adoptions as gravely immoral. To place adoptive children in a same-sex household, the Vatican said, "would actually mean doing violence to those children." So Catholic Charities was doing violence to children; the Boston archdiocese was involved in another form of child abuse.

Officials at Catholic Charities were remarkably unrattled by the public disclosure, however. Father J. Bryan Hehir, the head of the archdiocesan agency, explained that the Massachusetts government forbade discrimination against same-sex couples. If Catholic Charities violated that policy, he said, the agency would lose the government funding that subsidized its adoption program. "If we could design the system ourselves we would not participate in adoptions to gay couples, but we can't," Father Hehir reasoned. "We have to balance various goods."

The actual number of homosexual adoptions facilitated by Catholic Charities was quite low, the agency reported: only thirteen children had been placed in same-sex households, out of 720 adoptions the office arranged. If the Catholic agency had refused to cooperate with those thirteen placements, the other 707 adoptions might not have taken place. But this was a classic example of the flawed moral argument that the ends justify the means. If same-sex adoptions do violence to children, then Catholic Charities was justifying violence against *some* children by saying that *other* children would profit. Nor could the same-sex adoptions be justified by the claim that Catholic Charities was offering only "material cooperation" in an immoral policy; the Catholic agency was actively *carrying out* that policy and thus fully liable for the moral consequences.

In December 2005 the Vatican sent a directive to Archbishop O'Malley, telling him that Catholic Charities must cease all cooperation with same-sex adoptions. That same month the board of trustees of Catholic Charities—made up primarily of influential Catholic laymen—met to discuss the question. Unmoved by the clear orders from Rome, the trustees voted *unanimously* to continue arranging adoptions for homosexual couples. Peter Meade, a spokesman for the board, delivered his opinion that it would be an "unmitigated disaster" for the agency to stop serving gay couples.

Hoping to avoid a direct confrontation, Church leaders sought help from Massachusetts political leaders. They inquired about the possibility of a special exemption that would allow church agencies to arrange adoptions without following the statewide non-discrimination policy. Those inquiries were quickly rebuffed. Governor Mitt Romney voiced some sympathy for the Catholic position, but claimed that he did not have the authority to issue an exemption; the matter would have to go through the legislature, he said. On Beacon Hill, lawmakers made it clear that they would not be doing any special favors for the Catholic Church; the request for an exemption fell on deaf ears.

Now the choices were stark and simple. The Boston office of Catholic Charities could either stop placing adoptive children with same-sex couples and lose government funding, or continue the placements and effectively abandon any pretense of being guided by Catholic moral doctrine. Neither option was attractive. In March 2006 the agency found a way to avoid the dilemma. Catholic Charities announced that it would stop adoption services altogether. "The overwhelming majority of the time we reconciled the differences between our roots in the Catholic Church and our mission to serve the larger society," said Father Hehir. "But this time it was irreconcilable."

There was a faintly discordant note in that statement by the director of Catholic Charities: a hint that fidelity to Church teaching would often conflict with a "mission to serve the larger society." A convinced Catholic would say that the Church serves society best by spreading the faith, and that the social teachings of the Church—including, in this case, the injunction against same-sex adoption—point the way toward healthy public policy. If some political leaders perceive a conflict between the teachings of the Church and the welfare of the public, then the mission of Catholic activists is to change their minds. Throughout this crisis, however, Catholic Charities had sought not to change public perceptions, but to reach an accommodation with prevailing public opinion.

When it became evident that the Boston archdiocese would not openly defy Rome and the same-sex adoption placements would not continue, seven members of the board of Catholic Charities resigned in protest. The disaffected trustees said that the Church's refusal to participate in homosexual adoptions "threatens the very essence of our Christian mission."

There are two ways to interpret that statement. Perhaps these trustees—all intelligent members of the laity, presumably well informed about the faith—believed that the teachings of the Roman Catholic Church were incompatible with the essence of Christian mission. That would be an odd position for a Catholic to hold, to say the least. Or perhaps these Boston Catholics accepted the Church's argument that same-sex adoptions do violence to children, but believed that by stopping the adoptions the archdiocese would damage its overall mission in Boston.

The latter argument could be re-stated thus: It would be better to allow violence to a few children than to risk a public scandal that would harm the Church. Hadn't we heard that argument somewhere before?

PART V

RESTORATION

17

THE WRONG
EXPLANATIONS

The crisis that has stricken the Catholic Church in America is often described as a pedophilia scandal. That characterization is not accurate.

Pedophilia—a profound psychological disorder involving the sexual desire for young, pre-pubescent children—is fortunately rare. A few of the most notorious American clerics involved in the scandal, such as James Porter and John Geoghan, might be accurately classified as pedophiles. Because they molested scores of children, and because their cases came to prominence in the early days of the crisis, these deeply disturbed men were taken as emblematic of the larger problem in the American priesthood. But they were not typical.

Among the thousands of complaints lodged against American priests during the early years of the twenty-first century, the vast majority involved sexual relations with teenage boys. In some cases, to some extent, the boys may have appeared to be willing partners in the sexual activity. Since the teenagers had not reached the age of consent, and since the priests were exploiting their positions of authority and trust, the relationships were certainly abusive. But they cannot be classified as instances of pedophilia.

In a thorough study of sex-abuse complaints that was commissioned by the USCCB, the John Jay College of Criminal Justice issued a sweeping report in 2004 that covered more than 5,000 incidents. Of these, 81 percent involved priests with young male victims. Of those male victims, 90 percent were teenage boys.

Faced with that statistic, some analysts began to say that what had been seen as a crisis of pedophilia was really a matter of *ephebophilia*. (The term "ephebophilia"—which does not appear in standard diagnostic manuals for psychologists—refers to sexual attraction toward adolescents.)

Some commentators took comfort in using this new term. Other less pretentious observers concluded that the statistics proved what many Catholics had long suspected: the sex-abuse crisis was a crisis of homosexuality in the priesthood.

For several years Catholic scholars had been debating whether or not homosexuals should be ordained to the priesthood. A 1961 Vatican document addressed to the superiors of religious orders had said that men with a known homosexual inclination should not be admitted to seminary training. (That policy, which had fallen into desuetude, was reaffirmed by the Vatican and applied to all candidates for the priesthood in a new teaching document of 2005.) But many liberal Catholics argued that a homosexual who maintained a celibate lifestyle could be a fine priest. "Unless proven otherwise, there is no reason to believe that homosexual priests are any less likely to keep their promises of celibacy than heterosexual ones," wrote Father James Martin, a Jesuit journalist, in a November 2000 article in *America* magazine. That argument was central to the case in favor of ordaining men with homosexual impulses.

Even if homosexual priests are no more likely than heterosexuals to violate their vows, however, it stands to reason that if and when they do engage in sexual activity, their partners are more likely to be male. Thus the sex-abuse scandal had serious implications for the debate on homosexuality. Yet the National Review Board, in its first major report on the crisis, did not shrink from the obvious conclusion. "That 81% of the reported victims of sexual abuse by Catholic clergy were boys shows that the crisis was characterized by homosexual behavior."

From the earliest days of the scandal, when stories of abuse first appeared in the media, liberal Catholics and their friends in the world of journalism took pains to emphasize that there is no known connection between homosexuality and pedophilia. That is true, but irrelevant to most of the cases that the Church was confronting. The more relevant question was whether homosexual priests were more likely than heterosexuals to become involved with teenagers.

On that question, the report from John Jay College provided an interesting perspective. If 81 percent of the abuse cases involved male-to-male contacts, it would seem difficult to avoid the conclusion that homosexual priests—those attracted toward males—were disproportionately responsible for the abuse. In a fascinating study of the crisis entitled *After Asceticism*, the Linacre Institute used Bayes' Theorem—a standard statistical tool for studying the spread of epidemic diseases—to estimate the likelihood that homosexual priests would be involved in abusive behavior. The study concluded that if men with homosexual inclinations account for about 30 percent of the priests in the US, then the John Jay figures suggest that these homosexual priests are about *nine times* as likely as their heterosexual colleagues to be responsible for sexual abuse.

The number of homosexually inclined priests active in America is not an unknown factor, the Linacre study noted. If 81 percent of American Catholic priests are homosexually inclined, then the ratio of male-to-male abuse is unremarkable; the statistics would suggest that homosexual and heterosexual men are equally liable to engage in sexual abuse. If the proportion of homosexual priests is very low, on the other hand, then the disproportionate number of male sex-abuse victims is all the more noteworthy. If only 2 percent of priests are homosexual, the Linacre Center concluded, those few homosexuals are more than 120 times as likely as heterosexuals to be guilty of abuse.

The statistical calculations are imprecise, particularly because some key numbers—such as the proportion of homosexuals in the clergy—can only be guessed at. But the fundamental logic of the Linacre analysis is easy to follow. Most instances of sexual abuse involved homosexual acts. Presumably homosexual acts are performed by men with homosexual impulses. Therefore, priests with homosexual tendencies were responsible for most sexual abuse. It follows that either a) homosexuals are more likely to engage in abuse, or b) the number of homosexuals among the American clergy is so high that one would *expect* most abusive priests to seek male partners. In either case the figures show a crisis of homosexuality in the American priesthood.

Vatican officials had been alert to the question of homosexuality from the earliest days of the scandal. When Pope John Paul II summoned the leaders of the American hierarchy to Rome in April 2002, one of the key points on the agenda for discussion was the influence of a homosexual culture in the American seminaries. The joint statement released by the participating bishops at the end of that Vatican meeting also called for new emphasis on the moral teachings of the Church regarding sexuality, a message that could be read as a mandate for the American hierarchy to be more forceful in condemning homosexual behavior. But as we have observed, that aspect of the discussion in Rome was quietly dropped from the bishops' agenda before the Dallas meeting.

In Dallas the USCCB concentrated exclusively on the sexual abuse of minors. The final document produced at that meeting was awkwardly entitled a *Charter for the Protection of Children and Young People* in a tacit acknowledgement that the victims of abuse could not all be classified as "children." The Dallas norms set out disciplinary standards for priests who were involved in any sexual relationship with people, male or female, under the age of eighteen. But the bishops did not discuss, and the norms do not address, sexual misconduct by priests involving partners *over* the age of consent. When a priest pursues a sexual relationship with a psychologically vulnerable parishioner, he is guilty of abuse, even if that parishioner is an adult. And a priest who engages in consensual sexual contact with another man is guilty of grave misconduct, even if it is not abusive. But in Dallas the US bishops did not consider these sorts of clerical misbehavior; the scope of their attention was restricted exclusively to the abuse of "children and young people."

A more wide-ranging discussion of clerical misconduct might have led the USCCB to explore other questions, seeking a better understanding of the abusive behavior. When epidemiologists hunt for the source of a disease, they study not only the victims of the disease but also the people with whom they have been in contact in their homes and workplaces. When intelligence agencies discover an enemy spy within their own ranks, they carefully examine each bit of information that counter-agent furnished, and each contact he made, to root out the effects of his treachery. If the bishops had been determined to conduct a thorough study of sexual abuse they might have done similar investigations into the backgrounds of the priests who were accused. Who were there friends among the clergy? Where had they been assigned? Did they share vacation cottages with other priests or bishops? Who had been their seminary teachers?

At an even more basic level, an investigation into abuse might have compared the incidence of complaints in different dioceses. Were there any patterns to suggest that some bishops had been more successful than others in deterring abusive behavior? Were there some seminaries that produced an unusual number of molesters? Oddly enough the John Jay study did not break down the statistics on abuse by diocese, although those raw figures were obviously available to the researchers who compiled the report. Instead the John Jay account studies the incidence of abuse by geographical region—a factor that has no particular ecclesial significance. Nor did the John Jay study list the seminaries that produced the accused abusers.

There were, however, a few institutions that figured prominently in the lives of many serial molesters: the treatment centers to which these priests were assigned for therapy. In its report, the National Review Board criticized these centers for having repeatedly given clearance for abusers to resume parish work. Dozens of predators had received counseling at places like the St. Luke Institute in Maryland or the Servants of the Paraclete center in New Mexico, and returned to their dioceses with rosy reports from certified experts proclaiming their fitness for unrestricted ministry. The US bishops would have been amply justified in seeking to have some of these experts stripped of their licenses, but they did not. On the contrary, American bishops are still sending troubled priests to the same clinics.

What sort of approach did these centers bring to bear on the problems of abusive clerics? Father Stephen Rossetti, the president of the St. Luke Institute, has for years been the most influential figure advising the priests on the psychology of sexual abuse. In an article that appeared in *America* in 1995, he wrote the "priest-offenders have tended to be intelligent, high-functioning men, many of whom had otherwise exemplary ministries." Father Rossetti's sympathy for these priests, and his keen desire·to return them to ministry, was clear in that same article.

> But society hates and fears men who sexually abuse minors. We stereotype them; we claim they are all incorrigible; we wish to mark them as people not like ourselves. These men tap a deep well of fear and anger that goes beyond the facts of their crime. To reintegrate child molesters into our society will require us to face and overcome our own fears. To live in peace with child molesters will mean to let go of some of our own inner angers.

Father Canice Connors, a Franciscan priest, had preceded Rossetti as director of the St. Luke Institute before becoming president of the Conference of Major Superiors of Men. In that latter capacity he spoke out against the Dallas policy, saying that the bishops "have become one with the voices of the media, unreconciled victims, and a partially informed Catholic public in scapegoating the abusers."

Scapegoating the abusers? The fact that an informed priest could still perceive abusive priests as victims spoke volumes about the sympathetic attitude that misbehaving clerics could expect to find at the busiest treatment centers.

Not all priests found these centers so congenial, however. Beginning in the late 1990s, articles began to appear in more conservative Catholic publications charging that orthodox Catholic priests and seminarians were being sent to the same treatment centers to be counseled for vaguely defined problems such as doctrinal rigidity or "homophobia." Some of the clerics who were treated at these facilities—often against their wishes, under heavy pressure from their bishops or seminary rectors—reported that the centers showed open contempt for Church teachings on sexuality and sympathy for homosexual clerics.

These complaints about the treatment centers for troubled priests dovetailed neatly with another complaint that was being heard with increasing frequency: that diocesan officials were deliberately excluding conservative men from the seminaries and thus from the priesthood. Michael Rose offered a persuasive exposition of that complaint in his 2002 book *Goodbye, Good Men*. In many American dioceses, he said, seminary admissions committees were screening out candidates who said that they strongly supported Church teaching on the impossibility of ordaining women or the immorality of homosexual acts. The seminary gatekeepers did not openly dispute these teachings, Rose said; instead they announced that the conservative candidates were too psychologically "rigid" to be effective priests. Candidates who *dis*agreed with the Church's teaching on those issues encountered no such hurdles.

If a candidate for the priesthood survived the admissions tests, Rose continued, he might still face scrutiny during his years at the seminary. A student who was judged doctrinaire or insensitive could be discouraged or even dismissed from the seminary. Several young men, representing different dioceses, told Rose that when they complained about homosexual activities within their seminaries, they found *themselves* subject to disciplinary action rather than their gay classmates.

Defenders of the seminaries did their best to dismiss Michael Rose's book as the work of a conservative writer who brought a pronounced bias to his work. But Father Donald Cozzens, an influential liberal psychologist and former seminary rector, was honest enough to admit in 2000: "The disproportionate number of homosexually oriented priests and seminarians may well be a significant factor in the drastic reduction in the number of candidates for our seminaries." In his book *The Changing Face of Priesthood*, Father Cozzens indicated that he personally was not opposed to the ordination of homosexual men, but he saw a pronounced imbalance in the number of homosexuals in the American clergy. Cozzens concluded: "At issue at the beginning of the twenty-first century is the growing perception that the priesthood is, or is becoming, a gay profession."

That statement by Cozzens provoked a considerable reaction in Catholic publications. But the American hierarchy remained silent on the topic. The question of homosexuality within the priesthood or the seminaries was not a topic the bishops were prepared to discuss.

In 1996 an Illinois Catholic layman named Stephen Brady founded a new organization called Roman Catholic Faithful to counteract what he saw as the active subversion of Catholic parishes by clerics who rejected Church teachings on sexual morality. Doggedly exploring the ties among dissident priests, Brady uncovered a network of actively homosexual priests who communicated with each other through a crudely pornographic internet site entitled "Sebastian's Angels." On that site American priests (and one South African bishop, Reginald Cawcutt) exchanged notes about their sexual escapades and strategies for locating compliant young men. Horrified, Brady wrote to five American cardinals to alert them to the site's existence. Only one prelate replied, and that one—Chicago's Cardinal Francis George—told Brady that he did not want to view the Sebastian's Angels site because he feared it would be a temptation to sin.

Undaunted, Brady continued his investigation, and identified more than fifty priests who were active participants in the Sebastian's Angels exchange. He brought the activities of those priests to the attention of their diocesan bishops, asking for disciplinary action. Again most of his messages went unanswered. A handful of priests were suspended, and the Sebastian's Angels web site disappeared from cyberspace. The vast majority of these openly homosexual priests went unpunished, their activities unacknowledged.

The American bishops, it seems, were determined to avoid any discussion of priestly homosexuality, and still more determined to avoid grappling with the accusation that networks of homosexuals wielded great power within the clergy. At times that avoidance reached comical extremes. The future president of the USCCB, Bishop William Skylstad of Spokane, was questioned in 2002 about a police report that his predecessor, the late Bishop Lawrence Welsh, had tried to strangle a homosexual prostitute in his hotel room during a convention in Chicago in 1986. "Obviously he had a very serious drinking problem," Bishop Skylstad said.

Under police interrogation Bishop Welsh had admitted that he met the homosexual prostitute in his Chicago hotel room—although he denied trying to strangle him. "Certainly it's very sad behavior associated with that drinking," Bishop Skylstad told the Spokane *Spokesman-Review*. When the paper asked whether the former bishop's homosexual inclinations might have inclined him toward leniency to priest-abusers, Skylstad said: "Clearly, there was a drinking problem." Bishop Welsh did indeed have a drinking problem. But he had another problem as well: a problem that Bishop Skylstad did not want to acknowledge even in the face of overwhelming evidence.

In all their dealings with the sex-abuse crisis, the American bishops and their closest advisers have evinced the same sort of reluctance to admit the influence of homosexuality. They have shown no stomach for an investigation into the prevalence of homosexuals in seminaries or the influence of homosexual networks among the clergy. They have not explored the possible links between priests who prey on teenage boys and those who prefer slightly older men. They have not acted promptly on the Vatican's December 2005 directive saying that men with homosexual inclinations should not be accepted as candidates for the priesthood. In fact the most powerful voices within the American hierarchy argued against the Vatican plan to release that directive. The same voices have discouraged questions about the relationship between homosexuality and sexual abuse. Father Stephen Rossetti—still a top adviser to the bishops despite the many questions that have been raised about the St. Luke Institute—summarized his concern a year after the Dallas meeting: "What I'm afraid of is we're going into this witch-hunt for gays." There was no evidence in June 2003 that American Catholic leaders had any plans for a witch-hunt. There was, on the contrary, abundant evidence that the hierarchy would discourage any such investigation.

In November 2000, the monthly *Catholic World Report* published a cover story entitled "The Gay Priest Problem." That article, by a Jesuit military chaplain, Father Paul Shaughnessy, provoked more heated commentary than any other essay published during my twelve-year tenure as editor of the magazine. In his analysis, Father Shaughnessy concluded that homosexuals had a growing influence among the American clergy and wielded that influence to discourage any interference with their affairs. The problem, Father Shaughnessy argued, had reached a stage at which outside intervention would be necessary to bring about reform. He explained:

> The principal reason why the action necessary to solve the gay problem
> won't be taken is that the episcopacy in the United States is corrupt, and

the same is true of the majority of religious orders. In calling them "corrupt" I mean that these institutions have lost the capacity to mend themselves on their own initiative and by their own resources, that they are unable to uncover and expel their own miscreants. It is important to stress that this is a sociological claim, not a moral one. If we examine any trust-invested agency at any given point in its history, whether that agency be a police force, a military unit, or a religious community, we might find that, say, out of every hundred men, five are scoundrels, five are heroes, and the rest are neither one nor the other: ordinarily upright men who live with a mixture of moral timidity and moral courage. When the institution is healthy, the gutsier few set the overall tone, and the less courageous but tractable majority works along with these men to minimize misbehavior; more importantly, the healthy institution is able to identify its own rotten apples and remove them before the institution itself is enfeebled. However, when an institution becomes corrupt, its guiding spirit mysteriously shifts away from the morally intrepid few, and with that shift the institution becomes more interested in protecting itself against outside critics than in tackling the problem members who subvert its mission. For example, when we say a certain police force is corrupt, we don't usually mean that every policeman is on the take—perhaps only five out of a hundred actually accept bribes—rather we mean that this police force can no longer diagnose and cure its own problems, and consequently if reform is to take place an outside agency has to be brought in to make the changes.

Homosexual influence within the American clergy was not in itself the cause of the sex-abuse crisis. The corruption wrought by that influence was a more important factor. A very small number of priests preyed on children. A very large number of priests developed the habit of looking the other way, avoiding contact with any evidence of their colleagues' personal conduct. Actively homosexual priests did not want to be questioned about their Saturday-night activities, and they would not press their colleagues about their own affairs. For the sake of peace in the rectory, heterosexual priests learned to stifle any suspicions they might have.

Living a celibate life is a difficult challenge in the best of times, and particularly so in our sex-saturated era. For centuries Catholic priests worked to meet that challenge by growing in virtue and self-mastery. The priesthood had its own *esprit de corps*, like any other organization in which dedicated men work together toward a difficult goal. In seminaries young men would be introduced to strict patterns of discipline and expected to place great demands on themselves. Later, in parish ministry, they would hold each other to the same moral standards.

But the uncertainties of Catholic life after Vatican II eroded the old standards of clerical discipline. Seminaries relaxed their restrictions on their students, at just the time when the sexual revolution bombarded young men with provocative stimuli. Bishops and chancery officials eased their standards as well, allowing much greater latitude for priests in their choice of recreational activities. Within a few years the old norms of proper priestly conduct were gone, and no clear new standards established in their place.

The statistics of the John Jay report show that the incidence of sexual abuse by Catholic priests peaked in the 1970s as the consequences of the sexual revolution were settling in. But curiously enough, the priests most frequently accused of abuse were ordained in the 1960s. Many of these accused molesters were ordained to the priesthood before Vatican II began, and all of them received their seminary training prior to the general relaxation of standards that followed the Council.

Why were the men of this age cohort particularly apt to engage in sexual abuse? If they were inclined to molest children, why did they wait until a decade after ordination to act on their inclinations? One hypothesis is that they were trained in the seminary to meet standards that others set for them, and when those standards were set aside, they lacked the inner strength to discipline themselves. They were no longer surrounded by Catholics who held them to higher standards of moral conduct.

In the analysis of the sex-abuse scandal mentioned above, the Linacre Institute argues that this confusion about expectations was the root cause of the crisis. *After Asceticism* acknowledges the homosexual influence within the priesthood, then continues:

> But the ultimate cause of the scandal is not the sexual orientation of
> priests; it is a breakdown in traditional practices of spiritual formation
> and ascetical discipline. Here too the scandal among the clergy reflects
> the same phenomenon that has robbed the Church of public influence:
> the breakdown in understanding of what it means to be a Catholic or to
> be a priest.

18

THE
DASH-2 BISHOPS

S t. Augustine died in the year 430. He was the Bishop of Hippo, a diocese in North Africa that was besieged by Vandals in 429. Elderly
and infirm by that time, the great theologian had an opportunity to
escape from the city before the invaders broke through the last defenses.
Many other Church leaders fled, and St. Augustine encouraged the faithful to leave. But he stayed behind, explaining:

> When the danger is the same for bishops, clerics, and congregations,
> those who have need of others must not be abandoned by those whom
> they need. Let everyone withdraw to fortified places, but those who are
> forced to stay must not be abandoned by those who owe them the aid of
> the Church.

St. Augustine made great demands on his priests and his people, but
much greater demands on himself. Contrast his attitude with that of Bishop
Tod Brown of Orange, California. Early in 2004, Bishop Brown marched up
to his own cathedral carrying a document and a tap-hammer. In a theatrical
gesture that was obviously calculated to awaken memories of Martin Luther,
he posted the document, entitled "Covenant with the Faithful," on the
cathedral door. In that Covenant the bishop promised to be fully open with
the Catholic people of the Orange diocese, giving them a complete and
accurate accounting of the sex-abuse scandal. He followed up on that promise by releasing the names of all priests active in the Orange diocese who
had been accused of sexual abuse, whether or not the accusations were supported by reliable evidence. But there was one name missing from that list:
Tod Brown.

Bishop Brown's single accuser was not a terribly persuasive witness,
and the bishop denied the charge. It would be easy to conclude that the

bishop was innocent, and spared himself the trouble that would surely ensue if he publicized a false accusation. But he did not spare other priests of the Orange diocese who might have been equally innocent. And eventually the charge against him became public despite his silence.

Unfortunately Bishop Brown, not St. Augustine, typifies the response of the American bishops to the sex-abuse crisis. In their efforts to contain the scandal the American hierarchy has been willing to expose priests to the danger of false accusations, to close parishes and Catholics schools, and to sacrifice the religious freedom of the Church. But to this day the bishops have shown no willingness to discipline themselves or to call each other to account.

Before their memorable meeting in Dallas in 2002, most of the American bishops had allowed molesters to continue serving in parish assignments—in which, predictably, they continued to abuse youngsters. Why did the bishops fail to take action, to discipline the abusers and protect the innocent? Why did they defend the indefensible? And if there were a few bishops who resisted the pressure to tolerate sexual abuse, why did these stalwarts fail to criticize their aberrant colleagues? Some bishops must have been horrified by the realization that their colleagues were endangering the spiritual welfare of children in their dioceses; why did they not confront them?

Maybe they did. There is much to be said for a prudent, discreet approach. Maybe there were a few conscientious bishops who quietly pulled others aside and exhorted them to fulfill their pastoral duties. (I am aware of one instance in which a bishop privately confronted a prominent archbishop and urged him to resign, saying that the archbishop's homosexual activities were bound to bring scandal upon the Church. The archbishop denied the charges against him, and the bishop who had challenged him, lacking any direct evidence, had no choice but to accept the denial. The archbishop remained in office until he reached retirement age.) Still at some point the urgent need to protect young people should outweigh the desire to avoid public disagreements. It is natural for bishops to protect each other from embarrassment. But when that protection extends to cover negligence and duplicity, it becomes a sort of episcopal conspiracy against the laity: a form of corruption that threatens the integrity of the Catholic Church.

During the past several years, American Catholics have seen many bishops resign abruptly after being personally implicated in scandal.

Invariably these sudden resignations are explained to the public with a reference to a provision of canon law—canon 402-2—which provides for a bishop's resignation in case of illness "or other grave reason." That deliberately vague reason for a bishop's removal has been invoked so often that cynics have abbreviated the canonical reference, speaking of the "dash-2 bishops."

The "dash-2" clause allows the Vatican to accept a bishop's resignation without acknowledging the scandal that provoked it. So a bishop can leave office in good standing. His successor can pay homage to the retired bishop, thanking him for his long years of valuable service to the Church. Other bishops can continue to treat the "dash-2 bishop" as a respected colleague, overlooking the evidence of personal disgrace—just as in the past they ignored the evidence against the abusive priests.

In some cases a "dash-2" resignation has come without warning and only later have the faithful pieced together the evidence of misconduct that forced their bishop to resign before public exposure. But in many other cases the scandal had *already* come to light, and the reason for the sudden resignation is clear to all concerned; so that the "dash-2" reference accomplishes no purpose except to persuade the public that Church leaders are incapable of speaking the truth plainly.

In December 2002, when Cardinal Law's resignation was announced, Bishop William Skylstad issued a statement on behalf of the USCCB. "This resignation represents a significant step forward in the healing process, for abuse victims not only in the Boston diocese but in dioceses around the country," he said. "To restore trust and faith in our Church we must be held accountable. Today's action sends a strong message that all priests and bishops will be held accountable."

Those words sounded admirably clear. But notice that Bishop Skylstad did not explain *why* Cardinal Law's resignation would be a step forward. He said that bishops must be accountable, but did not indicate what actions Cardinal Law was being held accountable *for.* If Law was obliged to resign because he shuffled abusive priests from one assignment to another and concealed evidence against them, then scores of other bishops should have resigned for the same offenses. But in his statement on the Law resignation Bishop Skylstad deftly avoided identifying the actions that should be considered grounds for resignation.

In the five years that have passed since Law's departure, the American bishops have never said of a disgraced colleague: "We love our brother bishop, but we cannot tolerate his actions." Every "dash-2" bishop had been retired with full honors and treated with deference after stepping down. Not once has any American bishop explained that a colleague had shown himself unfit to hold episcopal office.

The evidence of gross misconduct among the American bishops is not difficult to find:

- Cardinal Joseph Bernardin died in 1996, well before the eruption of the scandal. But in November 2003 the Cincinnati archdiocese settled a long and bitter battle with local prosecutors by admitting that criminal conduct had been committed by archdiocesan officials who had "knowingly failed" to report sexual abuse there on several occasions between 1979 and 1982—under the leadership of then-Archbishop Bernardin. Earlier in 2003, the ex-priest Richard Sipe, who has written extensively on clerical abuse, made the provocative charge that he had spoken with homosexual priests who revealed that they had "partied" with the future cardinal in Cincinnati. Sipe went on to point out that Steven Cook, who had lodged and later retracted charges against the Chicago prelate, "did not ever retract his allegations of abuse, by anyone's account other than Bernardin's."

- Bishop Thomas Dupre resigned his leadership of the Diocese of Springfield, Massachusetts in February 2004, just one day after a local newspaper questioned him about charges that he had molested two young men years ago. After investigating reports of abuse by the bishop and other Springfield priests, the district attorney reported that the statute of limitations prevented him from bringing criminal charges. But he added the intriguing note that other jurisdictions might pursue charges—an apparent reference to reports that priests had brought young boys across state lines. Bishop Dupre—who never acknowledged the charges against him—has not been seen in the Springfield diocese since the day he resigned; his current whereabouts are not publicly known.

- Bishop Charles Grahmann saw his Dallas, Texas, diocese hit with legal damages of a record $119.6 million (later reduced to $31 million) for failing to control the known pedophile activities of a now-defrocked priest, Rudy Kos. Outraged lay Catholics sought the bishop's resignation, and in 2000 the Vatican appointed a coadjutor, Bishop Joseph Galante. But Bishop Grahmann refused to step down, and finally in 2004 Bishop Galante was transferred to a new assignment in Camden, New Jersey. Controversy continued to swirl around Grahmann, with repeated accusations that he has given pastoral assignments to priests after evidence of sexual abuse. He finally relinquished his post in 2007 after reaching the mandatory retirement age of 75.

- Bishop Robert Lynch of St. Petersburg, Florida, made a $100,000 severance payment to William Urbanski, who had left his job as spokesman for the diocese protesting that the bishop had sexually harassed him. The bishop denied the charges and insisted that the severance payment was not "hush money." But reporters investigating the case found that Lynch had showered Urbanski with personal gifts for nearly 5 years; the bishop had also awarded $30 million in no-bid construction contracts to another friend, David Herman—who, like Urbanski, is a muscular triathlete.

- Bishop John McCormack entered into an agreement with the attorney general of New Hampshire in December 2002 on behalf of the Diocese of Manchester, in which "the diocese acknowledges that the state has evidence likely to sustain a conviction" for the failure of diocesan officials to report sexual abuse of minors. Before becoming Bishop of Manchester, McCormack had been an aide to Cardinal Law in Boston, supervising clerical personnel, and in that role he had handled the cases of several notorious pedophiles. Under the terms of the agreement in New Hampshire, his diocese is required to submit regular audits of diocesan activities to law-enforcement officials.

- Bishop Thomas O'Brien resigned as head of the Phoenix, Arizona, diocese in June 2003, after his arrest in a fatal hit-and-run case that eventually made him the first American bishop ever convicted of a felony. Not long before the accident, in May 2003, he had signed an agreement with local prosecutors to avoid criminal charges for failing to report sexual molestation. "I acknowledge that I allowed Roman Catholic priests under my supervision to work with minors after becoming aware of allegations of sexual misconduct," Bishop O'Brien conceded. Later the bishop denied that he had hidden evidence of abuse. "To suggest a cover-up is just plain false," he claimed. An angry prosecutor shot back: "Is he revising history?"

- Bishop Anthony O'Connell succeeded Bishop J. Keith Symons (see below) in the troubled Diocese of Palm Beach, Florida. After three years there, he resigned, admitting that he had sexually abused students during his tenure as a seminary rector in Missouri twenty-five years earlier. The bishop said that the memory of his past transgressions had "always hung over me," but it had not dissuaded him from accepting the leadership of a diocese stung by the resignation of the previous bishop in similar circumstances.

- Archbishop Daniel Pilarczyk entered into an agreement with Ohio prosecutors in 2003, conceding criminal conduct in the Cincinnati archdiocese prior to his arrival. "Instances of child abuse that should have been reported to civil authorities were apparently not reported," the archbishop announced. But in February 2005, an investigative report by the local television state WCPO unearthed documents that proved Archbishop Pilarczyk and his aides were aware that one Cincinnati priest had abused children—but failed to report that abuse to civil authorities, as required by Ohio law. The current Hamilton County prosecutor was asked by WCPO why his predecessor did not prosecute the archbishop. "I don't know," he said flatly.

- Bishop Daniel Ryan resigned in October 1999 as head of the Diocese of Springfield, Illinois, citing health reasons. Neither the bishop nor the diocese has ever acknowledged the accuracy of evidence submitted by Roman Catholic Faithful to demonstrate that Bishop Ryan had preyed on young men. Even in retirement the former bishop continued to make headlines; in July 2004 police were summoned to his residence to restore order in an incident involving Ryan and two younger male companions.

- Bishop J. Keith Symons was the first US bishop to resign because of the sex-abuse scandal when he relinquished his title as Bishop of Palm Beach in June 1998. (He was replaced by Bishop Anthony O'Connell, who subsequently resigned for the same reason.) In admitting to the abuse of five altar boys, Bishop Symons said that it had occurred forty years earlier and insisted that he had subsequently lived a celibate life.

- Archbishop Rembert Weakland submitted his resignation as Archbishop of Milwaukee, as required under canon law, when he reached his 75th birthday on April 2, 2002. But there was no expectation that the resignation would be accepted quickly—until, just a few weeks later, a man named Paul Marcoux revealed that Weakland had paid him $450,000 to drop a sexual-assault complaint. The funds were drawn from the coffers of the Milwaukee archdiocese, prompting a local prosecutor to open a criminal investigation. Although no criminal charges were filed, Weakland asked the Vatican to speed up acceptance of his resignation; "I do not want to be an obstacle," he said. His resignation was formally accepted on May 24, 2002.

- Bishop Patrick Ziemann was accused of blackmailing one of his own priests in a bizarre case that came to light in July 1999. Father Jorge Salas, a priest from Costa Rica working in the Santa Rosa, California, diocese, charged that Ziemann pressured him to engage in homosexual acts by threatening that otherwise the bishop would reveal that Father Salas had been caught stealing parish funds. Bishop Ziemann resigned, admitting to a sexual relationship but saying that it was consensual. California authorities declined to prosecute, saying that there was insufficient evidence to support a case against the former bishop—whose mismanagement of funds had also left the little Santa Rosa diocese with a $16-million debt. In a lawsuit brought by Father Salas, the diocese eventually settled out of court, paying the priest $535,000.

Among the prelates on this inglorious list, two (Lynch and McCormack) remain in office as I write. One, Cardinal Bernardin, died in office and remains a revered figure among liberal Catholics. All of the others were allowed to resign, with a terse announcement citing Canon 402-2. In every case the resignation came *after* the public exposure of misconduct. Insofar as these bishops were held accountable for the activities, it was the mass media, not their brother bishops, who called them to account.

Why did the American bishops tolerate misconduct among their ranks, and thus increase the risk of scandal? One possible explanation is that bishops were cowed by the threat that even greater scandals might be laid bare. In a word, some bishops may have been subject to blackmail.

In 1992 an Arizona priest, Monsignor Robert Trupia, was accused of molesting an altar boy. Suspended from ministry and faced with the likelihood that his crime would become public knowledge, Trupia warned Bishop Manuel Moreno of Tucson that he was prepared to publicize "my direct knowledge regarding another bishop's activities, which knowledge was potentially of a highly explosive and damaging nature to the Church in Arizona." Bishop Moreno understood the message; Trupia was threatening to reveal that the late Bishop James Rausch, the former Bishop of Phoenix, had been an active homosexual.

In Boston the accused Father Paul Shanley had made a similar threat, saying that he had knowledge of misconduct by two Boston archbishops. But Trupia's threat, unlike Shanley's, pointed clearly at one prelate. And the public exposure of misconduct by Bishop Rausch would indeed have been explosive, not only for Arizona but for Catholicism throughout the United States. Before being assigned to the Phoenix diocese, Rausch had served as executive secretary of the US bishops' conference. There he had worked for, and eventually succeeded, the future Cardinal Bernardin, who had subsequently emerged as the most prominent Catholic prelate in America. If Bishop Rausch had been an active homosexual, he would himself have been subject to blackmail threats, and all his work on behalf of the US bishops' conference would be open to scrutiny.

Trupia's threat worked, at least temporarily. Bishop Moreno helped Trupia to escape legal responsibility for several years, until the statute of limitations had expired and prosecutors were forced to drop charges against him. Trupia left Tucson but remained on the diocesan payroll until 2004, when he was finally defrocked.

Was Trupia the only priest who won his bishop's silence through intimidation? We do not know. Given the number of bishops who were personally engaged in sexual misconduct, it is not unreasonable to think that others received similar threats. The blackmail hypothesis provides a logical explanation for behavior that is otherwise inexplicable: the bishops' willingness to risk the welfare of the faithful and their own reputations in order to protect abusive priests.

Whether or not they succumbed to blackmail, we do know that several bishops have entered into plea-bargain agreements with prosecutors, preserving themselves (and their predecessors) from criminal charges by sacrificing the autonomy of their dioceses. Under these agreements, public officials in New Hampshire, Ohio, and Arizona gained the power to watch over the activities of a Catholic diocese: a power that would ordinarily be unthinkable under the terms of the First Amendment. The public officials did not seize control over these dioceses, trampling on the principle of religious freedom; the bishops willingly ceded that control, as the price of escaping prosecution. Thus Bishops McCormack and Pilarczyk and O'Brien avoided the legal consequences of behavior which, they acknowledged, gave prosecutors adequate reason to press charges. But the agreements that they struck did not ony bind them personally; they also impinged on the freedom of the Church in their dioceses, the freedom of their successors as bishops.

In Spokane, Washington, Bishop William Skylstad entered into a troubling agreement of a different sort. In January 2007 the Spokane diocese reached an agreement with all of its creditors to emerge from bankruptcy. Under the terms of that agreement, the bishop promised to support statewide legislation that would eliminate the statue of limitations for the prosecution of child molesters. That legislation may have been a laudable reform, but Skylstad was promising the public support of the Catholic diocese in exchange for a tangible benefit: the discharge of diocesan debts. In effect it appeared that creditors had *bought* the support of the diocese for the legislation they preferred.

At the time he struck that agreement Bishop Skylstad was still serving his term as president of the USCCB. It was appropriately symbolic that Skylstad was elected to head the bishops' conference in 2004 at a time when his diocese was preparing to enter into bankruptcy proceedings. For years the American bishops have followed a set rotation for the top offices in the episcopal conference: when the term of a USCCB president ends, the vice-president is elected to succeed him, and a new vice-president chosen to wait in the wings. Thus when the term of Bishop Wilton Gregory ended in 2004, it was a mere formality that Skylstad, the incumbent vice-president, would take his place. An organization less fixed in its habits might have paused to consider whether a prelate whose diocese was facing the taint of bankruptcy would be the best public spokesman for the nation's bishops. But American Catholic bishops are not easily embarrassed; Skylstad's election proceeded on schedule.

Five American dioceses have now sought bankruptcy protection: the dioceses of Tucson, Arizona; Portland, Oregon; Spokane, Washington; Davenport, Iowa; and San Diego, California. In each case Church officials explained that the costs of sex-abuse settlements would exceed the available resources of the diocese. Not surprisingly, then, in each case the lawyers for victims of sexual abuse initially denounced the bankruptcy filing, claiming that the dioceses were using legal maneuvers to minimize the damages awarded to their clients. After contentious beginnings, the bankruptcies in Tucson and Spokane have been resolved amicably, and as I write there are reports that the case in Portland will soon be discharged as well, with a minimum of friction. But by choosing bankruptcy the bishops in each of these dioceses have courted serious danger for the Church.

The first danger is a loss of religious freedom. Under US law, during a bankruptcy proceeding a federal court assumes supervisory power over the financial affairs of the diocese. Since it is impossible to separate expenditures from policies, the court's control over spending entails a degree of control over the pastoral activities the Church. Any prudent pastor would zealously guard against such state interference in ecclesial affairs.

Perhaps a more serious practical concern in the bankruptcy cases involves the court's definition of diocesan assets. The typical American diocese is legally organized as a "corporation sole," with the bishop holding title to all assets—including parish churches, rectories, and parochial schools. Under the Code of Canon Law, the bishop holds these material assets as a trustee, acting on behalf of the parishes and parishioners. But a secular court is not bound by Church law, and from the perspective of ordinary state law the bishop, as head of the diocese, is listed as the owner of record. Thus a bankruptcy judge could rule that parish churches are the legal property of the diocese, and must be sold if necessary to meet diocesan obligations. Diocesan attorneys have argued strenuously against that conclusion, and to date no American court has ruled that a diocese must sell off parishes to pay abuse victims. But the danger cannot easily be dismissed. In filing for bankruptcy these bishops were taking a calculated gamble, putting their parishes at risk.

Today the American diocese facing the greatest problems and the prelate with the most uncertain future are both in Los Angeles. The largest ecclesiastical jurisdiction in the United States, with four million faithful and financial assets estimated at about $4 billion, the Los Angeles archdiocese is an attractive "deep pockets" target for victims' attorneys. And there is no shortage of alleged victims; more than five hundred people brought suit against the archdiocese on sex-abuse charges. Before those cases in Los Angeles were decided, plaintiffs' lawyers had already won huge settlements for their clients in the smaller California dioceses of Orange ($100 million), San Francisco ($66 million), Oakland ($56 million), and Sacramento ($35 million). The lawsuits in Los Angeles provided a spectacular final act in a decade of courtroom dramas.

As the head of the Los Angeles archdiocese, Cardinal Roger Mahony staged a dogged, protracted legal defense, battling against every new effort to extract information from the archdiocesan files. His legal tactics—like those of the bishops who filed for bankruptcy or accepted plea bargains—

showed a willingness to sacrifice the long-term welfare of the Church for the sake of the bishop's own reputation. In the legal maneuvering leading up to trials, lawyers for the Los Angeles archdiocese invoked an astonishing series of claims. First they claimed that the archdiocese should not be forced to yield files from priest-personnel records, because written communications between a priest and his bishop are protected by the same privilege that the law has traditionally applied to the confessional. There was absolutely no precedent in secular or ecclesiastical law for such a claim; sacramental confession never involves written documents, and the priest who hears confessions is forbidden from taking any action on the basis of what the penitent reveals—including, certainly, the preparation of memos for the personnel files. Still the lead lawyer for the archdiocese said that it would be "grave interference with the practice of Catholicism" if the court compelled release of those confidential files. But then within a matter of days the same lawyer announced that the files—which had previously been considered inviolate—would be handed over to insurance companies, since the insurers "are supposed to be on our side."

Cardinal Mahony said that he could not release the priests' files under any circumstances, because "it's the principle: the privilege." Another archdiocesan lawyer made the patently absurd claim that a three-way exchange of memos among a bishop, vicar, and priest were all covered by the same seal. He reasoned: "It's like having two priests in the confessional instead of one." Then the cardinal shifted his grounds and said that the files held in the chancery offices belonged to the priests, and thus the archdiocese did not have the authority to release them. At one point, in a related case involving a priest from Mexico, spokesmen for the archdiocese resisted pressure for the public disclosure of documents with an entirely different excuse, saying that they feared a legal crackdown on illegal immigrants. In this confusing and sometimes contradictory welter of arguments, the archdiocese claimed that internal files were protected by the First Amendment, the priest-penitent privilege, the California legal code, the priest-bishop bond, and the priests' own property rights. And yet when the same files were requested by the representatives of insurance companies, who were "on our side," the archdiocese was prepared to waive all those solemn rights and obligations. The conclusion was inescapable: The Los Angeles archdiocese, following the pattern set by American bishops over the past decade, was ready and willing to sacrifice the rights of the faithful—even imagined rights—to preserve the privileges of the hierarchy.

California courts rejected these flimsy arguments, one by one, and after months of contentious legal maneuvering, a trial date was set in July 2007 for the first of the victims' cases against the Los Angeles archdiocese. At last Cardinal Mahony would be forced to testify under oath about his administrative decisions—or so it seemed. But on the eve of the trial, the archdiocese announced that an agreement had been reached with representatives for all the victims. The main points of the settlement were the concessions by Mahony's lawyers that the long-disputed personnel files would be released (after having been vetted by a judge), and the archdiocese would pay a staggering $660 million in damages to the victims.

In his public statement announcing the legal settlement, the cardinal acknowledged that "these settlements will have very serious and painful consequences for the archdiocese." He continued: "This is not the fault, nor responsibility of the victims." True enough. But whose fault was it? Cardinal Mahony did not address that question; instead he went on to discuss the cutbacks that would be required in the archdiocesan budget.

The blame lay, of course, primarily on the priests who molested young people. (And it is of more than passing interest to note that several of the accused molesters were close associates of the cardinal.) But the blame also lay on the bishops who protected those predators and allowed them to continue associating freely with young people long after their vices were known.

By 2002, when the focus of attention was on Boston and Cardinal Law was under public scrutiny, this pattern of episcopal cover-ups had been fully exposed. Yet in Los Angeles, Cardinal Mahony had apparently learned nothing from his colleague's humiliation. In a shocking series of email exchanges during Holy Week (later leaked to the media), the cardinal and his top aides revealed themselves to be motivated by the desire to avoid disclosure rather than to protect children, to manage public perceptions rather than to defend the integrity of the Church. From that time forward, Cardinal Mahony and his legal team have followed the same self-serving strategy, fighting doggedly to prevent the disclosure of embarrassing information.

How much damage has been done to the credibility of the Catholic hierarchy through that needlessly prolonged legal process? Even the casual observer realized that this jumble of implausible and often contradictory legal arguments could be explained not by any defense of principle, but by the desperate motivation to avoid more damaging disclosures and to keep Cardinal Mahony off the witness stand.

Can anyone doubt that when the chancery files are finally opened, their contents will be even *more* damaging to Cardinal Mahony? A pattern had been clearly established in the Los Angeles archdiocese: information favorable to the cardinal was immediately aired; information that damaged his public standing was hidden from view for as long as chancery officials could maintain the shroud of secrecy. And the faithful were always left to wonder whether the archdiocese would ever reveal the entire truth.

Ironically, it was Cardinal Mahony who had been widely identified as the anonymous prelate calling for the resignation of the embattled Cardinal Bernard Law early in 2002. Now the cardinal in Los Angeles was facing the payment of legal damages five times as great as the payoff to victims in Boston. With a legal settlement reached on the eve of the first court date, the cardinal had been spared from testifying at a public trial, but the Church has paid an enormous price for the legal delays, and the cardinal's own credibility was tattered every bit as badly as Cardinal Law's had been.

Still Cardinal Mahony clung to his position, and two factors supported him in his quest to stay in power. First, after five years of saturation coverage, many Americans had grown tired of the sex-abuse story. The stories about archdiocesan neglect and connivance in Los Angeles were not read with the same shock and horror that had catapulted the Boston story into the headlines. Second, unlike Cardinal Law, Mahony enjoyed solid support in Los Angeles as the result of his political alliances.

In Boston's political battles, Cardinal Law had been identified with the unpopular Catholic position on issues such as abortion and same-sex marriage; he was viewed as an ideological foe by the liberal custodians of public opinion, led by the editors of the *Boston Globe*. Although his position made him immune from frontal attacks until the sex-abuse scandal broke, when that opportunity arose the media seized it with relish and criticized the cardinal mercilessly.

In Los Angeles, however, Cardinal Mahony's signature public issue had been immigration, and his posture on that issue—an unqualified support for the rights of immigrants, legal or illegal—had won him the sympathy of liberal commentators. The *Los Angeles Times* led a chorus of editorial criticism for the cardinal's treatment of the sex-abuse crisis, but that criticism never had the same savage edge that had characterized the media attacks on Cardinal Law. Moreover the Hispanic Catholics who now comprised roughly 70 percent of the faithful in the Los Angeles archdiocese looked upon the cardinal as a champion of their cause.

So Cardinal Mahony appeared likely to survive the scandal—at least unless or until more damaging revelations tumbled out of those personnel folders. Still, insofar as his survival depended on his political popularity rather than his pastoral leadership, he had enhanced his personal standing at the expense of true Church authority, and eventually he or (more likely) future prelates would pay the price. He had sought and won public approbation, but undermined the religious witness that was the only real basis for his public authority. The leadership of the Los Angeles archdiocese was headed down the same road that the Boston archdiocese had already traveled.

19

THE CHURCH
MILITANT

By the close of the nineteenth century Catholics had become the
most important group in Boston society, on the basis of their
numerical strength. But years would pass before the Catholic con-
quest was complete. The old Yankee elite, having controlled the region's
political and cultural affairs for so many generations, found it painful to
relinquish their power. Even the Catholics had some trouble realizing that
after years as a despised minority, they could now control the city.

A century later Catholics had ceased to be the most influential element in Boston society. But once again both the victors and the vanquished
were slow to recognize the new state of affairs. Church leaders still thought
of themselves as important public figures. Other community leaders preserved that illusion by treating Boston's prelates with great deference, acting out of habit rather than conviction. The sex-abuse scandal tore away
that façade of deference and exposed the weakness of the Church.

Today *former* Catholics constitute the largest religious bloc in the
Boston area. Some of these ex-Catholics have joined other religious bodies.
Others take no interest in religious affairs. Still others think of themselves
as Catholic, but they neither practice their faith nor honor its teachings. In
the opening years of the twenty-first century, *practicing* Catholics are once
again a small minority in Boston, barely tolerated by a society that finds
their views alien and potentially dangerous.

Like their predecessors in the 1800s, Church leaders now tacitly accept
the minority status of the Catholic community. Rather than risking conflict
by challenging the moral consensus of secular culture, they do their best to
protect the right of Catholics to maintain their own principles and pursue
their own devotions in private. To this day many Church leaders remain
convinced that the best way to acquire public influence is to persuade the

majority that Catholics are reasonable people, open to compromise—to hope for incremental change rather than to push for outright victory. That approach is bound to fail, just as it failed all through the late twentieth century.

Catholic public influence in Boston was built upon Catholic unity. The faithful were bound together by common beliefs, common discipline, and common worship. The Catholic population formed a distinct, identifiable social unit. It was possible to speak about "the Catholic position" on a public issue, and the more boldly that position was proclaimed, the more cohesive was the Catholic presence. As long as the clergy nourished the faith of the laity, and the hierarchy nourished the faith of the clergy, the influence of Catholicism continued to grow. Regular use of the sacraments and firm adherence to doctrine bred solidarity among Catholics: solidarity that could easily be translated into social influence and political power.

Yet from the first days of the Catholic ascendancy, Church leaders in Boston experienced the temptation to build up that influence and power for their own sake, rather than nurturing the religious solidarity on which they depended. Cardinals became preoccupied with the needs of the archdiocese as a secular institution, sometimes even to the detriment of the archdiocese as a community of faith.

Unfortunately the great crisis for Catholicism as a public institution in the late twentieth century came at just the time when solidarity among the faithful was under the greatest strain. In the years after Vatican II, the old unity of belief, discipline, and worship was shattered. The common sense of Catholic identity was lost. Rather than acknowledging a common creed and common worship, Catholics were being forced to choose competing theological views and liturgical experiments, all claiming to be authentically Catholic. At this historic moment, the sexual revolution challenged basic standards of private and public morality. Traditional Catholic teaching offered a strong antidote to the nostrums of the new morality, but now the Church was not prepared to speak with one clear voice.

To complicate matters, prelates who had grown accustomed to making political compromises discovered that they could, with only a *small* compromise on principle, reach a peaceful accommodation with the new ways of thought and avoid an open conflict. So Boston's archbishops made a series of tactical retreats, when they still might have rallied the faithful and revived the sense of Catholic identity by taking a principled stand and daring a public battle.

How much would Boston's history have been altered if Cardinal Cushing had offered a public critique of John F. Kennedy's speech to the Baptist ministers in Houston? If Cardinal Medeiros had announced that Catholic schools should always be open to new students, regardless of the city's busing policies? If Cardinal Law had joined Operation Rescue in blockading an abortion clinic? If Cardinal O'Malley had instructed Catholic Charities to stop placing adoptive children in same-sex households and prepare for a court challenge of the state's anti-discrimination law? The *Boston Globe* would have thundered in condemnation, we know; the editorials would have charged that the cardinals were being divisive. But such bold actions would have won the hearts of the most devout Catholics in the region, and thus strengthened the Church for the next public battle. Instead, in each of these cases Boston's top Catholic leaders chose to avoid confrontation. The *Globe* may not have applauded the cardinals' choices, but the *Globe* has never been the Church's friend.

In this book my focus has been on Boston. Because the Catholic presence was once so powerful in Boston and is now so weak, the story is a particularly dramatic one. But the same general pattern can be seen in other Catholic dioceses all across America. The fractured unity of Catholic communities after Vatican II sapped the public strength of the Church at just the moment when that strength was sorely needed. Bishops avoided open conflicts, fearful that their people would not follow them into battle. But that readiness to retreat in the face of public opposition caused still greater damage to the sense of shared Catholic identity and led to still further retreats.

Nor have Catholic leaders been alone in their willingness to retreat in the face of opposition on moral issues. Protestant and Jewish leaders have seen the same sort of erosion in their own public influence, especially when they have sought to uphold traditional moral precepts. Over the course of the past generation, defenders of Judeo-Christian morality have absorbed heavy losses in the sphere of American public affairs. Policies that would have been unthinkable just twenty-five years ago, such as the legal recognition of same-sex unions, are rapidly gaining public acceptance. Since there is no particular reason to expect a change in that trend, it is daunting to think about the changes the next twenty-five years might bring. Defenders of traditional morality—of marriage, the family, and the dignity of human life—often seem doomed to a continual rear-guard battle, struggling to yield ground as slowly as possible.

America remains an overwhelmingly Christian nation. Unlike their counterparts in Europe, most American Christians identify with a particular church and worship there regularly. Moreover, while the liberal "mainline" Protestant denominations have been shrinking in size, the conservative churches have been gaining followers. Still, the churches are under heavy pressure to abstain from involvement in public affairs.

The French Revolution brought the apotheosis of the notion that religious faith is an exclusively private matter. In the European countries where secular ideology now reigns supreme, private religious practice is tolerated, but public manifestations of faith are looked upon with deep suspicion if not hostility. Not surprisingly, when faith was removed from public life it gradually disappeared from private lives as well; the level of religious practice plummeted. So today Europe is a post-Christian culture.

It is not alarmist to question whether America is headed down the same historical path. In Boston, certainly, the Catholic faith once held unquestioned sway over the local culture, just as it had ruled the broader culture of Europe for generations. But eventually—in Europe and in Boston—Church leaders grew complacent in their authority, sought to align themselves with secular powers, compromised the distinctive characteristics of the faith, undermined Catholic unity, and finally found themselves unable to defend against the encroachments of their secular adversaries. Now other American religious leaders face the same temptations.

Certainly it is tempting for American pastors to ignore the problems looming on the horizon. Their congregations are still large and active. Pastors themselves are still highly esteemed in their local communities. But the cultural trends are adverse. Christians still account for a sizeable majority of American citizens. Yet on the single issue that has most clearly defined the social conflicts of the past thirty years, the question of abortion, Christians have steadily lost ground. In 1973, immediately after the *Roe v. Wade* decision, pro-life activists made it their goal to overturn the Supreme Court's ruling and outlaw abortion entirely. By 2004 the preferred presidential candidate of the pro-life movement openly stated that he could not foresee the reversal of *Roe v. Wade*. A majority of Americans may still oppose abortion, but that majority—if it still exists—has not been mobilized successfully. Conservative Christians form the majority, yet secular liberals have been winning the battles, just as they have won the battle for Boston.

Living in a culture that is sometimes openly hostile, Christians can be tempted to quit the public debates, accept the privatization of faith, and withdraw to their own enclaves. But in doing so they neglect the basic duty of every Christian to preach the Gospel. A living Christian faith is always evangelical. Or to put it differently, if Christians do *not* bear public witness to their faith, the corruption of the Church has already begun. In the Catholic Church, the Code of Canon Law stipulates that a pastor is responsible for the spiritual welfare of everyone within the boundaries of his parish, not only for the Catholics. A believer is responsible for the welfare of his neighbors, and he serves their welfare best by bringing them closer to Christ.

Alternatively, Christians can choose to remain active in public society but avoid confrontations, by accepting the premises on which the secular culture is based. Church leaders might hope to persuade their neighbors by the force of their arguments, without ever giving offense. But if the surrounding culture is truly hostile, even arguments can be seen as offensive—as today gay activists take offense when Christians say that homosexual activities are morally wrong. So Christian apologists are constantly tempted to yield on principle for the sake of public peace—and worse, to condemn those more rigorous Christians who do not make the same compromises.

Dietrich Bonhoeffer, the German Lutheran who was executed for his role in a plot against Hitler, saw the compromises that Christians leaders had made in their dealings with the Nazi regime and wrote about them in his book *The Cost of Discipleship*. "We justified the world," he wrote, speaking of his own Lutheran colleagues, "and condemned as heretics those who tried to follow Christ. The result was that a nation became Christian and Lutheran, but at the cost of true discipleship." Bonhoeffer continued:

> The price we are having to pay today, in the shape of the collapse of the organized Church, is only the inevitable consequence of our policy of making grace available to all at too low a cost. We gave away the word and sacraments wholesale, we baptized, confirmed, and absolved a whole nation unasked and without condition.... But the call to follow Jesus in the narrow way was hardly ever heard. Where were those truths which impelled the early Church to institute the catechumenate, which enabled a strict watch to be kept over the frontier between the Church and the world, and afforded adequate protection for costly grace? What had happened to all those warnings of Luther's against preaching the Gospel in such a manner as to make men rest secure in their ungodly living?

Bonhoeffer's words could be applied with only minor changes to the demise of Catholicism in Boston. Church leaders stopped making demands on themselves, on the faithful, and on the public at large. No doubt they were guided by the best of motives; they felt that their policies would strengthen the Church. But the sad results of their choices are now all too easily seen. And now other Church leaders are tempted to make the same choices, with the same likely results.

Questions about how a Christian should cope with the tensions of life in an unbelieving world are as old as the faith itself. "No one can serve two masters," Jesus told his disciples. "You cannot serve God and mammon." In his magisterial work *The City of God,* St. Augustine argues that a man's earthly priorities reflect his ultimate loves and loyalties. Is he a loyal subject of the Kingdom of God, who happens temporarily to be living in a civil society here on earth? Or does he give his first allegiance to the earthly city, making room for God when he can?

To serve the Kingdom of God involves real sacrifice on a material level. But then, to serve the Kingdom of Man involves sacrifice of spiritual goods. Which sort of sacrifice will a man choose to make? An important religious group will always have some influence on society, and the surrounding society will have some influence on the faith. For every believer, but especially for the religious leaders, the key question is: which influence will predominate? Will a Church leader strive to transform society, bringing it into line with the teachings of the Church? Or will he work to make his faith more acceptable in the eyes of contemporary society?

In Boston, too often, Church leaders have chosen the latter option. But the City of God can never be fully acceptable to the City of Man. An effort to make the Church acceptable damages both the spiritual welfare of the faithful and, ultimately, the social standing of the Church.

For the Catholic Church in Boston today, there is no earthly hope. In parish after parish the congregations at Sunday Mass are smaller every year—that is, if the parish itself survives the latest archdiocesan pruning. Parochial schools are closing. Empty buildings—cavernous Gothic churches, rectories, convents and schools—urgently need repairs, but the paltry collections are not even enough to keep up with the current fuel bills. Priests and nuns are aging, and precious few young people are entering the seminaries and convents to take their place. The congregations, too, are aging; the pews are dotted with gray heads, while young couples spend their Sunday mornings at home with the newspaper and the television programs that cater to serious-minded secular viewers by featuring discussions of current events.

The entire, massive structure of Catholicism totters along on borrowed time. But the trend is clear. That whole structure will come crashing down, perhaps within the next generation, unless there is some dramatic change. Yet the Church establishment gives no sign of changing, or even seeking to change. Quite the contrary; pastors and bishops alike studiously ignore the handwriting on the wall and pretend to conduct business as usual.

Catholic leaders today have resources that the twelve Apostles could never have imagined. They have undergone years of formal training, honing the skills for their ministry. They have access to every means of instant communication, including newspapers and electronic media. They control schools at every level, from kindergartens to universities. Their holdings in real estate alone are worth billions of dollars. Their flocks are (by reputation, at least) the most highly educated Catholic lay people in history. Yet the Church they guide is a shambles.

The Apostles were poor, uneducated, provincial. Yet their efforts brought the Gospel to every nation on earth. Today in comfortable suburbs, just down the street from the parish church, one can readily find people who, quite literally, have never heard the Gospel.

Tonight in suburban rectories, priests will filter into the den after supper, mix a drink, and turn on the television set. The rectory is a large, handsome building, with plenty of extra space for meetings. But few parishioners ever visit. Occasionally a young couple will drop by, to learn about the requirements for a church marriage. Many of those couples will already be living together, in flagrant defiance of Church teaching. But the priest will overlook the fact that they share the same address, preferring not to raise unpleasant questions. The priest is not in a position to ask the couple to make sacrifices for their faith, because he makes few sacrifices himself. His life is as comfortable as theirs.

More often than young couples drop into the rectory, a priest will be called out to visit an invalid parishioner, whose approach toward death reminds him of how quickly his congregation is aging. Or the priest might preside at meetings held by parish organizations (the Sodality, the Holy Name Society) whose membership is steadily diminished by old age.

Veteran priests remember the "glory days" of American Catholicism. They remember when every pew was packed for Sunday Mass; when scores of children graduated each year from the parochial school; when the parish was the center of the community's social life. Today, having assumed control of that once-proud parish plant, the pastor finds himself a forgotten man, living in splendid isolation in his rectory, wondering how to pay the repair bills for the empty school buildings.

In the convent around the corner, three or four nuns now live in a building designed to accommodate twenty women. Years ago the nuns served at the parish school. But that school has been closed for years now, and the nuns find jobs elsewhere. Perhaps they pursue ordinary professional careers—as day-care workers or secretaries. Or perhaps they still work for the parish, teaching the few children who still bother to attend the weekly religious-education classes. These nuns are approaching retirement age, in any case; most of the sisters in their religous order are already senior citizens. There are no young women joining the order, no new members to provide for the elderly nuns in the congregation. Nursing-home bills are mounting, and the religious order is facing bankruptcy.

Up and down the streets that surround the church, Catholic families live immune to the influence of their parish. On any given Sunday, less than one-fifth of the Catholic adults will attend Mass, and those who do attend regularly are disproportionately old. Young adults come to church on Easter and Christmas, for weddings and funerals. But their children know nothing about the faith; Catholicism is not a topic discussed at their dinner tables. In their personal lives, those who call themselves Catholics are indistinguishable from any other Americans. Even in matters on which the Church has a clear public teaching—matters such as birth control, abortion, and divorce—Catholics behave no differently from the American public as a whole. For the great majority of even those who could be termed practicing Catholics, the Church can command one hour of grudging, passive attendance in church each week—if that—and nothing more.

How can this aging, crumbling Church recover strength? With so little energy, such weak will, how can we overcome the world? When Catholics themselves neither know nor practice their faith, how can they be expected to preach the Gospel to all nations? Logically speaking, humanly speaking, there is no hope.

Fortunately, this situation is not new. The Catholic Church has never had any earthly hope.

Right from the beginning, the Church faced odds which were, from any logical viewpoint, insuperable. A dozen uneducated men, mostly fishermen by trade, from an insignificant captive nation in a remote and desolate part of the world, were sent out to preach the Gospel to all nations. They had no transportation, no efficient means of communication, no special skills in personal persuasion. Objectively speaking, they had no earthly hope of success.

No, the Apostles had something much more powerful than any earthly hope. Since they could not place their confidence in any logical process, or any material resources, they relied entirely on the power of the Holy Spirit. And they succeeded.

If the Catholic Church is nothing more than a human institution, it will not survive beyond the next generation or two. But then, if the Catholic Church is only a human institution, it does not *deserve* to survive. If, however, the Church is an institution founded by God—if it is the living Body of Christ—then she will certainly survive and flourish in spite of all earthly handicaps.

Then the task of loyal Catholics who live in America today is not to bemoan the fate of the Church or to cherish fond memories of bygone days, but to prepare a new offensive. Our goal is not simply to recapture the strengths that the Church enjoyed in the halcyon era of the 1950s, but to transform our entire society through the power of the Gospel.

With that ambitious goal in mind, our first task is to take stock: to identify the strengths within our Church as well as the weaknesses, the sources of renewal as well as corruption. We must ask ourselves where we are wasting our energy, and where more energy is needed. Above all else, we must recognize when we are relying on human strengths and earthly resources, and ignoring the power of the Holy Spirit.

The purpose of this book is to help with that first task, to take one small step on the road to Catholic renewal—or perhaps, more accurately, to take a compass bearing, so that we know which direction that road will lead in. This book is a study of Catholicism in America today, and more specifically of Catholicism in my native Boston. If it is a harsh portrait, I believe that harshness is justified. I love the Catholic Church. But love for the Church does not mean unquestioning love for every institution within Catholicism, any more than the love for one's spouse would extend to a cancer within the spouse's body.

When Church agencies begin to serve earthly aims, they become truly cancerous. They may grow rapidly and absorb tremendous amounts of energy—and they steadily drain real spiritual strength away from the Church. And in any case, the accumulation of earthly resources is pointless; that battle is already lost.

The Church as a whole is the Body of Christ, incorruptible. Individual organizations within the Church are very much corruptible, however, and in America today they are very much corrupt. Loving the Church means denouncing the corruption. Denouncing the corruption, in turn, means protecting the inner strength of our Church, clinging jealously to our one, last, infallible hope.

The same corruption that produced the sex-abuse scandal, the greatest crisis in the history of American Catholicism, remains widespread in the Church today. Indeed the corruption is more firmly entrenched now than it was in 2002 because the hierarchy has refused to acknowledge the most serious aspect of the scandal: the treason of the bishops.

Reform cannot begin until the corruption is acknowledged. And since the American hierarchy apparently cannot or will not recognize the corruption with itself, other Catholics must call the bishops to account and demand the sort of responsible pastoral leadership that the American Church has not seen for years. Under these circumstances lay Catholics who criticize their bishops are not showing their disrespect for the bishop's office. Quite the contrary. Those who revere the authority of a Catholic bishop should protect that authority—if necessary, even from the man who occupies the office.

American bishops of recent vintage have shown little interest in the use of their legitimate teaching authority. When they teach, loyal Catholics obey. But when they do *not* teach—when they remain silent in the face of grave abuses—how should a loyal Catholic layman react? Our faith teaches respect for the office, not the individual. If the bishop neglects the duties of his office, then deference toward him is misplaced. A loyal Catholic should protect the bishop's office by demanding that the bishop fulfills it. Failing that, a Catholic who loves the Church must demand that at a bare minimum his bishop refrains from debasing his office or bargaining away his authority to preserve his own comfort. Even if today's bishop is unworthy of his office, his authority should be protected for the sake of his successors.

Eventually, as the Holy Spirit guides the Church, a worthy successor will arrive to lead the reform. Once again the history of Catholicism furnishes enough examples of successful reform to bolster hope in even the grimmest of circumstances. When St. Peter Canisius was sent to Vienna in

1552, for example, 90 percent of the city's residents had abandoned the Catholic faith, and even among the remainder most were not actively practicing the faith. Many of the city's parishes had no pastor, and not a single priest had been ordained for the diocese in twenty years. Yet the great Jesuit preacher rallied the faithful few, confronted the enemies of the Church, and led the restoration that made Austria a bulwark of Catholicism for centuries to come. Perhaps even now another great saint is waiting in the wings, ready to lead the Catholic restoration in Boston.

But that restoration, if it does come, will not come without cost. To restore vigor and discipline to the Church, Catholic leaders will be required to make personal sacrifices and unpopular decisions—and to ask their followers to do the same. That is the mark of Christian leadership: the willingness to imitate the Sacrifice of Christ.

Cardinals, the leading prelates of the Catholic Church, traditionally wear red: the color of blood, the color of martyrdom. Their vestments bear witness—theoretically, at least—to their willingness to make any sacrifice for the welfare of the faithful. Pope Benedict XVI recalled that symbolism in March 2006, when he raised new prelates to the College of Cardinals for the first time in his pontificate. "I am counting on you," the Pope reminded the men to whom he was awarding red hats. He repeated the phrase frequently in his remarks at the ceremony: "I am counting on you." In 2007, during a visit to the Roman academy that trains clerics for service in the Vatican diplomatic corps, the Pope made the same point about how a readiness for personal sacrifice defines the nature of leadership in the Church. He told the aspiring diplomats that "whoever collaborates with the successor of Peter, supreme shepherd of the Catholic Church, is called to do his best to be himself a true shepherd: ready, like Jesus the Good Shepherd, to give his life for his flock."

Just prior to his election as Roman Pontiff, the future Benedict XVI made another perceptive point about the nature of Christian leadership in the early years of the twenty-first century. In Europe particularly, said then-Cardinal Joseph Ratzinger, faithful Christians should "recognize themselves as a creative minority." Christians today should not delude themselves, he reasoned; in Europe today they are a minority, in a society that has lost contact with its Christian heritage. And yet, he continued, "The future of a society often depends upon creative minorities."

A creative minority: That phrase could accurately be used to describe the loyal Catholics of Boston after years of scandal. The same could be applied, actually, to the Catholic presence in Boston some two hundred years ago. Catholics formed only a small minority in the early nineteenth century, despised and oppressed by a hostile majority. But they were bound together by the strong bonds of a shared faith, determined not merely to endure but to spread that faith. They were confident that they could overcome all opposition, and eventually they did. With the power of faith it could happen again.

FURTHER
READING

Parts IV and V of this book explore topics that have not received much attention in previous works: the price of the sex-abuse scandal (as measured in terms of Catholic influence in public life) and the prospects for recovery. But readers who are interested in a fuller treatment of the themes covered all too briefly in Parts I–III will find many excellent books available. Herewith just a few recommendations:

Part I: The Catholic Century

For an overview of Boston Catholic history, see *Boston Catholics*, by Thomas H. O'Connor (Northeastern, 1998), a book marred only by the author's invariably conventional approach. A much livelier treatment, critical of Cardinal William O'Connell's career, is *Militant and Triumphant*, by James M. O'Toole (Notre Dame, 1992). For a treatment of anti-Catholicism in America, with many references to the rich history of that bias in Boston, see *The Persistent Prejudice*, by Michael Schwartz (Our Sunday Visitor, 1984).

To understand the unique role that James Michael Curley played in Boston's political and social history, one might read the very unflattering biography *The Rascal King*, by Jack Beatty (Addison-Wesley, 1992). But those who knew him best generally agree that Curley was captured wonderfully in a work of fiction—not his autobiography *I'd Do It Again* (Prentice-Hall, 1957), which probably qualifies in that genre, but Edwin O'Connor's memorable *The Last Hurrah* (Little Brown, 1956).

The Kennedy family has been the subject of many different books. Among those that treat the family's deleterious influence on the Catholic culture of Boston are Peter Collier's *The Kennedys: An American Drama* (Encounter, 2002) and Thomas Maier's *The Kennedys: America's Emerald Kings* (Basic, 2004).

There is no satisfactory book-length account of the controversy surrounding Father Feeney, but *The Loyolas and the Cabots*, by Catherine Goddard Clarke (Ravengate, 1950), gives the understandably biased perspective
of the woman who led the group that challenged the Boston archdiocese,
and Abbot Gabriel Gibbs, OSB, has now added, in *Harvard to Harvard*
(Ravengate, 2007), the more detached perspective of those who endured
the crisis and were reconciled with the Church.

The social upheaval caused by busing in Boston's public schools has
also been the subject of many books; probably the best is *Common Ground*,
by J. Anthony Lucas (Knopf, 1985)

Part II: Shifting Foundations

Scores of excellent books have been written about the problems that
emerged within the Catholic Church after the Second Vatican Council.
The most accessible, to someone looking into the topic for the first time,
might be *What Went Wrong with Vatican II*, by Ralph McInerny (Sophia,
1998)—a book written in a disarmingly simple style that nevertheless handles the most serious theological issues. *Catholicism and Modernity*, by James
Hitchcock (Servant, 1979), is another very readable treatment of whether
the faith influences the culture or vice versa.

Philip Trower's *Turmoil and Truth* (Ignatius, 2003) helps readers to
understand how a bogus "spirit of Vatican II" came to triumph over the
actual teachings of the Council. In *The Crisis of Authority* (Regnery, 1981),
the late Monsignor George Kelly traces the effects of theological dissidents
through the Catholic universities of America into public life.

The Naked Public Square, by Father Richard John Neuhaus (Eerdmans,
1986), notes the shrinking space allocated to religious arguments in modern
public discourse. And in *The Catholic Moment* (Harpercollins, 1990) Father
Neuhaus explains how the Catholic tradition could play a vital role in the
revival of public discourse, if allowed to do so. In *The Long Truce* (Spence,
2001), A. J. Conyers makes a very convincing argument that the notion of
tolerance was introduced into political theory as an argument in support of
state power.

Part III: The Collapse

Jason Berry set the standard for reporting on the sex-abuse scandal with the
stunning *Lead Us Not into Temptation* (Doubleday, 1992). Notice that his
book was published a decade before the crisis was allegedly "discovered" in

Boston. When the scandal did peak that year, Servant Press put out a very useful collection of essays entitled *Shaken by Scandals*, edited by Paul Thigpen, offering a variety of perspectives from loyal Catholics suffering through the crisis.

Betrayal (Little Brown, 2002), the work of the *Boston Globe* investigative team that ferreted out the truth about the sex-abuse crisis in Boston, is the definitive resource for any treatment of that story, and I leaned on the *Globe's* reporting heavily in writing this book.

Commissioned by the US bishops, the John Jay College of Criminal Justice produced its study *The Nature and Scope of Sexual Abuse of Minors by Catholic Priests and Deacons in the United States, 1950–2002* (USCCB, 2004), which is as dry as the title suggests, but packed with useful information. An entirely different approach—highly personal, including very personal anecdotes and conveying the emotional devastation wrought by abuse (not for the faint of heart)—is *Sacrilege*, by Leon Podles (Crossland, 2007).

Goodbye, Good Men (Regnery, 2002), by Michael Rose, recorded how conservative candidates are systematically barred from American Catholic seminaries, while homosexual candidates are protected as they advance into the priesthood. By far the best examination of the psychological and pastoral issues involved in the handling of deviant priests is *After Asceticism*, a sadly unrecognized resource published by the Linacre Institute (2006).

ACKNOWLEDGMENTS

The ideas that form the backbone for this book began stirring in my mind more than a decade ago, long before the eruption of the sex-abuse crisis. At the time I was editor of *Catholic World Report*, and veteran readers of that monthly magazine will surely recognize many of the themes developed in these pages. I am grateful to Father Joseph Fessio, SJ, my old publisher, and to Ignatius Press for giving me the freedom to pursue those ideas, both in the magazine and on my own.

My current colleagues have been equally supportive. Thanks to Peter and Jeff Mirus of Trinity Communications (the online publisher of Catholic World News) for encouraging my work on this book, and making every effort to accommodate my writing schedule.

The Faith & Reason Institute in Washington, DC, appointed me as a non-resident fellow while I worked on this book. Thanks to Robert Royal for arranging that appointment. For donations that helped to underwrite that position I am grateful to the Strake Foundation. Special thanks are also due to the many readers of Catholic World News who contributed to the project, and especially to Leon Podles, John Joyce, and Tim Daly. Abbot Gabriel Gibbs, OSB, and my friends at St Benedict's Abbey provided both material support and more valuable spiritual sustenance.

Many friends and colleagues were generous with their time and advice as I worked through this project. C. J. Doyle of the Catholic Action League of Massachusetts was an invaluable resource; I relied heavily on both his political analysis and his encyclopedic knowledge of Boston's Catholic history. Father Paul Mankowski, SJ, and Father Jerry Pokorsky reacted to my ideas, critiqued portions of the manuscript, and offered encouragement throughout. Rick Cross provided some special insights into the psychology of aberrant behavior and the practical benefits of Christian asceticism. Many other friends, particularly in the Boston archdiocese, offered suggestions on the express condition that I should not reveal their names; nonetheless they should know that I am grateful for their help. They— and the others listed above— should be absolved of responsibility for any excesses or shortcomings in my work.

The staff of Encounter Books has been attentive and unfailingly professional. Special thanks to Roger Kimball, Heather Ohle, Lauren Powers, and Alexandra Mullen Kimball for making the process of preparing this book for publication so easy and enjoyable.

My wife Leila and our children have all contributed mightily to this project in a variety of ways. I am grateful for their patience, endurance, and unflagging enthusiasm for my work. If I tried to give adequate thanks to Leila— who is my most perceptive critic and most reliable proofreader, as well as the heart of an extraordinarily happy household— I'd need to write another book.

INDEX